W9-BTH-645

TRAUMA
TRESSES
& TRUTH

TRAUMA TRESSES & TRUTH

Untangling Our Hair
Through Personal Narratives

EDITED BY LYZETTE WANZER

Lawrence Hill Books
Chicago

This publication is made possible in part by grants from the Center for Cultural Innovation, San Francisco Arts Commission, and California Humanities, a National Endowment for the Humanities partner. Significant support has also been provided by Intersection for the Arts and Shuffle Collective.

Copyright © 2023 by Lyzette Wanzer
Foreword © 2023 by Afiya Mbilishaka
Each essay remains the copyright of its listed author
All rights reserved
Published by Lawrence Hill Books
An imprint of Chicago Review Press Incorporated
814 North Franklin Street
Chicago, IL 60610
ISBN 978-1-64160-670-7

"The Ancient" by Iris Crawford was performed at the 2020 AfroSolo Arts Festival and previously appeared on the author's website.

Excerpts of "Toward Decolonizing Our Roots" by Lyzette Wanzer previously appeared as "Twisted" in *Guernica Magazine* (2014) and in *Civil Liberties United: Diverse Voices from the San Francisco Bay Area* (Pease Press, 2019).

"Peinate el Pelo" by Carmen Bardeguez-Brown previously appeared in *Centro Voices* (Center for Puerto Rican Studies, 2015).

"solstice in solidified sugar" by Dr. Raina León previously appeared in *The Ascentos Review* (June 2020).

Library of Congress Control Number: 2022941628

Cover design: Dubelyoo
Interior illustrations: Sal Steiner
Typesetter: Nord Compo

Every effort has been made to contact the copyright holders for the images that appear in this book. The publisher would welcome information concerning any inadvertent errors or omissions.

Printed in the United States of America
5 4 3 2 1

To Mrs. Mary Simmons of SBS
and
Dr. Gordon M. Wickstrom of F&M,
who believed in me first and catalyzed the best in me

People . . . write books about baseball, and people can intellectualize the discussion around baseball. So if you can do that, why not Black women's hair, which has a history, which has political meaning, which is so deeply layered, and which I think the world doesn't know enough about?

—**Chimamanda Ngozi Adichie**, novelist

It is axiomatic that if we do not define ourselves for ourselves, we will be defined by others—for their use and to our detriment.

—**Audre Lorde**, writer and civil rights activist

CONTENTS

Part I: A Critical Lens

Part II: The Pilgrimage

Part III: Intimate Encounters

Part IV: The Unshackled Chronicles

FOREWORD

MY MOTHER WASHED MY HAIR in the bathtub every Sunday night, usually around seven, after family dinner. Our bathroom had a white tub with mustard-yellow stickered stripes for grip. Within that bathtub, my mother would apply tear-free shampoo and offer me tiny scalp massages to lather the bubbles throughout the waist-length hair plastered to my six-year-old body. Once the coconut-scented shampoo covered all my strands, she would say, "All right, it is time to lean back." I would do my reverse crunch into the tub until my ears were submerged in the lukewarm bath water. She would rub and rub some more with her powerful hands, always adorned with baby-pink or fire-red manicured nails. Then would come my favorite part: she would let me pick the number of braids that I'd wear for the week! As the youngest child, there were very few things that I had choice over. In my mind, owning the agency to determine the number of braids that I would wear was quite empowering. Each week I anticipated the question: "Afiya, how many braids do you want this week?" I would shout "Two!" or "Four!" but my favorite number was three. And please believe, my mom knew how to work three braids. Sometimes she'd part from ear to ear and divide the top of my crown right in the middle, using my nose for reference and then making one braid along my occipital bone. Other times she would divide the fractions to have an L shape and slick back parts of my hair to the rear. Or she would connect the braids, so that every braid neatly poured into the next. I didn't know it then, but I was learning a bit of geometry, too, in this weekly ritual.

I had no sense of how long this process took. I just knew that I enjoyed resting between my mom's legs while she sat on her bed or on the living room couch among the larger family. I cherished this time. I felt special and loved.

Sadly, this family self-esteem rite was tested consistently outside my home. The biggest tests took place under the command of stopwatches at swim meets.

I was a Black girl swimmer, and at the pool, my wet curly hair drew questions and criticism. White and Asian swimmers, teammates and competitors alike, had too many questions about my hair. The locker-room mirror became a research lab on Black hair.

"Why does your hair curl like that?"

"Can you use a comb on your hair?"

"Are you putting grease from a chicken on your hair?"

"Does your hair have a smell?"

And of course: "Can I touch your hair?"

I never knew to whom they reported their findings, but I began to board the school bus with a towel covering my wet hair rather than endure the inquisition. I hated the queries in their words and eyes as I attended to my hair. I noticed that washing my hair in the locker room did not give me the same emotional satisfaction as did my earliest memories of my mom washing my hair. While wearing a towel on my head on a bus did raise a few eyebrows, I positioned myself to be "mysterious" rather than a specimen. Memories of Mom's hair-washing ritual infused me with the strength to reject my peers' attempts to dictate my self-concept and hair story. I was then—as I am now—the only person who could choose how I wanted to feel and think about my hair.

What happens when someone gets to choose how they tell their hair story? We feel seen. We feel consideration, agency, recognition, and, above all, comprehension. As a clinical psychologist, hairstylist, and hair historian, I engage in work that centralizes hair as an entry point into mental health and wellness. Over the last twenty years, I've heard thousands of hair stories on my therapy couch and in my salon chair. My passion for collecting and affirming hair stories has created opportunities for healing at both the individual and the community levels. I have testified to Congress on the CROWN Act (Creating a Respectful and Open World for Natural Hair), I have developed occupationally specific mental-health first aid for hair-care professionals, and I have published over twenty articles in the past three years on PsychoHairapy. PsychoHairapy is a therapeutic technique that uses hair as an entry point into mental-health services. I founded and designed this community-based storytelling method to alleviate hair trauma.

Storytelling is a traditional healing modality our African ancestors employed to decipher the universe's mysteries, unify art and science, conduct intergenerational cultural transmissions for survival, and honor the spiritual realm. Lyzette Wanzer honors this tradition as a master storyteller and editor. While her award-winning publications offer a timeless archive to honor Black lives in America, Wanzer has now conjured a book fashioned for the souls of African American and Afro Latina women searching for connections while combating cultural, psychic, and aesthetic trauma. During the height of the COVID-19 pandemic, in the wake of summer 2020's racial unrest and uprisings and in the midst of continuing (and underreported) police violence against women of color, Wanzer organized sacred spaces for women across the African diaspora to birth community through processing the emotional significance of self-concept through hair.

Trauma, Tresses & Truth offers vivid vignettes of individual and collective episodic memory. There is an urgent need for collective healing that invites Black and Brown women to tell their stories from the crown down. Stories about hair can offer narrative therapy for both writers and readers alike. While narrative therapy as a practice is credited to New Zealand–based family therapists Michael White and David Epston, retelling important stories has served as a healing modality for millennia. White and Epston recognized within a therapeutic context that we all carry internalized and evolving self-narratives that influence how we feel, think, and behave. Some stories are healing, while others are problematic. Narrative therapy invites people to reauthor problematic stories. Narrative therapy differs from other therapies in that the storyteller is regarded as an expert. And therapists recognize these stories—which the authors constructed from early childhood—as energy that individuals harbor within themselves for an entire lifetime. Hair stories serve as opportunities for self-reflection and externalization of the multiplicity of problems American society projects onto Black natural hair. While contending with the preponderance of white American paradigms, the scope and sway of the battle is enough to overwhelm even the most skillful, stalwart, intrepid social activist. But examining the norms of white hegemonic appearance can render the problems more approachable. We begin to unearth the bevy of falsehoods and racism that yielded the nearly ubiquitous Natural Hair Story.

Natural hair stories are ancient. As documented on papyrus and pyramid walls, our ancestors used Black hair for sacred healing rituals for centuries. Our hair served as a love offering to deities. Our hairstyles spoke life into family connections through birthing rituals, rites of passage, marriages, and even funerals.* Through years of colonization and enslavement, Europeans desacralized our natural hair, referring to it in derogatory terms like *wool* or *fur*, terms that dehumanized women and men of African descent. From the time of the inaugural Middle Passage abductions, Black Americans were denied and divorced from the respect, attention, care, and time to practice their ancient hair and beauty rituals. It is then—during the time of legalized chattel slavery in the Americas—that the stories of Black hair became fixated in trauma, humiliation, ignorance, and misuse. *Trauma, Tresses & Truth* seeks to unseat and decolonize our natural hair stories, redirecting entire eras of grief into rediscovery, rebirth, and reclamation of our ability to choose our hair stories.

Afiya M. Mbilishaka, PhD
Clinical Psychologist and Hairstylist
Founder and CEO of PsychoHairapy LLC
March 14, 2022

---

* Ayana D. Byrd and Lori L. Tharps, *Hair Story: Untangling the Roots of Black Hair in America*, 2nd ed. (New York: St. Martin's Griffin, 2014).

PREFACE

I OWE THE IDEA for this book to audience members at the 2020 AWP Conference in San Antonio. After the conclusion of my panel of five authors, with each of us reading an essay excerpt concerning our experiences wearing natural hair, several attendees asked me where they could purchase the associated book. (Kim Coleman Foote, one of the contributors in this book, was the first one to inquire about buying the then-nonexistent anthology.) Although at first I wasn't convinced that my panel idea had legs as a book, the 2020 summer of racial reckoning following the Breonna Taylor and George Floyd assassinations changed my mind. I spent much of that summer being enraged, my days fraught with unhealthy, unrelieved gavel-to-gavel fury that compromised my everyday functioning. I found it difficult, sometimes impossible, to operate in a normal manner. The coronavirus lockdown exacerbated the situation, and eventually protests here in San Francisco led to a curfew as well. In the midst of feeling impotent, I realized that my pen was the one weapon I could wield. So in July 2020, when national demonstrations approached an acute zenith—and as the president urged white supremacists to "stand back and stand by"—I began writing the *Trauma, Tresses & Truth* book proposal. The writing process was a sound way for me to channel my fury and sense of futility. Writing also enabled me to surface the erasure of Black and Black Latina women and girls in the police-reform and Black Lives Matter movements. Note how women's injustices have been largely subordinated to those of men in those movements. Beyond Breonna, beyond Sandra, there's also Korryn Gaines, Tanisha Anderson, Michelle Cusseaux, India Kager, and so many others who seldom draw the same journalistic attention as Tamir Rice, Eric Garner, Alton Sterling, Michael Brown, or Philando Castile.[1] As a topic at the intersection of racial injustice and Black feminism, a book on natural hair seemed potent, timely, and curative.

While organizations around the nation hurried to establish equity seminars and plaster solidarity platitudes on their websites, I wrapped up my book proposal. In August I began shopping it to publishers, and by the end of October I'd received offers from five different presses. However, even after signing the book deal with Chicago Review Press, I was *still* feeling angry, nearly every day. The August 2021 Trauma, Tresses & Truth: A Virtual Natural Hair Conference emerged as my conception of a healthy, correlative solution. Several of this book's contributors served as panelists, as did authors, artists, and speakers from around the country and Canada. Registrants attended from nine US states, Brazil, Canada, and Kenya.

In 2019 Los Angeles Board of Supervisors member Holly Mitchell, a Democratic state senator at the time, introduced SB 188, the CROWN Act. California's State Assembly passed it on a unanimous vote, and Governor Gavin Newsom signed the bill into law on July 3, 2020, a date now known as National CROWN Day. This bill made California the first state to officially prohibit race-based hair discrimination and extend protection to natural hairstyles in work and educational environments. The bill, in part, states, "Workplace dress code and grooming policies that prohibit natural hair, including afros, braids, twists, and locks, have a disparate impact on black individuals as these policies are more likely to deter black applicants and burden or punish black employees than any other group."

New York City Human Rights Commissioner and Chair Carmelyn P. Malalis pulled no punches in expressing the same sentiment:

> Policies that limit the ability to wear natural hair, or hairstyles associated with Black people, aren't about "neatness" or "professionalism"; they are about limiting the way Black people move through workplaces, public spaces and other settings.[2]

New York became the second state to pass anti-hair-bias legislation.

I hope that in 2021 you had an opportunity to celebrate the second National CROWN Day. The hashtags #PassTheCrown and #TheCrownAct were trending in the days leading up to July 3. The day of events kicked off with an online workout routine, a mural reveal,[3] and a live-streamed awards ceremony honoring trailblazing Black women in a range of industries, including business, entertainment, and community. Guests included *Ebony* magazine CEO Michele

Thornton Ghee; Dr. Kizzmekia S. Corbett, immunologist and lead who worked on the COVID-19 vaccine; and women's basketball player Joy Holmes-Harris.

Throughout this book, I capitalize *African American*, *Afro Latina*, and *Black*. And although the *New York Times* says it does not regard its "stylebook as an instrument of activism," in this book, I'm treating these terms in precisely that way: as a form of cultural assertiveness and activism.[4] I do not capitalize *white* in this volume, as a form of protest against white-supremacist websites and publications that do capitalize that word and because Afro Latina and African Americans have been lowercased, hyphenated, or expunged for far too long.

In 2022 we celebrated the third National CROWN Day and the second official Juneteenth federal holiday. My wish is that you will share this volume with your colleagues, students, family, and friends as we lean in to whatever vicissitudes and triumphs the coming year holds for us.

For further discussion about the debate concerning *Black* versus *black* in writing, see the following:

Appiah, Kwame Anthony. "The Case for Capitalizing the *B* in Black." *Atlantic*, June 2, 2021. https://www.theatlantic.com/ideas/archive/2020/06/time-to-capitalize -blackand-white/613159.

Perlman, Merrill. "Black and White: Why Capitalization Matters." *Columbia Journalism Review*, June 23, 2015. https://www.cjr.org/analysis/language_corner_1.php.

Tharps, Lori L. "The Case for Black with a Capital B." *New York Times*, November 18, 2014. https://www.nytimes.com/2014/11/19/opinion/the-case-for-black-with -a-capital-b.html%20[https://perma.cc/V8G7-DUE.

Wong, Brittany. "Here's Why It's a Big Deal to Capitalize the Word 'Black.'" *HuffPost*, September 3, 2020. https://www.huffpost.com/entry/why-capitalize-word-black_l _5f342ca1c5b6960c066faea5.

Works Cited and Notes

1. I owe a debt to the African American Policy Forum's 2020 and 2021 Critical Race Theory Summer School for making me aware of the #SayHerName campaign. Learn more at https://www.aapf.org/sayhername.

2. Melkorka Licea, "After Years of Discrimination, Women Embrace Right to Natural Hair," *New York Post*, July 8, 2019, https://nypost.com/2019/07/08/after-years-of -discrimination-women-embrace-right-to-natural-hair.

3. See Candice Taylor's mural at https://twitter.com/lexjuareztv/status/1413605333 453451273/photo/1.
4. Nancy Coleman, "Why We're Capitalizing Black," *New York Times*, July 5, 2020, https://www.nytimes.com/2020/07/05/insider/capitalized-black.html.

ACKNOWLEDGMENTS

THIS BOOK WOULD not have been possible without guidance, assistance, and encouragement from so many of my colleagues, partners, and friends. Some have been instrumental in shaping my approach to this project, while others shared their ideas, time, and generosity of spirit.

I first want to thank my Father God for giving me the fortitude to persevere with this project in the face of numerous challenges, including ridicule from several white men who left sarcastic remarks on my social media accounts about a topic they viewed as imprudent and comical. I thank my contributors for their perseverance with the project from conception to realization and for their attendance at multiple strategy and planning meetings. I express my appreciation for their moral support and encouragement. I want to thank the authors, speakers, and panelists who contributed to the larger Trauma, Tresses & Truth project, specifically to the inaugural August 2021 virtual conference. I thank the artist Dubelyoo for designing such an arresting book cover, one that diverged from and significantly improved upon my original cover concept.

I extend a special thanks to Sal Steiner, the artist who has contributed the intricate natural-hair sketches throughout the book. I discovered Sal's powerful *Headscapes* series in early 2020 and fell in love with the almost tactile attributes of his drawings. Once I decided to embark on this book, I contacted him to express my interest in hiring him to contribute sketches. Only at that time—and to my great surprise—did I learn that Sal was Caucasian. I'll admit that, as I contemplated the implications of hiring him, his race gave me pause. But I loved his work so much that I moved forward with commissioning his sketches. I thank him for his courage and boldness for not backing away from a potentially controversial project.

For bolstering me throughout this process and helping me believe this was an idea both timely and meritorious, for writing support letters, and for reviewing grant-application drafts, I thank Dr. Barbara B. Adams, Christopher D. Cook, Taryn Edwards, Constance Hale, Miah Jeffra, Laird Harrison, Susan Ito, Saila Kariat, Brenda Knight, Amy Kweskin, Mary Ladd, Michael Larsen, Roberto Lovato, Eileen Malone, Tara L. Masih, Kathleen McClung, Alvenson Ikemba Moore, Caroline Paul, Bridget "BQ" Quinn, Shizue Seigel, Jesus Sierra, Krista Smith, Allison Snopek, Truong Tran, Preeti Vangani, Stephanie Wildman, Dr. September Williams, Ellen Woods, and, most especially, my beloved younger sister, Veronica Wanzer.

Thank you to those organizations that have partnered with this project since its 2019 inception, supporting project-related panels and events or providing administrative assistance and practical insight: Association of Writers & Writing Programs, the Authors Guild, Bayview Opera House, Intersection for the Arts, Museum of the African Diaspora, National Writers Union, Popular Culture Association, and the African American Center of the San Francisco Public Library. I'd like to give a special shout-out to Shuffle Collective, in whose inaugural literary cohort I gained the fortitude, fuel, and encouragement to sow and grow my book proposal. The collective's members have served as both thought partners and cheerleaders. Tess Bliven and Anuj Nijhawan have founded a wonderful, one-of-a-kind organization in support of artists and culture bearers.

I want to thank my senior editor, Kara Rota, for seeing the possibilities in my Trauma, Tresses & Truth concept, for agreeing to take on a rather controversial topic, and for nurturing the writing and publishing process.

I owe a debt of gratitude to the funding agencies, application reviewers, and program officers who believed in this project enough to support it with grant and fellowship dollars: California Humanities, a National Endowment for the Humanities partner; Center for Cultural Innovation; San Francisco Arts Commission; and Yerba Buena Center for the Arts. Collectively, these organizations' funding laid the formative ground for my writing, production, and research. Thank you!

INTRODUCTION

AFRO LATINA AND AFRICAN AMERICAN women's natural hair—braids, Afros, dreadlocks, and other styles—has always been political and, today, remains persecuted. We have always known that our natural hair resides on the lower end of mainstream society's beauty-assessment scale. We recognize that the policing of our hair is part of a system of racial apartheid. We realize that various hegemonic institutional policies have been weaponized against our hair. White heteropatriarchy gets systematized while we get erased.

The essays in this collection turn a lens on how, why, and the myriad ways in which the Black body remains misread and misunderstood. Particularly relevant during this time of emboldened white supremacy, racism, and provocative othering, this work explores how writing about one of the still-remaining systemic biases in schools, academia, and corporate America might lead to greater understanding and respect.

This book focuses on women, but we all remember Andrew Johnson, the high school wrestler who had to cut his dreadlocks or else forfeit an opportunity to win not only the match but also a division title. The referee, Alan Maloney, said Drew's hair (Andrew's nickname) was "unnatural" and had to be rectified in a ninety-second time-out. If you haven't seen the video, do so. Regardless of who you are, you will feel much humiliation and embarrassment for this young man, who has been damaged by this incident. Days afterward, these descriptions appeared in the online magazine the *Undefeated* (now called *Andscape*): "Since that awful day in December when a referee had forced the sixteen-year-old wrestler to either cut his dreadlocks or forfeit his match, he felt as if the world was constantly watching him, especially in his small New Jersey town. Watching and whispering about things beyond his control." A little later in the article we read this heartbreaking account:

But now Drew had a new problem. One night, he had grabbed a pair of scissors from the kitchen and hacked at what remained of his dreads, then asked his little sister to finish the job. Drew loved his hair but was tired of it causing so much trouble. Tired of being treated differently and made into something he was not. Tired of looking in the mirror and seeing the referee, Alan Maloney, looking back.

Read the entirety of senior writer Jesse Washington's article in the September 18, 2019, issue of the *Undefeated*, an online newsletter exploring the intersections of race, sports, and culture.[1]

In another instance, Catastrophe Management Solutions (CMS) in Mobile, Alabama, made an offer for a customer-service position to Chastity Jones. As she neared the end of the interviewing process, she learned of an attendant proviso: she must cut off her dreadlocks. When Jones refused to do so, CMS rescinded her employment offer. The white HR manager had told Jones that dreads tended to get messy, although: "I'm not saying that yours are, but . . . you know." The Equal Employment Opportunity Commission helped represent Jones at the Eleventh Circuit Court of Appeals. The judge dismissed the case because he ruled that, unlike skin color, hair was a "mutable characteristic." If Jones wanted the job, all she had to do was comply with the company's grooming policy which, CMS contended, wouldn't have allowed white employees to wear dreadlocks either. CMS's grooming policy said, "All personnel are expected to be dressed and groomed in a manner that projects a professional and businesslike image while adhering to company and industry standards and/or guidelines. . . . Hairstyles should reflect a business/professional image. No excessive hairstyles or unusual colors are acceptable."[2]

I write this introduction during a pandemic-delayed Olympic year, when the 2020 Games occurred in summer 2021. As an avid sports fan, particularly of gymnastics, track and field, and all the aquatic events, I paid particular attention to the pre-Games Olympic swim-cap fiasco. In early July 2021, right around the celebration of the second National CROWN Day,[3] the International Swimming Federation (a.k.a. FINA) banned a swimming cap, called the Soul Cap, that two Black British men invented in 2017. The men, Toks Ahmed-Salawudeen and Michael Chapman, were taking a swim class when it occurred to them that swimmers of African descent might benefit from a cap designed with extra room at the top to accommodate Afros, braids, dreads, knots, twists, and 4C hair.* They wanted to make their cap available to swimmers at the 2020 Summer Olympics. When any vendor wants to introduce clothing or equipment for an Olympic Games, it must file an application with the particular sport's National Governing Body. In this instance, that body was FINA, which denied the application. I located the specific citation that FINA used to back its denial, in its Requirements for Swimwear Approval text. Section 4.3.1, Swim Cap Design, states, "The swim cap shape shall follow the natural form of the head." FINA determined that the Soul Cap does not conform with this mandate.

The funny thing about the cap contention is that the larger Soul Cap could, potentially, amount to a competitive *dis*advantage, owing to its size and less-streamlined configuration. In any event, FINA became the subject of voluminous media backlash, as evidenced by headlines such as these:

- **ABC News:** NATURAL HAIR SWIM CAP REJECTION SPARKS CONVERSATION ON CODED BIAS, GATEKEEPING, AND REPRESENTATION
- **Yahoo:** THE BAN ON SWIMMING CAPS FOR BLACK WOMEN IS JUST ONE EXAMPLE OF RACISM AT THE OLYMPICS
- *Today Show*: OLYMPICS BANS SWIM CAPS PREFERRED BY BLACK ATHLETES WITH NATURAL HAIR
- The *Los Angeles Times*: THE OLYMPICS ARE POLITICAL, INCLUDING RULES ON SWIM CAPS
- Even *Vogue* got in on the argument with: WHY THE RULING AGAINST SWIM CAPS FOR AFRO HAIR AT THE OLYMPICS IS A STEP BACKWARD FOR SPORTS

This book illuminates two predicaments: first, the absurdity of trying to enforce white hair-care standards on Black women; and second, the muted but invasive means by which society's institutions and inherent structures shame our hair from infancy through adulthood.

Before readers delve into the essays, acquiring some sense of history about The CROWN Act will help. In 2019 then senator Holly J. Mitchell of California drafted and sponsored antibias legislation called the CROWN Act, also known as SB 188, wherein CROWN pulls double duty as another word for

---

* This hair chart from Black Hair Information provides a great guide on hair types: https://blackhairinformation.com/general-articles/hair-type-chart-discover-hair-type.

our heads—also, perhaps, a nod to the queendom of our foremothers—and an acronym meaning Creating a Respectful and Open World for Natural Hair. (The acronym has since acquired an additional meaning: Creating a Respectful and Open World with No Racism). The fact that Mitchell felt the need to introduce such a bill reveals the longstanding hegemonic triumph of a dominant Eurocentric beauty ideology in America. On July 3, 2019, California became the first state in the nation to pass this antidiscrimination law. Since that time, nearly thirty other states and municipalities have introduced some variant of this bill. The crux of the bill's language is the provision that "ensure[s] protection against discrimination in the workplace and schools based on hairstyles, by prohibiting employers and schools from enforcing purportedly 'race-neutral' grooming policies that disproportionately impact persons of color."

The founding CROWN Coalition members that helped pass the CROWN Act in California are Dove, National Urban League, Color of Change, and Western Center on Law & Poverty. Dove is the soap and cosmetics company we all know. The National Urban League is a civil rights organization founded in 1910, with branches in thirty-seven states. If you've participated in any marches or demonstrations or signed online petitions, especially since 2016, you likely are familiar with Color of Change. It is an online organization that leads campaigns against injustice, prison expansion, criminalizing the poor, and white supremacy. The Western Center on Law & Poverty aims to ensure that low-income Californians receive equitable treatment in civil court, criminal court, and housing-protection matters. As of this writing, the CROWN Coalition has burgeoned to eighty organizations.

The CROWN Act is law in the following states, effective as of the listed dates:[4]

- California (July 3, 2019)
- New York (July 12, 2019)
- New Jersey (December 19, 2019)
- Virginia (March 3, 2020)
- Colorado (March 6, 2020)
- Washington (March 19, 2020)
- Maryland (May 8, 2020)
- Connecticut (March 4, 2021)
- New Mexico (April 5, 2021)

- Delaware (April 13, 2021)
- Nevada (April 19, 2021)
- Nebraska (May 5, 2021)
- Illinois (January 1, 2022)
- Oregon (January 1, 2022)
- Maine (April 20, 2022)
- Tennessee (May 27, 2022)

On March 18, 2022, the House of Representatives passed the CROWN Act at the federal level by a 235–189 vote. Attention now turns to the Senate, where Democratic New Jersey senator Cory Booker reintroduced a companion bill on March 27, 2022.

———————————

This book is divided into four sections, with a poem or hybrid piece opening each. Section I, "A Critical Lens," features essays that examine investigative, analytical angles while interweaving and highlighting the authors' personal stories. In "Toward Decolonizing Our Roots," I interlace personal vignettes with examinations of the manners in which natural-hair discrimination disproportionately affects, targets, and seeks to corral Black women in nearly every environment imaginable, including the armed forces. Regis Fox tells us about an appalling encounter—laden with an inordinate amount of hubris—with staff at her daughter's day-care center in "The Swiftness Black Women Know." Shatima Jones's "Black Hair Matters" recounts her semester teaching university courses in the midst of twin pandemics: the turbulent 2020 summer and COVID-19. She came to new terms with her hair during the pandemic lockdown. In "Natural's Not in It," Margalynne Armstrong chronicles her natural-hair calculus through the lens of a legal and academic career odyssey.

Section II, "The Pilgrimage," contains narratives charting crusades for, or excursions into, the liberation and Black joy of rocking our natural hair. In "Hair Politics: An Afro Puerto Rican Womyn's Untangled Narrative," Bárbara Abadía-Rexach shares aching sociocultural commentary from her vantage point as a dark-complexioned Puerto Rican woman: "I live as a Black Puerto Rican Womyn, and writing about my hair hurts." Early in her essay, Kim Coleman Foote reveals that, as a young girl, she learned that "Black was anything *but* beautiful." She tells how a life-changing college semester abroad in Ghana flipped the script for her in "Naturally: A Hair Journey to Africa and Beyond." In "Another Layer of Our Freedom," Lyndsey Ellis examines the many messages—both voiced and silent—she internalized about her hair from elementary school days and the consequences that reverberated downstream through those childhood years to adulthood. And Adrienne Oliver considers history, media advertisements, and the snare of social conventions that have induced Black women to engage in contortionist attempts to make their hair "fit in" in "'Fro Fatigue and Other 4C Woes."

In "Intimate Encounters," section III, the authors shepherd us into the core of family relationships, delineating the bonds, fissures, and unanswered questions that crystallize in direct consequence with the regard relatives hold for natural hair. MK Chavez situates us in the vivid sights and scents of the Mission, San Francisco's celebrated Chicano/Mexican American cultural district, in "Pelo Liso y Pelo Malo." She details her confusion, pain, and struggle as an Afro Latina daughter yearning for her father's acceptance. In "Self-Care and Sanctuary in Black Women's Salons," Sherry Johnson describes the childhood bonding and amity that developed—as they did for so many of us—with a mother (or for some of us, a grandmother, aunt, cousin, or older sister) during the course of getting her hair done. In many ways, her hair transitions along with her relationship with her mother, who experiences mental decline. Sulma Arzu-Brown's "My Locs, Her Locs" transmits as a measured contemplation of her elder daughter's decision to transition out of her locs. In "My Curls, My Crown," Priscilla Ferreira introduces us to her loving, supportive father who did her hair every morning before school, whose "gentle touch on my hair every morning was his way to disavow the abrading violence of the belief that my hair was ever unpleasant." Her story ends with a radical, emancipatory sacrifice that doubles as an offering.

The "Unshackled Chronicles," section IV, closes the essays with poignant chronicles of journeys from wresting our hair from majority-culture conformity to embracing it in its natural state as liberation, self-acceptance, and celebration. In "Power Struggle," Jasmine Hawkins probes the diminishing manners in which—gripped in the throes of fear, doubt, and unending quests for assimilation—"our mothers pressed out more than hair." Jewelle Gomez's triumphant narrative relates how she managed to countenance the shame, racism, and self-hatred that has descended through generations of Indigenous and Cape Verdean ancestors in "In the Kitchen." In "Beauty Is Pain: A Hairstory,"

Kelechi Ubozoh regales us with episodes from the days when she pined for a crest of Shirley Temple curls, to mother-daughter clashes with the abhorrent hot comb, to the manifold challenges she negotiated during her school years, eventually embracing the versatility and vivacity of her "comb-breaking Nigerian hair." In "Hair Chronicles of an Afro Puerto Rican," Dahlma Llanos-Figueroa details the destructive impact of long-ingrained lessons of inferiority and confronts both sorrow and rage when she experiences intrafamilial prejudice, warnings, and harsh judgments from the very people she expects to accept her as she is. When Black people foist Eurocentric beauty ideals on other Black people, whose position are they reinforcing? Finally, in "Turning the Lens Rightside Up," I explore the reasons why hair discrimination affects Black and Brown women in such incommensurate ways—and exacts such a searing toll for us—relative to men.

Afro Latina and African American women aren't the only people to suffer sustained hair discrimination. While blogging about this topic, I received emails and tweets from South Asian and biracial women. An American Jewish woman spoke to me about her burden of living with "Jewish hair," a construct with which I had been wholly unfamiliar. A Native American man explained how he had been turned down for and dismissed from jobs because he refused to cut his long hair, even though he wore it in a single neat braid down his back. As these employers' demands were at odds with his tribal values, he had difficulty finding employment in his field. A woman of Middle Eastern descent wondered whether I might broaden the scope of the book to include Persian and Arab people who, she informed me, also experience pressure regarding the grade of their hair. I also heard from Afro Asians and other multiracial people.

The book closes with a reader discussion guide and a resource guide. The discussion guide, geared for senior high school and university students, is based on a series of reflections that lend themselves to discussion issues or written assignments: "Personal Experiences," "Outside Readings," "Attending School or Work While Black," and "Dialectic Topics." The resource guide contains suggestions for additional reading, including a section for children's books, along with lists of natural-hair festivals and events; organizations; salons with particular expertise in natural hair care, treatment, and styling; a sampling of topical film titles; and a reference list for readers planning to make the leap and "go natural." These listings are more illustrative than comprehensive; I include them to demonstrate the breadth of resources that cater to the natural-hair community. I hope the guide will prompt you to unearth further resources in your local sphere or perhaps even galvanize you to start your own endeavor.

Finally, though this is a book about Black women's experiences, let's not forget our men. As I write this introduction in late 2021, California is facing the first test of its inaugural CROWN Act. Jeffrey Thornton of San Diego has filed a lawsuit against Encore Global, a company that was prepared to extend him a job offer *if* he cut his dreadlocks. Mr. Thornton wears short locs and said that a hiring manager told him that, in order to work in the San Diego office, he would have to cut his locs away from his ears and shoulders. What makes this case intriguing is that Thornton, an audiovisual technician, worked for four years for this very same company's Florida office—with no problems regarding his hair. Thornton has retained counsel and seeks both a company policy change and a formal apology. It remains to be seen how this example of discrimination litigation will resolve. Perhaps by the time this book is in your hands, The CROWN Act will have secured its first legal victory.

Lyzette Wanzer, MFA

For more information about the Trauma, Tresses & Truth project, see: Shuffle Collective. "Trauma, Tresses & Truth: Untangling Our Hair Through Personal Narrative." https://shuffle.do/projects/trauma-tresses-truth-untangling -our-hair-through-personal-narrative.

For more information about the related conference, see: Trauma, Tresses & Truth Conference. https://trauma-tresses-truth-untangling -our-hair-thro.heysummit.com.

Works Cited and Notes

1. Jesse Washington, "The Untold Story of Wrestler Andrew Johnson's Dreadlocks," *Andscape*, September 19, 2019, https://andscape.com/features/the-untold-story-of -wrestler-andrew-johnsons-dreadlocks/.
2. EEOC v. Catastrophe Management Solutions, NAACP Legal Defense and Educational Fund, November 18, 2016, https://www.naacpldf.org/case-issue/eeoc-v -catastrophe-management-solutions.

3. The CROWN Coalition has established July 3 as a holiday commemorating the inaugural signing of the nation's first CROWN Act legislation. In 2021 the coalition hosted the inaugural CROWN Awards.

4. This list was compiled in December 2021 and updated in March 2022. Note that Washington, DC, maintains that its Human Rights Act of 1977 already provides hair-discrimination protection, even extending to beards. District of Columbia councilmember Brianne Nadeau, who is white, introduced a DC CROWN Act in fall 2020, requesting that the specific phrase *protective hairstyles* be added to DC's Human Rights Act.

PART I

A CRITICAL LENS

THE ANCIENT

Iris Crawford

Photo by Oladimeji Odunsi on Unsplash

When entering a Black woman, you enter the ancient,
Ever see a Black woman in the sunlight?
She shines so radiantly that it's hard to tell whether she is reflecting
light or absorbing it.
The sun shines on Black women whose names we do not say enough.
Makeba of Ethiopia gives us her strength.
Nefertiti of Egypt gives us her beauty.

3

Nandi of South Africa gives us the ability of standing in our self-worth.
And Aminatu of the Sahara gives us our unwavering courage.

We carry their memories.
Mother Earth's bounty is in our hair.
Our veins reveal the journey of our foremothers.
All the little chocolate drops that come from our wombs
are nourished from our breasts.
The evolution of creation rests in our souls.
I am ancient.

TOWARD DECOLONIZING OUR ROOTS

Lyzette Wanzer, MFA

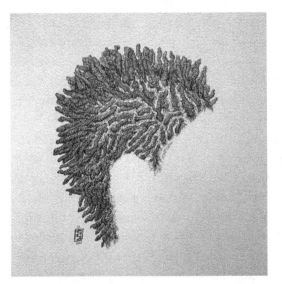

IT WAS JUST MY THIRD DAY ON THE JOB; I was still learning to use the fax machine, a newfangled contraption that everyone in the office viewed with diffident deference. My coworkers pined for the IBM Wheelwriter in the center of my desk; they all still used Selectric typewriters. I was a newly minted office manager in a Wall Street office, my first leadership role and "real" job after several years of temping as a girl Friday and desk clerk at various Manhattan firms. It seemed that all of New York City was of the opinion that liberal arts degrees weren't good for much else than answering phones, taking messages, and typing carbon copies. But this role provided a chance for me to shed that misconception and initiate a true career path.

Irene, who shared a large office with me, was my office assistant, a thin, young woman with long dark hair and bangs that covered her eyebrows. She cussed under her breath as she struggled to realign paper in the dot matrix printer. I could see blue veins in the translucent skin on her slim hands.

"You'll wind up having to do this a few times every day," she told me. "Rare is the day when this this thing doesn't jam."

I laughed and walked over to help. "The trick is to *press* the paper holes onto the base, not just align them," I said. I bent over the printer to demonstrate. "Put a finger on either side of the holes, press down, then slide your fingers down the margins. This won't stop jamming altogether, but it buys you a little more time before the paper comes off track."

The company was small, comprising eight employees. Coworkers had taken me out for lunch on my first day, minus one team member who was on vacation. I was told that the absent team member had a fifty-five-gallon aquarium in his office filled with guppies, angelfish, and mood lighting. As Irene and I were tinkering with the recalcitrant printer, he knocked on our door and walked in. A portly man in his late thirties with a shock of russet curls and sporting a bright white shirt and a polished silver watch, he came over to introduce himself with a nutcracking handshake. I returned to my desk and politely inquired about his vacation. We made small talk, then business-speak, back to small talk. Only so much to be said about the weather, the traffic, and the mayor. A column of silence rose between us. His gaze alighted on my head. "How did you get your hair like that?" He reached across my desk and ran all five fingers of his right hand through my shoulder-length braids.

I seized his arm mid-arc, gripped it just hard enough to signal my spirit and knocked it away with a fisted hand. I stared at him, letting a new, foul silence shroud us for several seconds. Three-quarters of letting a lance hit its target is timing. "If you want to touch my hair," I said, "you *ask* first. And when you *do* ask, I'll say no."

Shock and puzzlement leaped through his features. I read the question marks and a flash of apprehension in his eyes. He flushed several shades of red, pivoted, exited.

The 1980s. Braids and dreadlocks are prohibited in the workplace at: Atlanta Urban League, Chicago Regency Hyatt, downtown DC Marriott Hotel, Washington DC Metropolitan Police Department. In the US Army, African Americans could not wear braids until 2002.

"Do you wash those?" She, a fellow straphanger, blonde, on New York's uptown Lexington Avenue express. Although we didn't know one another, we waited in the same area of the subway platform each morning and often wound up riding together, exchanging nods and smiles.

"Wash what?"

"Your braids."

I wrinkled my brow and tilted my head, affecting a perplexed posture. I was wearing dreadlocks at the time. "These aren't braids."

"Yeah, they are."

"No, they're not."

"What do *you* call them?"

"Dreads."

"Dreads?"

"As in dreadlocks."

"Do you wash them?"

"Of course I wash them. It's my hair. You wash yours, don't you?"

"I didn't know you were Rasta."

"I didn't either. Thanks for enlightening me."

For over four hundred years, Black women's hair has been the target of erasure efforts, demarginalizing us both as African Americans and as women. The various institutional modalities of policing Black women's (and men's as well) hair are a form of racist politics. Despite structural denials to the contrary, our natural hair remains a heretical war zone. Policing of both Black bodies and our natural hair is a form of structural oppression. This is not such a surprising revelation when you consider that law is, itself, a form and site of politics.

In her 1990 essay "Is Your Hair Still Political?" Audre Lorde explains how an immigration officer's objections to her dreadlocks nearly cost her a vacation in the British Virgin Islands. Natural hair, whether in the form of braids, Afros, dreadlocks, or other natural styles, has always been political. Unfortunately, despite our being well into the twenty-first century, the response to Lorde's question is a most disheartening, definitive Yes. Black women's natural hair remains political and persecuted. Our current twin pandemics of COVID-19 and racism have surfaced, even more, the precarity of Black lives. Writing about the many disquieting, execrable, and prejudiced experiences vis-à-vis Black women's hair illuminates two conundrums: the absurdity of trying to enforce white hair-care standards on African American women and the muted but invasive means by which society shames our natural hair from infancy through adulthood.

———————

I'm in my high school's infirmary. My math teacher dispatched me there in the middle of class when she noticed sweat beads jeweling my face. I sit in a small room, marveling that though I'm in a clinic, the room is devoid of any semblance of care or comfort. The chair's metal legs are cold, a gadget in one corner beeps, an array of menacing devices hang along the far wall, and a stench of illness and caustic cleansers rinses over me. Outdoors, the temperature is in the seventies, but in here, I'm wearing two sweaters and shivering. My throat is blazing. My skin is clammy. I'm sporting a Jheri curl but can't even feel the juicy locs lapping my forehead. The nurse standing over me in unrelieved white, including wavy white hair and a crisp nurse's hat, asks me to describe my symptoms. I tell her my head feels like a melting candle with a low wick. Shadows of bafflement and astonishment scud across her face. The school, predominately white and private, has a bucolic campus, a dress code, a swimming pool, no graffiti, and a two-hour entrance exam. I've seen that fazed look on faculty faces—instructors were faculty here, not merely teachers—directed at me numerous times in the school's spartan classrooms. I know what the look means, and I'd normally take a little wicked pleasure in their shock at my precise, creative diction, but I'm too sick to care. The nurse inserts a thermometer under my tongue and stands beside my chair as we wait. All I want to do is slide into one of the infirmary beds and go to sleep. I feel a sudden pressure in the center of my scalp, a series of dabs. I tilt my head up to see the nurse leaning over my hair with an expression of wonder, her mouth slightly ajar, her eyebrows arched. I slide down in the chair to ease away from her pawing. She laughs warmly and says, "I just *had* to touch it!" We're in New York, but a southern accent coats her syllables. She withdraws the thermometer and declares I have a fever of 101. I tell her I want to call my mom and go home. I want to tell my mom I need to return to public school.

First-generation American Jheri Redding, a Caucasian man who rose to pioneering prominence in the cosmetics industry in the mid-1980s, first concocted the brew that would become the germ and mainstay of the Jheri curl style. He was a cofounder of Redken, a popular shampoo brand that still exists today. So great was his impact on the beauty industry that Redding's nickname was "the Godfather of Hair," and he eventually earned induction into two esteemed cosmetology associations' halls of fame: the North American Hairstyling Hall of Leaders and the National Cosmetology Foundation. His salon was equal parts chemistry lab, kitchen, and school. He introduced the idea that hair was a protein, and created the first batch of pH shampoos, creme rinses, and conditioners. He authored a book titled *The Anatomy of a Permanent Wave*.[1]

Black entrepreneur Comer Cottrell took Redding's perm curl product and fine-tuned the recipe and application so that it could accommodate African American hair. In 1979 he debuted his Curly Kit. This package, consisting of curl activator and moisturizers, became a hit with Black Americans. The kit contained an affordable way for them to maintain a style reminiscent of white folks' curls, in their own homes, without expensive marathon salon visits. Before long, other beauty brands created copycat kits in bright-hued boxes that lined the shelves of hair and cosmetics aisles in drug and grocery stores. My family swore by Soft Sheen's Care Free Curl kit. The number of male Black entertainers sporting the style made the Jheri curl all the more attractive and trendy: Eazy-E, Ice Cube, Michael Jackson, Lionel Richie, and Edmund Sylvers.

The Jheri curl, however fashionable and time-saving, bore with it a host of challenges. The fundamental rule for keeping the permanent curls in was to keep the hair moist around the clock. For me, this meant sleeping with a plastic cap on my hair every night and saturating the curls every morning with a trifecta of sour-smelling chemicals, each in a different bottle. My curls were simple to conserve; exhibited a contemporary, mainstream appearance; and bounced with every step I took. But I had to be hypervigilant about where I laid my head.

There were the sleepover incidents when my plastic cap slipped off during the night, leaving a slick, slippery residue on my hosts' pillowcases. There were the blind dates I went on when men would want to run their hands through my hair but dared not. There was the mortifying modern-dance-class episode in college, during which my instructor slipped and fell, face-down, on a circular greasy patch my head had left on the studio floor after our warm-up session. She managed to get up and lead a series of exercises, but after the first set, she turned to me and asked me to "clean up your hair stuff from the floor" so that it wouldn't endanger other students as the class progressed. The other students stared at me, the only Black student in the studio, as I headed to the bathroom for a fistful of paper towels. There are countless other occurrences that are so smarting to recall, the eye of my memory averts itself. Despite the eggshell-walking I had to do during my Jheri-curl days, I was willing to withstand the ignominy and inconvenience because my hair didn't look or behave like African American hair. It resembled and comported itself, by and large (as long as you didn't touch it), like everybody else's.

I can't remember her name; I can't remember the year. I recall she was in Boston, and I know it was the 1990s. She tended the front desk of a tony hotel, the kind of place with pearly shampoo bottles in the bathroom, sumptuous, pressed robes on the door hook, pillowed gold-foil Godiva squares. She sported a new, intricate pattern of braids. Guests traced her glimmering plaits with their eyes; they complimented her.

Management did not.

Management was alarmed.

Management, in fact, demanded that she remove the braids and return to her perm, a style befitting a post at her lacquered mahogany station.

Ms. Boston was fire. She left her braids *in*. Dismissal followed. She sued under Title VII. I can't remember her name, and she wouldn't know mine, but the night her story aired, I began growing out my relaxer. Having withstood a combined thirty years of the terrorizing hot comb, the interminable relaxer salon appointment, and the succulent Jheri curl era, I chose Senegalese Casamance braids. I stood in solidarity with Ms. Boston, yoking the miles, shoulder to shoulder, sister to sister.

Race men and women may easily have straight, soft, long hair by simply applying Plough's Hair Dressing and in a short time all your kinky, snarly, ugly, curly hair becomes soft, silky, smooth, straight, long and easily handled, brushed, or combed.

Ad in the *New York Age*, May 3, 1919[2]

From grammar and high schools to corporate boardrooms and military squadrons, Black and Afro Latina natural hair continues to confound, transfix, and enrage members of white American society. Why, in 2023, is this still the case? Why have we not moved beyond that perennial racist emblem? And why are women so disproportionately affected? Why does our hair become most palatable when it capitulates—and has been subjugated—to resemble Caucasian traits as closely as possible? Who in our society gets to author the prevailing constitution of professional appearance? How do we, as Black women (and men as well) encourage course correction and alter the prism through which our hair is interrogated? *Which* differences make a difference? And when?

A 2016 Perception Institute survey[3] of Black and white women found that although the majority of both Black and white respondents exhibited bias against natural hair, white women "showed explicit bias" against women who wear natural hairstyles, while one in five Black women "feel social pressure to straighten their hair for work—twice as many as White women." One concept to bear in mind when considering the aforementioned questions I posed is this: hierarchies marked by race are ideologically inflected ways of enforcing the majority culture's status quo.

———

The United States Air Force has a regulation, AFI36-2903 DRESS AND PERSONAL APPEARANCE OF AIR FORCE PERSONNEL, which in part, discriminates against African-American women serving in the Air Force. The code was recently updated to include a ban on ... "dreadlocks." Female personnel with neat, clean, professional well-kept hair are being forced to choose between cutting their hair and treating it with chemicals to conform to this regulation. ... This leaves women with hair that is in no means a distraction or a detriment to their duties, subject to disciplinary action.
—Letter to representatives on **Going Natural** website[4]

My stylist, the soothsayer. Sugarcoater not. She pulled no punches. Warned me outright about the beginner phase, the in-between phase, the neither-here-nor-there phase. The need for patience. She ushered me in one January, and we began. She shared stories about schisms among stylists who wear natural hair and those wearing weaves and perms. Within the natural collective, additional rifts cracked along client lines: if the stylist serviced natural clients but wore a straightened style herself, she was a preachy poser whose hands were out of synch.

It's essential to realize that white American society hasn't had to live as racialized beings, making it difficult for that sector to acknowledge race as an inherent part of systems. Mainstream American society considers whiteness to be the typified barometer. The Caucasian standard is, implicitly, the baseline against which all other standards are measured. And this is precisely the type of metric that problematizes our natural hair.

In *Slavery and Social Death*, Harvard sociologist Orlando Patterson says, "Hair type rapidly became the real symbolic badge of slavery, although like many powerful symbols, it was disguised, in this case by the linguistic device of using the term 'black,' which nominally threw the emphasis to color. No one who has grown up in a multiracial society, however, is unaware of the fact that hair difference is what carries the real symbolic potency."[5] Sakilé Camara would recapitulate his perspective nearly thirty years later: "Hair, like skin color, is a social marker that distinguishes Blacks from others and has essentially functioned as a way to position some outside the sanctified realm of beauty and acceptance since slavery."[6] And the language in California's CROWN Act concretized both Patterson's and Camara's sentiments: "In a society in which hair has historically been one of many determining factors of a person's race, and whether they were a second-class citizen, hair today remains a proxy for race. Therefore, hair discrimination targeting hairstyles associated with race is racial discrimination."

My stylist smiled. I couldn't quite cannonball, so I dipped a toe in: braids out, spartan crop of Nubian twists in. Strangers on streets and in trains, in cafés and on elevators, commented.

"I see you're just getting started."

"That'll take forever. Did you know you can get instant ones?"

There are many paths to dreadlocks, including the immediacy of instant techniques. I wanted not just the style, but the journey. The quest and the emancipatory process, however fraught with angst it might be. Shortcut methods would exclude any trial that might accompany my odyssey. I needed the complete compass. In electing this organic pilgrimage, I was embracing, with abrasive candor, my need to confront the web of supervision and surveillance Black women's hair endured on a daily basis, courtesy of racial politics and its concomitant hierarchical maintenance structures. I was seeking to repel rules and standards that implied that our hair—*my* hair—bore an innate legal inferiority. I was brandishing stereotype threat,[7] daring someone to call me out on it. I was flaunting hair alteration as a cultural script, to borrow Nina Ellis-Hervey's locution.[8] In short, I was acknowledging my hair as a vector of power.

Rastafarians and others with dreadlocks made eye contact with me, nodded, smiled, sometimes spoke in bookstores, post offices, theaters, shops, trains, festivals, restaurants, libraries, galleries, parks, airports, clubs, and at Kinko's. Assumptions spurred their spontaneity. My political, philosophical, spiritual stance? They never asked. They thought they knew.

> Dreadlocks (n.): from dread + locks. The style is said to be based on that of East African warriors. So called from the dread they presumably aroused in beholders . . . dread also has a sense of "fear of the Lord."
> —**Online Etymology Dictionary**[9]

———————————

Though I'd worn various braided styles and TWAs ever since the time of the Boston hotel affair, I've worn deadlocks for the past eight years. One month ago, as I was walking my dog in my San Francisco neighborhood, I passed a white man draped in scruffy loose garments. His eyes followed me as I walked past him. When I reached the middle of the block, he called out, "I like your snakes! They're really pretty!"

Since only I, he, and my dog were on the block at the moment, I knew he was addressing me. I ignored him. My dog stopped to do his business. As I scooped it up in a doggie bag and walked on, the man called out again in rapid-fire speech, to my retreating back: "Your snakes. I really like them! They're so neat. I like the color."

I felt the involuntary dip in the center of my tongue that perennially preceded an obscenity-laced remark issuing from my mouth. By the grace of God, I checked my spleen. I didn't acknowledge the man. I continued strolling with my dog, no slower and no faster than before, and turned the corner.

———————

In 2009 Luke Visconti's Ask the White Guy column on DiversityInc (a company of which Visconti is both founder and CEO) featured a topic called "Do Blacks Need to Relax Their Hair to Get Promoted?" As recently as 2019, the comments section was still active. A few gems drew my attention:

> Having struggled with the decision to go natural for over 5 years, I took the leap, the comments, and the questions as I continued to climb the corporate ladder.

> As a woman of color who wore her hair in a short afro for many years, I decided to don a new hairstyle which was more in line with mainstream society. . . . One M.D. went as far as to say that now I truly looked professional and was much prettier than he originally thought I was.

> For my next job, I straightened my hair for the interview. I'd already interviewed with many firms with my natural hair pulled back or in braids and guess what happened! Yeah, the first time I straightened my hair was the first time I got a job offer.

Another commenter responded to the above with this:

> You should have stuck it out. I think after awhile they would have got used to it.

And the most scintillating observation of the bunch:

My hair doesn't do my job, *I* do.

If you are an optimist—a staunch one—it's quite likely that you feel the Black hair politics of earlier decades are passé, even gauche. After all, we are well into the twenty-first century and, with a raceless Gen Y blooming, we're all grown up. Structural inequities continue to exist, of course, alongside educational disparities and myriad other unresolved race complexities. But what happened to Ms. Boston in the early 1990s wouldn't happen today, right?

It certainly *shouldn't* happen today.

But we know that it does. While Ms. Boston had the ability to act on the courage of her convictions, not everyone does. Many women cannot afford to contest the status quo for fear of losing their jobs or losing opportunities to advance at their jobs. Women may desire to "go natural," but they must consider a breadth of plausible consequences before they can do so. How will changing their hair impact their income stream? Upward mobility? The ability to be seen, heard, and respected in meeting rooms? This perception assessment concerning our hair is perversely preponderant for African American and Afro Latina women. How many women of other races must perform this tightrope calculus before deciding whether to sport a new hairdo in the workplace? Tina Opie and Katherine Phillips make this astute observation with regard to these laden decisions:

> Afrocentric hair makes race salient (Maddox 2014) which may trigger negative stereotypes of Blacks. In turn Blacks may engage in social identity–based impression management strategies (i.e., deemphasize social identity traits that signal group membership) to manage the impact of these negative stereotypes on others' perceptions of their competence and character (Roberts 2005). Concerns about professional image construction may lead Black women to conform to Eurocentric appearance standards and suppress identity traits.[10]

United States District Court, S. D. New York.
Renee ROGERS, et al., Plaintiff, v. AMERICAN AIRLINES, INC.,
R. L. Crandall, President of American Airlines, and Robert Zurlo,
in his capacity as Manager, Defendants.
Plaintiff is a black woman who seeks . . . damages, injunctive, and
declaratory relief against enforcement of an American Airlines grooming policy . . . that prohibits employees . . . from wearing an all-natural
hairstyle.[11]

During this case, the court—incredibly—discussed how Rogers could retain her
job by covering her braids with a wig to comply with the airline's grooming
policy. She filed a challenging action. Rogers worked as an airport operations
agent, which involved heavy involvement with customers. The court's decision
illustrates one example of how often law drives inequality through margin-
alization of our identity traits. This despite, way back in 1896, the *Plessy v.
Ferguson* case containing language that, on its surface, appears to be concerned
with protecting minorities from hostile legislation: "[The government] shall
not permit the seeds of race hate to be planted under the sanction of law."[12]
But whom is this language fooling, really? We know very well that our bodies,
including our hair, are not cloaked in the same equal legal and civil protections
that heteronormative bodies enjoy.

———————

In March of 2013 *HuffPost*'s Black Voice column ran the article BLACK WOMEN
WORRY THAT THEIR NATURAL HAIR COULD AFFECT JOB EMPLOYMENT OR
RETENTION.[13] During that same year, Georgia State University hosted a sym-
posium titled "Black Women, Their Hair and the Work Place—A Dialogue."
Panelists included Natasha Daniels, a legislative analyst for the City of Atlanta;
James M. Bailey, CEO for Operation HOPE's Atlanta market; Pam Beckerman,
human relations vice president for the Metro Atlanta Chamber of Commerce;
and Donnita Raglin, leadership and professional development director at Clark
Atlanta University. Despite the fact that these conversations are happening
in more open, navigable spheres, the hair politics have moderated little. If
you are an optimist, your bullish suppositions splintered on March 31, 2014,
courtesy of the US Army.

Without regard for whether natural styles truly interfere with military head-gear or present an unkempt, unprofessional appearance, the army uncorked a bale of directives with regard to hairstyles. The regulation, known officially as AR 670-1, earmarked all-natural African American female coifs with imperial measures:

> The Army . . . issued new appearance standards, which included bans on most twists, dreadlocks and large cornrows, all styles used predominantly by African-American women with natural hairstyles. More than 11,000 people have signed a White House petition asking President Barack Obama, the commander in chief, to have the military review the regulations to allow for "neat and maintained natural hairstyles." . . . The changes and several other Army appearance modifications were first published . . . in the *Army Times*.[14]

Sergeant Jasmine Jacobs—in 2014 a member of the Georgia Army National Guard—is the woman who began this petition. At the time, she was part of the 31 percent of Black women in the army. The *Washington Post*, in its April 3, 2014, She the People: Changing the Conversation column, stated that "the petition states that . . . '[t]hese new changes are racially biased and the lack of regard for ethnic hair is apparent.'"[15] Subsequently, Sergeant Jacobs did interviews with National Public Radio (NPR), MSNBC, *Time*, and *USA Today*. In the April 18, 2014, issue of the *Chicago Sun-Times*, in an article titled CONGRESSWOMEN UPBRAID ARMY, SAY HAIRSTYLE RULES ARE UNFAIR, Sergeant Jacobs said, "White females can wear their hair as it naturally is. We want to be able to wear our hair professionally as it naturally is, the way other females are able to wear their natural hair."[16] In support of her, sixteen women of the Congressional Black Caucus sent a joint letter to Secretary of Defense Charles Hagel.

Sometimes, you let the hair do the talking.
—**James Brown**

I'm at a 2019 Thanksgiving potluck dinner at a friend's house, with nearly twenty people in attendance. I've brought homemade apricot cream cheese cookies and a bottle of Moscato d'Asti. Other than the host's housekeeper, I am the only Black person there. The housekeeper, Isla, is not relegated to a subservient role; rather, she joins us in the parlor for hors d'oeuvres and chatter in between checking on the ham, fish, and fifteen-pound turkey in the home's sumptuous kitchen. Isla's skin is the color of sorrel, and she sports a crown of tapered natural spirals, but her head is shaved down to stubble on both sides above her ears. Her accent conjures up honeyed memories of ginger beer and *ponche crema*, drinks that my mother's Trinidadian friend gifted my family during my childhood. When a lull opens in the conversation, Isla smiles and says to me, "I love your dreads. They're beautiful."

I return her smile and say, "Thank you." Though I'm wearing a brown beret on my head to complement my brown and gold outfit, my hair hangs loosely about my shoulders.

All the guests turn to look at me, nodding and murmuring their admiration. Isla asks me, "But that's not your hair, is it? Where did you get the extensions?"

The smile recedes from my face like a retreating ocean wave. "These aren't extensions," I say. "It's my hair."

"That's your real hair?" Isla asks. Her eyebrows arch on the question.

"Yes, it's mine," I reply.

Isla nods, appearing surprised and impressed. The lull returns.

"When I first started, they were tiny two-strand twists," I add, feeling compelled to expound. "I've been growing these out for nearly five years."

"They're gorgeous," one of the men says, reaching for a small container of ceviche. "I wish I could wear dreadlocks."

I look at Isla. "Where are the rest of your curls?" The question arcs from my mouth like a ribbon of viper venom, this time without the advanced warning of a tongue dip.

The guests' gazes swivel to Isla. She throws her head back and laughs, a wild, rocking chord that reverberates in the small parlor. "Oh, I just shave it off," she says. "So I only have to maintain the top. My hair is too much bother. I'm busy. I don't have time for it."

It takes care and attention and time to handle natural hair. Something we have lost from our African culture are the rituals of health and beauty and taking time to anoint ourselves. And the first way we lost it was in our hair.

—**Harriette Cole**, quoted in *Hair Story*[17]

Sergeant Jacobs's petition was unsuccessful; she failed to obtain the minimum one hundred thousand signatures by the April 19, 2014, deadline. But that is not the point. Had she made the signatures goal, the White House would have been obliged to address the issue through an official statement. An army spokesperson at the Pentagon, Lieutenant Colonel S. Justin Pratt, in remarks to *HuffPost*, said, "The requirement for hair grooming standards is necessary to maintain uniformity within a military population. . . . In addition, headgear is expected to fit snugly and comfortably, without bulging or distortion . . . and without excessive gaps."

Straightening is whitening. Whitening is bettering. Therefore, straightening is bettering. It is bettering in that it makes Black women more acceptable in environments dominated by Whites.
—**Adele Morrison**[18]

Let me be clear: The headgear decree made, and still makes, unqualified, logical sense. We are talking about our soldiers' protection and safety. Given the nature of business in the armed forces, there is no such thing as outright security. If you have a loved one or significant other in any branch of the military, you in particular understand the import of safety without compromise—as far as is possible within the work our military performs.

But, how could we square Lieutenant Colonel Pratt's remarks with Sergeant Jacobs's interview with *Army Times*: "I've been in the military six years, I've had my hair natural four years, and it's never been out of regulation. It's never interfered with my headgear." Sergeant Jacobs wears twists—which meant that suddenly, per AR 670-1, her hair was now out of regulation.

AR 670-1, in the supposed interests of setting professional presentation standards, might not warrant a second look were it not for its appearing to primarily—if not exclusively—target Afrocentric hairstyles. Upon reading the entire regulation, I found the following aspects to be among the most vacuous. I had quite a few questions about these criteria.

The following is with regard to female braids:

- "Must be of uniform dimension, small in diameter (approximately 1/4"), show no more than 1/8" of scalp between the braids."
- → *Question:* Will someone be making the rounds with a ruler to ensure compliance?
- "Ends must be secured only with inconspicuous rubber bands."
- → *Question:* What's inconspicuous? Black bands? Navy? White? Gray? Tan? Brown? Green? All of these? None of these?
- "When braids are not worn loosely, but braided close to the scalp, braids must start at the front of the head."
- → *Question:* Why? What's the principal rationale for this qualification?

With regard to female cornrows (yes, interestingly, cornrows *were* permitted):

- Cornrows must start at the front of the head and continue in one direction in a straight line and end in a consistent location at the back of the head.
- → *Question:* Consistent location. Does that mean a single location? "Back of the head" can be either a single location or multiple locations.

With regard to twists:

- "Defined as twisting two distinct strands of hair around one another to create a twisted rope-like appearance."
- "Although some twists may be temporary . . . they are unauthorized."
- → *Question:* So, as long as twists are temporary, they will be tolerated, albeit unauthorized? What's the time span for "temporary"?

- "This includes twists worn against the scalp or worn in a free-hanging style."

And finally, with regard to dreadlocks:

- "Any style of dreadlock (against the scalp or free-hanging) is unauthorized."
- "Any unkempt or matted braids or cornrows are considered dreadlocks and are not authorized."
- → *Question:* How on earth can braids be considered dreadlocks? They are entirely different styles and processes. Who made this ludicrous determination?

Just these few aspects that I've cherry-picked shed more heat than light. There were, we're told, African American women on this regulatory panel. Which stylists did they consult to arrive at these definitions? Braids, whether matted or not, are not dreadlocks. Cornrows are a style of braids—not twists—so why aren't they included under the female-braids section? What makes them warrant their own subsection? What about braids whose ends don't need securing with "an inconspicuous rubber band," such as Casamance braids? What about the raft of other braids that aren't even addressed here, like box braids, tree braids, micros, goddess, fishbone, waffle, spider braids, cage, Iverson, Ghana, pixie, rope, crown, and four-strand braids?

The whole affair spawned several headline riffs in media vehicles:

- PENTAGON VOWS TO UNTWIST BLACK HAIRSTYLE CONTROVERSY (World News Network)
- A HAREBRAINED REGULATION (the *Dish*)
- CONGRESSWOMEN UPBRAID ARMY FOR UNFAIR HAIRSTYLE REGULATIONS (*Chicago Sun-Times*)
- ARMY HAIR RULES: UNKEMPT INTENTIONS (*Spectator*)

Less cute and more direct:

- WHEN BLACK HAIR IS AGAINST THE RULES (Black Politics on the Web)
- ETHICS VS. ETHNIC? SOME SOLDIERS CALL HAIR RULES UNFAIR (Headline News)
- HAS THE ARMY DECLARED WAR ON BLACK WOMEN'S HAIR? (*Beyond Black & White*)

A recent report ... showed a 26 percent decline in relaxer sales over the last five years, with an uptick in sales of natural hair products.... In the past 12 months, nearly three-fourths (70 percent) of Black women say they currently wear or have worn their hair natural (no relaxer or perm), more than half (53 percent) have worn braids, and four out of 10 (41 percent) have worn locks.
—**Mintel report** referenced in the *Washington Post*[19]

In summer 2014 Secretary of Defense Chuck Hagel walked back the army's, navy's, and air force's draconian hairstyle requirements for women of color. Service members may now choose from a range of acceptable braided and twist styles. In December 2015 the marines allowed both locs and twists. In 2017 the army revised its dreadlocks ban. That same year, *Vogue* published a celebratory article entitled NEW ORDER, featuring Black servicewomen wearing natural styles in uniform.[20] In 2018 the navy went further, permitting service members to wear dreadlocks in uniform. It took the first two decades of the twenty-first century for the military to grow up a bit and acknowledge that its outmoded grooming standards had never been formulated with Afro Latina or African American women in mind.

The problem with black hair is that it's confusing for white people. That's why people are always asking to touch it. They don't get it. . . . Up until recently, the Transportation Security Administration was

able to take a black woman and search her hair because it seemed "different." . . . At schools, girls' [and boys', by the way] natural hair has been deemed a problem and they've been penalized with threats of expulsion. . . . And yet nothing is done about white people and their mullets. . . . For black men, the longer the hair is, the scarier it is. . . . White people like black people to have hair as boring as theirs.
—**D. L. Hughley**[21]

Black women continue to have a convoluted relationship with their hair. While the CROWN Act has been a notable step in the right direction, the fact that it is a state, and not currently a federal, law means that African American and Afro Latina women remain at risk of hair bias, discrimination, and insidious, punitive measures. As of the time of this writing, fourteen states have enacted some version of the CROWN Act. That's progress, but I still see a glass half-empty: thirty-six states lack legislation protecting this basic civil right. Furthermore, in March 2021, before the 2022 bills, a federal bill was introduced in Congress, courtesy of House Representative Bonnie Coleman, and in the Senate, by past presidential candidate Cory Booker. Although the bill passed the House, it tanked in the Senate. Booker remarked on this battle:

Implicit and explicit biases against natural hair are deeply ingrained in workplace norms and society at large. This is a violation of our civil rights, and it happens every day for black people across the country. You need to look no further than Gabrielle Union, who was reportedly fired because her hair was "too black"—a toxic dog-whistle [sic] African Americans have had to endure for far too long. No one should be harassed, punished, or fired for the beautiful hairstyles that are true to themselves and their cultural heritage. Our work on this important issue was enhanced by the tireless advocacy of my colleagues in the Congressional Black Caucus, CROWN Coalition advocate Adjoa B. Asamoah, and the NAACP Legal Defense and Educational Fund.[22]

In states that don't have a CROWN Act, some individual municipalities and cities have enacted their own form of the legislation, such as Ann Arbor, Cincinnati, Louisville, New Orleans, Philadelphia, Saint Louis, among several others. Our culture is shifting, be it ever so ploddingly.

Everything I know about American history I learned from looking at Black people's hair. It's the perfect metaphor for the African experiment: the toll of slavery and the costs of remaining. It's all in the hair.

—**Lisa Jones**[23]

For weeks, my coworker distanced himself from me, until the day we boarded the same crowded elevator. Our eyes met across the grid of heads and hats and helmets. Neither of us blinked. He gave a small nod, small smile, touched the brim of his derby. I nodded back sans smile. When we alighted, we walked single file in silence. As we passed the vending machine, he spoke: "Nice day today."

"Yes, it is."

"Supposed to rain tomorrow."

"Is it?"

"What do you make of Giuliani's plan for Times Square? I think it sucks."

"I agree."

"It'll turn the place into a Six Flags for tourists."

"I hope not."

"Worse than the Vegas strip."

"I guess we'll find out soon enough."

"Well, here we are. Another day, another dollar." He dashed ahead to open the door for me.

"Appreciate it."

"You bet. Isn't today the building's ice cream social?"

"Think so."

"You going?" He spoke to my back as I headed for my office.

"Maybe. Depends how much work I get done."

"I'm going."

I slid the key into my door lock.

"Might be a good way for you to meet other tenants in the building."

"That's a thought." I turned the knob.

"Well, have a good one."

"You too." I shut my door.

Works Cited and Notes

1. "Jheri Redding Hair Products," Lemelson-MIT, n.d., https://lemelson.mit.edu /resources/jheri-redding.

2. "Plough's Hair Dressing" ad, *New York Age*, May 3, 1919, Newspapers.com, https:// www.newspapers.com/clip/4265054/ploughs-hair-dressing-ad-new-york-age.

3. The Perception Institute conducts a number of empirical studies concerning discrimination. The particular study I'm referencing here is the Good Hair study. Learn more at https://perception.org/goodhair.

4. Toshia Shaw-Lacy, "The Politics of Natural Hair," Going Natural, December 22, 2009, https://going-natural.com/the-politics-of-natural-hair/.

5. Orlando Patterson, *Slavery and Social Death* (Cambridge, MA: Harvard University Press, 1982).

6. Sakilé Camara, "Conformed and Disrupted Black Bodies in Intraracial Interactions: Deliberations on the Wearing of Natural Hair," in *Interracial Communication: Contexts, Communities, and Choices*, ed. Deborah Brunson, Linda Lampl, and Felecia Jackson Jordan (Dubuque, IA: Kendall Hunt Publishing, 2010).

7. This a term Claude Steele raised in "Thin Ice: 'Stereotype Threat' and Black College Students," *Atlantic Monthly*, August 1999, 44, 46.

8. Nina Ellis-Hervey et al., "African American Personal Presentation: Psychology of Hair and Self-Perception." *Journal of Black Studies* 47, no. 8 (2016): 869–882.

9. Online Etymology Dictionary, s.v. "dreadlocks," https://www.etymonline.com /search?q=dreadlocks.

10. Tina Opie and Katherine Phillips, "Hair Penalties: The Negative Influence of Afrocentric Hair on Ratings of Black Women's Dominance and Professionalism," *Frontiers in Psychology* 6, article 1311 (August 31, 2015): https://doi.org/10.3389 /fpsyg.2015.01311.

11. Rogers v. American Airlines, Inc., 527 F. Supp. 229, 233 (S.D.N.Y. 1981).

12. Plessy v. Ferguson, 163 U.S. 537 (1896), no. 210.

13. Julee Wilson, "Black Women Worry That Their Natural Hair Could Affect Job Employment or Retention," *HuffPost*, March 5, 2013, last updated March 13, 2013, https://www.huffpost.com/entry/black-women-natural-hair-at-the -workplace_n_2811056.

14. Jesse J. Holland, "Black Women Worried About Army Hair Regulations," Yahoo! News, April 4, 2014, https://news.yahoo.com/black-women-worried-army-hair -regulations-203052619--politics.html.

15. Nia-Malika Henderson and Bethonie Butler, "Army's Ban on Twists, Other Natural Hairstyles Sparks Calls of Racial Bias," April 3, 2014, https://www.washingtonpost.com/blogs/she-the-people/wp/2014/04/03/armys-ban-on-twists-other-natural-hairstyles-sparks-calls-of-racial-bias/.

16. Mary Mitchell, "Congresswomen Upbraid Army, Say Hairstyle Rules Are Unfair," April 18, 2014, https://chicago.suntimes.com/politics/2014/4/18/18585889/congresswomen-upbraid-army-say-hairstyle-rules-are-unfair.

17. Ayana D. Byrd and Lori L. Tharps, *Hair Story: Untangling the Roots of Black Hair in America* (New York: St. Martin's Griffin, 2014).

18. Adele M. Morrison, "Straightening Up: Black Women Law Professors, Interracial Relationships, and Academic Fit(ting) In," *Harvard Journal of Law & Gender* 33, no. 85 (2010), https://heinonline.org/HOL/LandingPage?handle=hein.journals/hwlj33&div=7&id=&page=.

19. Henderson and Butler, "Army's Ban on Twists."

20. Chioma Nnadi, "New Order: A Trailblazing Generation of Black Military Servicewomen Is Embracing the Natural Hair Movement," *Vogue*, October 4, 2017, https://www.vogue.com/projects/13535484/army-ban-on-dreadlocks-black-servicewomen-military-natural-hair-portraits-twists-braids-afros.

21. D. L. Hughley and Doug Moe, *How Not to Get Shot: And Other Advice from White People* (New York, William Morrow, 2018).

22. Cedric Thornton, "Cory Booker Announces Federal Bill That Bans Natural Hair Discrimination," *Black Enterprise*, December 9, 2019, www.blackenterprise.com/cory-booker-announces-federal-bill-that-bans-natural-hair-discrimination.

23. Lisa Jones, *Bulletproof Diva: Tales of Race, Sex, and Hair* (New York: Anchor, 1997).

THE SWIFTNESS BLACK
WOMEN KNOW

Dr. Regis Fox

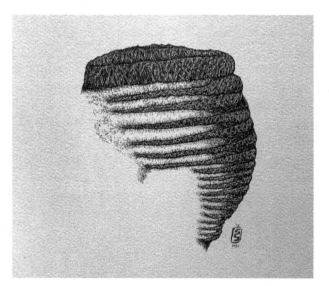

Black mothers . . . are scared not of *talk* of race but of the impact of racist oppression. We're scared because we have no choice but to release our beloved creations into environments—doctor's offices, hospitals, daycare facilities, playgrounds, schools—where white supremacy is often woven into the fabric of the institution and is both consciously and unwittingly practiced by the people acting in loco parentis.[1]

—Dani McClain, *We Live for the We:
The Political Power of Black Motherhood*

AS A BLACK WOMAN mothering a Black girl, I feel a connection to the sentiments of journalist and activist Dani McClain. Her insights above provide context for me as I grapple with what I can only call the swiftness: A swiftness that my mother knows. A swiftness that my grandmother knows. A swiftness that my girlfriends of color, in their capacities as biological mothers and "other-mothers," know.[2] Even more fitting, McClain opens her book, *We Live for the We*, with a passage from Audre Lorde's classic book of essays, *Sister Outsider*. Forty years after the initial publication of Lorde's words, McClain draws upon Lorde's perceptions of the latter's relationship with her son, especially Lorde's recognition of Black motherhood as embodied fortification against practices of Black dehumanization.

Lorde's and McClain's vulnerability helps me process the swiftness with which whiteness objectifies Black youth, the dizzying pace at which intrusive white onlookers first scrutinize, and repeatedly touch, my infant daughter by way of legitimizing her beauty, only to stigmatize her as inordinately Other before her second birthday. Lorde's and McClain's truths encourage me to address how a white gaze propels Black girls from small bodies fondled at will and petted without consent, to excessive bodies in need of containment when occupying (white) space. For many Black girls, their status as "too much" corresponds directly with their hair and that hair's violation of mainstream norms of being, beauty, and bodily presentation.

―――――――――――

When my daughter was a few days shy of seven months old, my husband and I enrolled her in a local day-care center in our midwestern town for three days per week. The start of the academic year was approaching, and, as a professor at a nearby university, I could no longer stay home with her full-time. Research and teaching obligations beckoned. As any parent—and first-time parent, in particular—will likely admit, the initial separation was tough. For weeks, I speed-walked out of the facility after morning drop-off, shedding tears alone in my car. Though the predominantly white, suburban educational center featured a live video feed to all student classrooms, I found myself worrying about what might happen to my child who had never been outside of my care or the care of trusted family members. I struggled with visions of what cameras stationed around the building might not pick up: an aide's quick, hard shove to the floor; an illicit touch during a diaper change. It felt difficult to entrust the care of my baby, who at the time could neither walk nor talk, to strangers. Instead of relief, a tinge of uncertainty pricked my heart as I read the words printed at the top of her daily report: "Rose had a good day!"[3]

To our surprise, our little one thrived in her new setting. The transition did not seem to rattle her or to dim her light much at all. Despite being younger and smaller than most of the other children when she started, she was quick to pick up on things. She adjusted to taking bottles from teachers and support staff, and began to sleep comfortably in the nursery, despite unfamiliar, and sometimes wailing, babies nearby. This place was beginning to feel like a space where Rose could grow to define herself *for* herself. I soon found myself crying less often at morning drop-offs. As I watched the top of my daughter's bald head from the window, as she inched closer and closer to newfound infant friends before crawling out of sight, I couldn't help but smile.

At fourteen months old, Rose transitioned to the toddler room across the hall from her original class. I marveled at all she had learned to do since her arrival just a few months prior, including walking and communicating her feelings through all manner of gesture and sound. She took a wide range of new skills along with her to the toddler room, and a smidge more hair. Her father and I loved watching her little curly Afro take shape alongside her growing personality. We each saw a bit of ourselves, and of our respective families' stories, in both her ringlets and her frizz, in her kinks and in the impossibly straight strands woven in between.

"She got that hair from me!" declared my grandmother on more than one occasion, inspecting her great granddaughter's tresses. Jima, as we call my grandmother, claimed Rose's hair texture mirrored what her own had been as a child.

"No," Rose's paternal great-grandmother determined. "Rose looks just like her aunt!"

For my part, I saw my story in my baby's lack of edges. Soon after I gave birth to her, the edges of my hair, especially around my temples, fell out in sizable chunks. I knew Rose's edges would eventually come in full and thick because she'd stolen mine! Her thin edges also made my daughter's forehead more pronounced, another feature linking her to her mama. Drawing on my own journey, on lessons learned from years of forcing my hair to look and act contrary to its coily nature, my husband and I decided to keep things simple with Rose's hair: regular cleansing, moisturizing, detangling, and a baby wash 'n go. Rather than pulling her patches of short hair into tight plaits, or piling on products resulting in cakey residue, on most days I misted black vanilla leave-in conditioner on her hair, worked it through her curls, and just let her be.

While I handled morning drop-offs at day care, my husband did the pickups. One evening, as I returned home from a long day on campus, I sensed from my husband's expression that something was wrong. In her high chair sat my one-year-old, a well-worn rubber band corralling her wayward curlicues into a tiny, misshapen ponytail at the top of her head.

"Mommy home!" Rose squealed.

Tears welled in my eyes as I proceeded to ask my husband a question to which I already knew the answer. "Did you do Rose's hair like that?"

"No. *They* did," he confirmed.

When my husband had attempted to obtain more information about the day's activities, he was met with a smile and a familiar refrain: "Rose had a good day!"

My anger and pain, I knew, stemmed from a few places. The first was purely hygienic. What comb or brush had been used on my daughter's hair? Had the same hair supplies been used on every child in the classroom? What if one of the other kids had lice?

My husband picked up where my exasperation left off: "Where did this rubber band even come from?" He wound up having to cut the tangled band out of Rose's hair with scissors during her bath time.

Secondly, the day-care staff's actions violated cultural norms. Black hair care, in many instances, necessitates intimacy between Black people. Access to our tendrils requires consent. And it requires knowledge about the character and dimensions of our hair. My emerging confidence in the largely white employees at the day care began to crumble. They had deviated far from the appointed curriculum, manipulating Rose's hair without bothering to secure permission from her parents first. How often had this happened? What messages might she be internalizing about whether her hair should be tamed—and, if so, why, where, and by whom?

Over the previous few months, I'd gathered from brief conversations with the day-care staff that the actions of the underpaid, young workers constituted unwitting manifestations of white supremacy, as McClain details in the epigraph.

That is, I imagine that—in their view—they were enacting a pedagogical framework of tolerance, association, and concern. As they shifted the shared grooming instruments from one small head to the next, not stopping to account for racial or ethnic differences, but merely to rinse the comb under lukewarm water (a practice I later witnessed in another classroom), they attempted to cultivate an ethos of equal treatment and a spirit of sameness. No child would be left out of this extracurricular hairdressing exercise. All one-year-olds' hair mattered.

But white politics of inclusion often culminate in Black harm, especially against the more vulnerable among us. Nursery rhymes and other games associated with sensory development, recognition of body parts, and with coloring and portraiture, that appear color-blind on their face, frequently rely on implicit bias. They bolster racial power and privilege, reinforcing standardized expressions of gender, class, sexuality, and ability. By the end of a full day, including both recess and nap time, with a rubber band entwined in her curls, pieces of Rose's already fragile, still-developing hair broke off.

In *Pushout: The Criminalization of Black Girls in Schools*, Monique W. Morris posits, "The politicization (and vilification) of thick, curly, and kinky hair is an old one. Characterizations of kinky hair as unmanageable, wild, and ultimately 'bad hair' are all signals (spoken and unspoken) that Black girls are inferior and unkempt when left in their natural state."[4] Morris's assertion corroborates what I know to be true as a Black woman with natural hair, raised by a Black woman who has worn natural hair for the majority of my lifetime. Morris elaborates further: well-intentioned deeds and outwardly discriminatory protocol alike "can also reinforce internalized oppression about the quality of natural hairstyles on people of African descent."[5] By no means monolithic, Black beauty and authenticity do not necessitate donning natural hair. Moreover, a single ponytail fashioned without approval may, for some, reflect benign intentions. Still, repeated, subtle attempts to tweak or rework one's identity trigger a cumulative effect, demeaning and diminishing Black experience over time.

For instance, the day-care staff's hairdressing scheme also reinforced problematic colorism hierarchies, whereby light-skinned African American children with straighter or "more manageable" hair, those with textures more closely aligned with Eurocentric beauty standards, are prized over the hair textures of those bearing darker complexions. Indeed, although at first glance the activity appeared to involve every child in the room, I began to notice a pattern on those days when my schedule permitted me to pick Rose up from day care. A dark-skinned African American boy, one I recognized as one of the few other students of color at the school, bore none of the signs of messiness or poststyling entanglement that other boys and girls did. I soon realized that it was the light-skinned children—those presenting as Caucasian, Asian American, Latinx, or biracial—frolicking around with elastic banded 'dos. Toddlers with deeper skin tones, denser hair, or both, did not evidence the staff's imaginative styling.

I flashed back on some of Rose's recent behavior. I noticed in church that Rose would squeeze her petite frame behind my husband or behind me in a pew. She'd then adopt the role of beautician, running her fingers through our hair. With a heavy hand, she'd try to rearrange our tendrils and lay them smooth, something we'd assumed she'd picked up from a miscellaneous story or song. It dawned on me that she was likely mimicking the conduct of her white teachers. She was mirroring their invasive contact with the bodies of others, imbibing and reproducing racialized codes of worthiness and attraction.

––––––––––––

I spend my days writing about and informing students of ongoing realities of racial violence in the United States, and yet, some time elapsed before I felt ready to confront the day-care center's management about my daughter's hair. Part of me feared what might happen to Rose in retaliation. From my earliest days of motherhood, white women associated with Rose's care, such as her first pediatrician, dismissed my parenting concerns as unimportant or irrational. As a result, I lacked assurance that I could function as an effective advocate for my daughter's needs. I anticipated that my assessment might not be heard for what it was: a strategy to engage all students in respectful, culturally competent terms. I suspected I'd be reduced to little more than an "angry Black woman."

My suspicions weren't baseless. In addition to touching Rose's hair, staff members had already attributed unfounded animosity to Rose since her arrival in the toddler classroom. On two separate occasions, a young teacher, who had been known to compliment my daughter's intelligence, referred to her as having an "attitude." In both cases, she and I were walking in opposite directions down the school's slim front corridor. The first time she spoke to me of Rose's temperament, I was speechless. I assumed that she couldn't possibly be speaking to me. But the second time, the young woman paused just long enough to lift her fingers: "That Rose has an at-ti-tude," she snapped with each syllable and laughed, inviting me in on the joke, before bouncing on her way. This time, I could not remain calm. Labeling Black girls as indignant and irritable, while mismanaging their hair without assent, work in tandem to perpetuate disparagement and exclusion. I spoke directly to day-care management the next day.

Usefully, a friend of mine and mother of three Black boys shared her perspective on the situation with me. She was a doctoral student in human development and family studies, and she helped me sort through my feelings and evaluate the aforementioned teacher's treatment. Fourteen- to eighteen-month-olds, my friend explained, are transitioning into a psychological space in which they seek to distinguish themselves from others and to establish autonomy. Likewise, they are determining the boundaries of social community, figuring out whether the people surrounding them are trustworthy and capable of protection. Accordingly, on their pathway to meaning-making, they may come up against perceived constraints, and they may question efforts to influence or redirect their burgeoning worldview. My friend also reminded me of the ways my husband and I were raising Rose in a highly verbal household environment, one in which she was encouraged to assert herself, using the power of her voice and evolving language skills to communicate her desires. Raising an eighteen-month-old daughter, McClain laments in *We Live for the We*, "It's only a matter of time before too many of my daughter's actions are misinterpreted as dangerous or defiant just because she's a black girl. Someday soon enough she'll be reprimanded harshly by someone who doesn't recognize her fierce and courageous spirit for what it is."[6] Racial and gender stereotypes can distort one's capacity to recognize developmentally appropriate behavior or to recognize the critical-thinking skills parents intentionally hone within Black youth. The consequences of this failed recognition can be devastating.

A complicated array of motivations undergirded the teacher's reactions to Rose, including place-based anxieties tied to specific racial dynamics in our midwestern town, as well as practices that education scholars refer to as *age compression*. Morris explains, "The assignment of more adult-like characteristics to the expressions of young Black girls is a form of age compression.

Along this truncated age continuum, Black girls are likened more to adults than to children and are treated as if they are willfully engaging in behaviors typically expected of Black women."[7] The day-care teacher did not judge my daughter as taking part in age-appropriate modes of discovery. Instead, she mischaracterized Rose as too loud and too aggressive, before Rose had attained adequate vocabulary and speech proficiency to fully articulate compliance or dissent. "This compression is both a reflection of deeply entrenched biases that have stripped Black girls of their childhood freedoms and a function of an opportunity-starved social landscape that makes Black girlhood inter-changeable with Black womanhood," adds Morris.[8] A misconstruing of the emotional and intellectual capacities of Black girls and Black women alike, age compression incites further violence.

In widely reported cases in 2007 and 2012, police handcuffed and arrested six-year-old kindergartners Desre'e Watson of Florida and Salecia Johnson of Georgia for having tantrums in their classrooms. Just a few years older than my and McClain's daughters, these girls experienced severe trauma in the very setting where adults should be most equipped to appraise child-hood development and mental health and to implement procedures with holistic well-being in mind. In 2009 a teacher at a Milwaukee elementary school called seven-year-old Lamya Cammon to the front of the class and cut off one of her braids as punishment for playing with her hair in class.[9] In 2013 the administration at an Orlando school threatened twelve-year-old Vanessa VanDyke with expulsion if she did not cut or straighten her natural hair.[10] According to Morris's research, "Black children are 19 percent of pre-school enrollment, but 47 percent of preschool-age children who have had one out-of-school suspension. Black girls are 20 percent of female preschool enrollment, but 54 percent of girls receiving one or more out-of-school sus-pensions."[11] Significantly, for Morris, "three core issues" drive such statistics, two of which correspond to my daughter's treatment at her day-care center: "the perceived 'bad attitude' of Black girls"[12] and "the criminalization of Black girls' appearance."[13]

Again, I struggle with the swiftness. I remember telling myself, *She's not even two years old. Not even two years old.*

I wonder when my own mother first encountered the swiftness. I wonder when the white people in her midst first touched us, her two Black daughters, without asking, handling us under the guise of good intentions or the premise of authorizing our attractiveness. Had we been Rose's age? Older? Younger perhaps? Did our mother wrestle with how to speak up for us or whether to remain silent? Did she find the swiftness exhausting? If so, how had she coped with the fatigue?

By the time I reached high school, my mother no doubt had ample experience navigating social dilemmas like these and shielding us against racial and gender animus, subtle and overt. One instance in high school, in particular, stands out to me for the way she rejected age-compression practices leveraged at Black youth, an episode when she thwarted my predominantly white high school's hyperpunitive response to ill-advised, though not atypical, teenage antics.

At the time, I was an AP student with an excellent academic record, one that would eventually secure me a full-ride college scholarship. I also participated in varsity cheerleading throughout the football and basketball seasons. The only Black member on the squad, I often mingled with white superiors and counterparts, while sporting a conventional suburban cheerleading 'do. For me, this meant freshly relaxed locs, pulled back and away from my face. In fact, I had been begging my mom to permit me to chemically straighten my hair for years. She'd finally relented. As an adult, I can see that my choice of cheerleading hairstyle was all about safety and belonging. Contrary to my present-day natural, asymmetrical cuts, those unassuming buns and high, soft ponytails ensured that I did not take up much space. As the aforementioned scenarios in Florida, Georgia, and Wisconsin indicate, white authority too often regards taking up space with big hair as distracting and disorderly. Black girls make themselves smaller, literally and figuratively, to evade criminalization. While I have always maintained pride in my heritage, the styles of my youth allowed me to conform with aesthetic dictates my white teammates exemplified, codes customary within the institutional culture.

In the spring and summer of my first two years of high school, I also ran track. A decent middle-distance runner, especially in the eight-hundred-meter race, I no longer represented the only Black face on the team. Many of my closest Black friends ran as well. One humid day, a group of us lingered by the locker rooms after a grueling practice. Physically drained and drenched in sweat, we waited for the last fleet of school buses to take us home. "Wanna take a dip in the pool to cool off?" someone offered up. He didn't have to wait long for a response. Though there was no lifeguard on duty, and technically, it was after hours, we didn't care. We headed to the pool and leaped in, still clothed in our colorful jerseys and shorts embellished with the school mascot.

Splashing around in the school's Olympic-size arena, I remember feeling weightless, carefree. We cackled at one another's belly flops and emitted giddy squeals as we catapulted backward off diving boards. Our exhilarating escapade did not last long. Within minutes, a member of the after-school disciplinary patrol arrived on the pool deck. We got out of the water slowly, instinctively forming a line at the edge of the pool. In turn, the frowning, white woman security officer surveyed us. Soiled practice uniforms clung to our black bodies. Our manes—now unfettered—generated small puddles at our feet. When her gaze passed over me, the woman paused, perhaps recognizing a disheveled, kinky-curly version of the school's single Black cheerleader, the one with whom she conversed on a regular basis when she patrolled our home football games.

"In-school suspensions for *all* of you," she bellowed, stalking toward the end of the line to collect our names in her small yellow notepad.

Upon learning of my suspension, my mother immediately requested a meeting with the principal. At the conclusion of the closed-door session, I received word that the decision mandating my in-school suspension had been reversed. Today, my mom only vaguely recollects this event, conflating it with too many others in which she says she simply did what she had to do. But the memory has always stayed with me, and it carries increasing weight as I find my voice as the mother of my own daughter. In speaking with the white administrator that day, my mom countered the swiftness. She undermined the dominant narrative, which sought to render her Black girl not as a teen who went for a swim with friends without permission—as teens will do—but as a co-conspirator in a mob of Black students. My mother refused to accept the security officer's attempt to label me as excessive or expendable, recognizing ways in which such designations would follow me far beyond my time in high school.

I also remember my mother's regret that day that her advocacy did not have a wider impact. On the ride home, we spoke of privilege—tied to education and perceived class status, but also to colorism—and of other mothers who could not show up that day for their own children in the same ways she had. We lamented that the disciplinary sanctions my peers faced remained in place. Because of my mother's example, I know I must be vigilant about potential obstacles hampering my ability to speak up on Rose's behalf. And I must remain mindful about aspects of my identity that make my advocacy more legible than that of others.

My mom carried something else with her into the school administrators' meeting that day, too. She bore the distinct hallmark of having integrated a private swim club just a few miles away from my high school, when she was still an elementary schooler herself—an elementary schooler with a Black mother unwilling to submit to the swiftness. In the early 1960s my grandparents, mother, and uncle constituted one of two Black families residing in their predominantly white suburban township. For a year, they had visited a local swim club as registered guests of their white next-door neighbors. Subsequently, my grandparents applied for a family membership to the private club, but the organization's board of directors rejected their application. Board members, including a man who was my grandparents' neighbor and the father of the friends who had invited them to the club over the course of the previous year, endorsed the position of the club's owner. The owner believed that Black community members should fund and develop separate recreational spaces.

Back then, my mom wore her thick brown hair parted down the middle, with one big plait on each side of her head and bangs. I can picture my grandmother watching my mom's braids bobbing as she waded around the pool with her friends, unaware that the smiling white grown-ups around her had determined she was undeserving of regular admittance to the facility. Mom's frizzy hair, like her fuller body and lively family, resembled those of her white peers, but not closely enough. Her hair represented difference. For club management and members, this difference was a threat.

While my grandmother, Jima, says that my Rose gets her hair from her side of the family, my hope is that the inheritance doesn't end there. Jima appealed the board's decision, eventually exposing the club's segregationist, prejudicial treatment to local radio and television stations. Mounting public pressure compelled swim-club leadership to acquiesce, resulting in my mom and uncle gaining full club membership. My grandmother rejected the viewpoint that her children were unworthy of spaces bound by white rules of containment. She challenged the notion of her children as unworthy of just being kids. They belonged there, in all their natural-headed glory.

Jima herself never frequented the swim club again, albeit a public facility still in existence today, still just down the street from our high school, with its own closely surveilled pool grounds. Recently, I asked my grandmother why she never went back. Smilingly, she professed, "I don't know how to swim."

———————

The policing of my daughter's hair cannot be extricated from intraracial respectability politics. I've noticed a swiftness of a different sort extending from African American relatives and acquaintances. Some folks invoke conservative gender norms, situating Rose as flawed, but redeemable. "Don't worry. My daughter was bald for those first few years, but now she has a head full of long, beautiful hair. It will grow in," they encourage me. And I cannot exempt myself from perpetuating such politics, either. During Rose's first year, I found myself interjecting, before anyone else could offer a comment about her appearance, "Her hair is still growing in!" Such comments preempted scrutiny from family and friends during get-togethers and other social outings. Over time, as her uneven, curly Afro continues to develop, Rose's hair has provoked a range of euphemistic questions, which suggest, when it is all said and done, that "that girl needs to get her hair done." Work remains to be done, then, inside and outside of our communities.

Hence, McClain's book could not feature a more apt excerpt from Lorde's essay "Man Child: A Black Lesbian Feminist's Response," at its outset: "Raising black children—female and male—in the mouth of a racist, sexist, suicidal dragon is perilous and chancy. If they cannot love and resist at the same time, they will probably not survive."[14] As I become more experienced as a Black mother, I realize that I want to raise Rose so thoroughly convinced of her brilliance, her beauty, and her belonging that her sense of self cannot be easily displaced. Certainly not by white women in educational facilities, whether a smiling preschool teacher, or a scowling, high school security officer. And not by a police officer. Not by anyone.

I want to raise her to style her hair big and wild or pressed and straight or any other way, because it is her hair and because she understands that regardless of her self-presentation, she is loved. I want her father and me to raise her to ask questions when her surroundings seek to place limits upon her and her peers. I want her to understand misnaming and other violence that may attend her speaking up.

I know this to be easier said than done. But I will do everything I can to ensure that forty years from now, Rose is not struggling, as have generations of women before her, with how to intervene in the swiftness. My prayer is that she'll be too busy living out our primary charge to her: to just be herself.

Works Cited and Notes

1. Dani McClain, *We Live for the We: The Political Power of Black Motherhood* (New York: Bold Type Books, 2019), 8.
2. I borrow the concept of "other-mothers" from scholar and activist Alexis Pauline Gumbs.
3. Names have been changed or omitted in this narrative to preserve anonymity.
4. Monique W. Morris, *Pushout: The Criminalization of Black Girls in Schools* (New York: New Press, 2018), 92.
5. Morris, 92.
6. McClain, *We Live for the We*.
7. Morris, *Pushout*, 34.
8. Morris, 34.
9. "Teacher Cuts Off Girl's Braid in Front of Class," WISN 12 ABC, updated December 11, 2009, https://www.wisn.com/article/teacher-cuts-off-girl-s-braid-in-front -of-class/6296650#.
10. Clare Kim, "Student Will Not Face Expulsion for Her 'Natural Hair,'" MSNBC, November 27, 2013, https://www.msnbc.com/the-last-word/school-backs-natural -hair-threat-msna221071.
11. Morris, *Pushout*, 57.
12. Morris, 57.
13. Morris, 58.
14. McClain, *We Live for the We*.

BLACK WOMEN MANEUVERING NAPPY

Judy Juanita

MY TEENAGE GRANDSON HAS been pursued by white girls. I want to warn him that, even in the twenty-first-century, ultracosmopolitan, Oakland–San Francisco Bay Area, his precious brown body is a war zone and those love pellets are bullets. But I'm just a grandma, albeit one who learned the hard way that the Black body is a war zone and the Black skull, the helmet.

How one wears Black hair, one's helmet, one's protective combat headgear, is the subject of hot debate within the family and the community. Appearance and success are intertwined in the Black population where Eurocentrism, a major character in the Black narrative, still prizes pale skin, pale hair, and pale eye color.

Black women have had to overcome the oppressive hold of dark-skin prejudice and straight-hair preference, the rigid, almost prescriptive mixture of colorism and intraracism. As barriers fell, new images and role models replaced old ones. But this great feeling of independence, intelligence, and enhanced attractiveness took time: centuries, not years.

As early as 1619 Africans first arrived to the Americas as indentured servants. However, Virginia farmers and planters quickly recognized the utter usefulness and physical endurance of the imported Africans. They pushed to change state laws to ensure African servitude would be lifelong. Enslaved Blacks were forced to conform or restrict their appearance and behavior to whatever the slave owners deemed serviceable and marketable. Thus began the centuries-long struggle of Black women making their nappy hair work as they labored.

A plethora of illustrations, diaries, and letters from those who lived in those times before photography provide insight into what enslaved African women wore on their heads. Picture after picture shows the African enslaved woman wearing head rags, head cloths firmly pressing down the hair and tied mostly in the back. Even the original Black Statue of Liberty had her head wrapped.[1]

Dr. Anna Arabindan-Kesson noted that it was "common to read about the gorgeous headdresses worn by black women, their brilliant colour and intricate arrangements, a vivid gesture that was both a remembrance of, and connection to, an African heritage." She also notes, however, that the slave owners were careful to dress up their slaves for market.[2]

We have been a part of the workforce in the fields, the big house, the marketplaces: sewing, cooking, planting, harvesting, often keeping our thick, coiled hair under wrap. There were even Negro codes governing our dress and hair. South Carolina law required masters to clothe slaves in accordance with the Negro Act of 1735. For the hair, sunbonnets were required; annual clothing distributions from plantation owners included palmetto hats and turbans.

Conformity to Eurocentrism's oppressive hold is intertwined in our population with survival and success, never more so than with our hair. The examples here of Black women manipulating their hair shows that we take our nappy hair and figure it out: Madame C. J. Walker (1867–1919), my late friend and movie icon Vonetta McGee, newscaster Melba Tolliver, and the sisters of the Black Panther Party.

Our hair texture has been manipulated chemically, with heat or with the barber's clippers, to fit a prevailing societal requirement. To be able to earn our keep, to be accepted by our peers, we could not simply pull our hair into a ponytail. We had to texturize, clip, press, shape, alter the hair—or risk being fired, shunned, relegated, ostracized, or ignored.

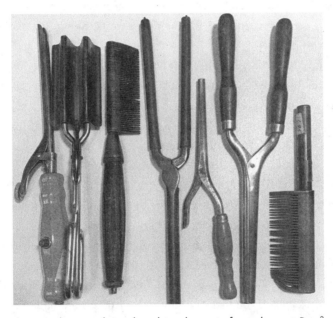

Antique hot comb and curl implements for sale on eBay[3]

Madame C. J. Walker invented the Walker System, a manner of grooming that promoted hair growth and conditioned the scalp via her shampoo, her pomade, strenuous brushing, and heated iron combs. She never claimed to have invented the hot comb. Madame Walker widened the fingers of the comb, and she popularized the comb by refining it. By 1914 there was enormous competition, even hot-comb wars, to address the market of Black women who had to go to work.

By 1974, movie star Vonetta McGee had starred in *Thomasine & Bushrod*, an underrated film classic. Vonetta and I became buddies in 1967 while students at San Francisco State University, in the Black theater scene with Ed Bullins, Danny Glover, and Marvin X. She broke into film in Italy and then led the Black film breakthrough in Hollywood in the 1970s. In *Thomasine & Bushrod* she showed the natural beauty and strength of an unadorned Black woman of the plains—and a sophisticated criminal. But Vonetta did her own hair, makeup, and clothing, as she'd always done, even sewing her own clothing for fashion shoots. She knew exactly what she wanted to project.

Stills from the movie show her hair chemically untreated, her nappy edges showing. The film's producer and writer, Vonetta's partner Max Julien, similarly wears the Afro. At one point in the film, Max's character, a bank robber, loses his nerve, and Vonetta's character slaps the mess out of him. This is an allusion to Harriet Tubman's famous warning to the escaped slaves who wanted to turn back during the difficult underground journey: "If you turn back, I'll shoot you."

Vonetta starred in *To Sleep with Anger* by Charles Burnett, a Black auteur. She lets her edges show the way her hair grows naturally.

She's not masquerading gelled-down baby hair, which is the current Hollywood trend for evoking a mixed racial heritage (while trashing the African part of that heritage). Vonetta was working with these unsung Black directors who were conscious of the Black cultural legacy they were building.

In a press photo for *Blacula*, she wears a short natural for the role, after one of her several bouts with cancer. She had lost her hair to cancer treatments and told me that when it grew back she intended to never wear it short again. She didn't prefer it. But at the moment it served her well in her career. But working for Hollywood studios once again in Clint Eastwood's *The Eiger Sanction*, she was back to wigs. White actors wore wigs as a matter of course. However, their wigs mimicked the texture and shape of their natural hair. Black actors were required to have hair like white people's, unlike their own, a form of cultural denial to put it lightly—or cultural oppression, to give it a truer name. This adherence to white hairstyling also promulgated employment discrimination against Black hairstylists, who were nonentities in the industry.

In 1971 newscaster Melba Tolliver's Afro got her fired from WABC-TV in New York. In an interview, she said, "The day before I was supposed to cover Tricia Nixon's wedding at the White House, I got my hair changed to a natural—previously, I'd been having it straightened—and can you believe they actually told me I couldn't appear live in the studio unless I changed my hair back to the way it used to look? They said I looked less attractive—less feminine. But it was their standard of femininity, not mine."[4]

I was a worker bee in the Black Panther Party and the Black Power movement in the 1960s and 1970s. I saw firsthand the breakthrough of the color caste in the Black community via the Black is Beautiful movement, which ended unhealthy limitations on physical appearance for Black women (far more than for Black men). In the Black Panther Party, many women, including me, wore the natural, the Afro, and were often photographed at rallies, protests, and events. We braided it at night for length and sway. Barbers had to shape it with care, and we patted it down each day before spraying to hold it in place.

A helmet is a form of protective gear worn to protect the head and the brain. Soldiers wear helmets. More specifically, a helmet complements the skull in protecting the human brain. It's not a stretch to say the Afro hairstyle was a key element in overcoming centuries of brainwashing, the inferiorization of the Black mind. The Afro was more than a ceremonial or symbolic hairstyle. It was akin to helmets worn by police, hazmat workers, astronauts, pilots, workers facing dangerous conditions. The national, unprecedented hunt for Angela Davis—after the prisoner escape and courthouse killings of George and Jonathan Jackson, and others, in 1970 northern California—demonstrated the power and fear that the Afro instilled in white society. The FBI put a whole nation on alert, giving permission to profile, harass, and arrest any Black woman wearing a natural.

The Black lesbian community has taken the battle to new levels with new stratagems. Kinsey Clarke says, "In Black lesbian communities, cultural aesthetic standards are the driving force behind our signifiers: locs, fades,

Author, second from the left, in 1967 at SFSU.
Jerry Varnado

high-quality wigs, and natural hairstyles are some calling cards, as are nail styles and the language we use to identify ourselves."[5]

Thus, the struggle over, and weaponization of, Black hair in the fight for justice continues. The Black woman historically has not been afraid of showing who she is ethnically. But she's had to be careful where and when to be courageous.

Works Cited

1. Furious [pseud.], "The Original Statue of Liberty Presented to the U.S. Was a Statue of a . . . 'Black Woman,'" *Urban Intellectuals* (blog), April 19, 2013, https://urbanintellectuals.com/the-original-statue-of-liberty-presented-to-the-u-s-was-a-statue-of-a-Black-woman/. Note that this claim remains a contested one. Many reputable historical websites cite a 2007 installation for this statue—known as Lady Liberty—on the island of Saint Martin, which would, of course, mean that this statue could not be the original. However, commentary on both sides of this issue continues to define this statue as either debunked rumor or buried truth.

2. Anna Arabindan-Kesson, "Dressed Up and Laying Bare: Fashion in the Shadow of the Market," Princeton University Department of African American Studies, News, August 9, 2019, https://aas.princeton.edu/news/dressed-and-laying-bare -fashion-shadow-market.

3. eBay, photograph, https://i.ebayimg.com/images/g/nngAAOSw1kxeGobu/s-l300 .jpg. The sales listing is no longer available.

4. Barbara Campbell, "Melba? She's the Toast of the Town," *New York Times*, February 18, 1973.

5. Kinsey Clarke, "For Black Lesbians, Artificial Nails Can Be an Important Signifier," *FLARE* (blog), *Fashion*, August 26, 2019, https://www.flare.com/identity /Black-lesbians-artificial-nails.

BLACK HAIR MATTERS: TEACHING AND LIVING RACE AMID CIVIL STRIFE

Dr. Shatima Jenique Jones

I HAVE TAUGHT MY SIGNATURE courses (De)Tangling the Business of Black Women's Hair, and Black Experiences in Literature, Movies, and Television several times. But teaching during the fall of 2020 was a uniquely peculiar experience.

Amid a combination of crises—the COVID-19 health pandemic, police-brutality murder cases, the era of Trump, climate change, and the California fires—the summer of 2020 left me traumatized. The concoction of these catastrophes meant that a lot of us found ourselves suddenly at home, unable to avoid learning and talking about the issues that underlay these events, many of which have plagued our country since its establishment.

The Black Lives Matter movement, in particular, formed the basis of my most difficult conversations with close family members and friends, all of whom would identify as liberal. The silence on the issues by my in-laws, who are white, was resounding. It did not occur to them to check in with me, the one adult Black person in their family, to see how I was dealing with the situation. And once we finally did talk, our conversations involved a refusal to hear me, along with denial, defense, attacks, critiques, and a whole lot of tears, including mine (and it is rare for me to cry in front of others). But there were a lot more tears from the white women involved.

On my side of the family, which is all African American, I had difficult conversations with relatives about the most productive (code for *respectable*) way for Black people to protest. I had to challenge their newfound concern for Black-owned businesses and companies that service predominately Black neighborhoods. I had to push them to distinguish looters and rioters from peaceful protesters. Some family members also asked me to be more forgiving of my partner's side of the family, something I have not been inclined to do. The summer of 2020 was an unexpected, unfortunate, but necessary litmus test for my inner circle.

On one hand, I was grappling with new questions about what it means to be a Black woman in an interracial marriage with a white man whose politics align with mine, but whose kin remain, for the most part, willfully ignorant of their white privilege. On the other hand, as a Black woman who had experienced upward socioeconomic mobility—I was a first-generation college graduate and first-generation homeowner—I did not feel beholden to the same kind of respectability politics that my parents and less-educated (not to be conflated with less-intelligent) family members apparently did. Just as I was the only Black person to eat at my in-laws' dinner table, my husband was the only white person to ever dine in the homes of my side of the family.

I found solace in trying to complete my book, *The Headmasters of Brooklyn: Barbering, Blackness, and Brotherhood.* My writing felt like the most accessible form of activism; I understood it as an opportunity to say something enlightening about Blackness, Black masculinities, and Black communities to a wide audience. I also felt empowered while writing my book, especially in the face of a pandemic that is pushing more and more women out of the paid workforce.

The thought of teaching in this context was beyond daunting. Here I was, a Black woman writing about Blackness, mothering two young children with absolutely no childcare, tasked with teaching two courses centering Blackness during a moment in which the Black Lives Matter protests were reaching their crescendo—all while adjusting my pedagogy to remote learning. I was unsure that I could get myself together enough to resemble a professor. While I always encourage students to ask questions, with the primary purpose of sharpening their critical-thinking skills, I was less confident this semester that I would have answers for them about what it means to be a Black person in the United States today.

Once I realized that it would be several months, instead of weeks, that my family and I would live in quarantine in upstate New York, I wanted to braid my hair. I usually have a professional stylist braid my hair before a beach vacation. With braids, I can enjoy playing in the water and spend time sightseeing rather than caring for my hair. Any other time, I like the freedom to style my hair differently by the day, according to my mood and the activity.

When I teach, I tend to draw a partial line in the front middle of my hair, slick down the sides, and tie it into a low, centered ball. To achieve a casual look, I style my hair into a high, bouncy ponytail, using a colorful scarf as a headband. For date night with my husband, I usually wear my hair loose with a partial flat twist on the front side. When I write, I cover my head with a hoodie or cap, which juxtaposes my body's finiteness with the limitless freedom of my words on the page.

I was not going on a beach vacation in the summer of 2020. Yet, I wanted my hair in braids. Amid the chaos of the world, I thought that braids might protect my hair from my inability to devote as much time to it and my limited knowledge on how to best care for its overall health. Braids would also give me some stability over my hair while I processed the upheavals in the world and in my life. Under quarantine, I did not desire versatility with my hairstyles; the constraint and restriction of braids felt appropriate.

But I dared not travel to the African hair-braiding salon on Fulton Street in Brooklyn, where at least two women would simultaneously braid brown and blonde streaks into my hair for hours. The two-hour drive back to New York City and the risk of contracting COVID outweighed my yearning for braids. Instead, I was forced to think about, spend time with, and take care of my hair—just as I now had to deal with so many other personal adjustments and matters, some of which had remained unresolved for too long.

––––––––

The first time I taught my college course (De)Tangling the Business of Black Women's Hair, I stood at the head of the table, organizing my handouts and reviewing my notes. As students trickled in, a funny thing happened. There were smiles, a couple of loud high fives, and even a few hugs. The students' collective joy and excitement were palpable. I thought to myself, *These students must know each other.* But most of them did not.

Students lingered after class to tell me that I was their first Black professor at New York University (NYU), even though they were juniors and seniors. They were relieved that I was a Black woman teaching this particular topic and would have been disappointed otherwise; they were excited about being in a classroom full of Black and Brown people for once. One student even asked to take a photograph with me and thanked me for offering the course. I had designed the course for *any* NYU student, and I was well aware that fewer than 6 percent of this elite private university's undergraduates identified as Black.

A diversity of perspectives and experiences is always present in my classroom. Our Blackness is complicated by our multiracial backgrounds, nationalities, skin tones, hair textures, classes, genders, sexualities, religious beliefs, ages, body types, and so on. The intersection of these identifications shapes our daily encounters and informs how we navigate and understand the social world. I encourage the non-Black students to realize the value of their perspectives in the class discussion, despite suddenly finding themselves in the "minority" demographic. I also encourage them to realize the particular power they have, by virtue of not identifying as Black, to address, outside my classroom, the social problems associated with Black women's hair. My classroom is an inclusive intellectual space where one's personal experience counts as a data point, a valid perspective, and a useful framework through which we can better understand the topic at hand.

Too many people still make assumptions that an afro implies some sort of militancy or that wearing dreadlocks means a predilection for smoking pot.
—**Lori Tharps**, journalist and coauthor of *Hair Story: Untangling the Roots of Black Hair in America*

Students in these courses express that they "feel seen" in the classroom in ways they had not before. Some students who discuss traumatizing racial encounters they have experienced, or who identify as queer, bisexual, or gender nonconforming, preface their remarks by signaling that this is privileged information that they have seldom, if ever, shared with classmates. In turn, their peers show empathy and support for one another. Through applause, hugs, and sometimes tears, we then work to situate their individual experiences in a macro, structural context.

Because we all share and become vulnerable during the course, students are able to hear, see, and appreciate each other for the important and courageous work they are doing. We can debate about Blackness, race relations, power, and inequality in respectful and meaningful ways that bring about new and more nuanced understandings. We are able to recognize and bond over our common experiences. And our differences help us come to new realizations, including of our own implicit biases, whether of our own privileges or of the struggles of others.

Almost immediately after I began teaching it, (De)Tangling the Business of Black Women's Hair took on a life of its own. At faculty mixers, colleagues would remark, "*You* teach that class? I've heard so much about it!" A student who praised my course was featured in a social media post that received thousands of likes and around one hundred endorsements. Students were so inspired by my course that, during my first year there, they asked me to be the keynote speaker at NYU's Black Graduation. And more recently, Medium, an independent online media outlet, listed (De)Tangling as one of the most innovative courses offered nationwide for the 2019–2020 academic year. I had not anticipated how well others would receive my course, nor the many ways that I would evolve through it.

———————

Within my first year of teaching (De)Tangling, I went natural.

I had worn a perm, a chemical straightener, all of my adult life until that point. Ms. Roseanne, my lifelong beautician, began caring for my hair when I was eight or nine years old. She continued doing so for close to three decades. She would spend hours perming my hair, washing and conditioning it, rolling it with the wire rollers and keeping them in place with plastic, pink straight pins. I would sit under the dryer for at least two hours. Then she would take the rollers out of my hair, grease/oil my scalp, and spray my hair with light sheen oil. It was an all-day event! Most often, this ritual occurred in a salon or in my home, though a few times in Ms. Roseanne's home, and once in a Maine hotel, where she washed my hair in the bathroom sink the night before my wedding. Ms. Roseanne is like a godmother to me.

With a roller set, I did not have to do much with my hair for months at a time. I would keep my curls tight, and just bunch it up with a hair tie for days. As the curls fell or loosened up, I wore them in a ponytail. As my curls loosened even more, I wore my hair out, combing it through. My hair would have a bounce to it, the sort of look I have after I get a wash, set, and wrap at a Dominican salon. Once the big curls straightened out, I would put greater thought and effort into styling my hair into a single loose braid on one side, fixing it into buns, or wearing it out partially. I loved how my hair looked after getting a perm: healthy and versatile. I appreciated the time it gave me to focus on other aspects of my life, like my family and career. I loved my relationship with Ms. Roseanne and with my hair.

However, Ms. Roseanne was growing older. Despite her retirement from salon work in 2008, at age sixty-eight, she vowed to continue doing my hair. Thereafter, she would commute two hours, riding the bus and subway from her apartment in Coney Island to mine in Greenwich Village. She lugged a small suitcase full of hair supplies curated just for me. As it became more difficult for her to make the trip, it became hard for me to rationalize asking her to do so.

And as I taught (De)Tangling, some of the material struck me in unexpected ways. When we covered Chris Rock's film *Good Hair*, the students and

I were very critical of it. However, one moment was powerful enough to give me pause: the scene where a white scientist places a toxic chemical onto a metal can and the chemical is so caustic it burns a hole through the can. The scientist is shocked to learn that this same chemical is a key ingredient in Black women's hair relaxer. The stunned scientist asks, "Why would anyone want to do that?" The rational response and astonishment from an outsider about the hair care practices of some Black women, along with scientific research that has found correlations between relaxer use, fibroids, and other medical conditions common among Black women, made me consider going natural.

But the deciding factor was that, at the time, I was a mother to a fairly light-skinned biracial son (and now the mother of two sons). He would spend significantly more time among white and other non-Black people than I had at that age. Motherhood changed, and continues to change, me. As I taught students about the significance of Mamie and Kenneth Clark's infamous, groundbreaking doll-test study and about the Black is Beautiful movement, for instance, I made a conscious decision to let my son see me in all my Blackness, my Black womanhood. I wanted him to see that nothing about me, and by extension him, has to be changed for any reason, that we should find pride and beauty in those aspects of our identity and culture that we embrace as Black.

I have been natural for seven years now. I still do not have time to sort through the overwhelming amount of products on the market. I still do not have a hairstylist, though Ms. Roseanne calls me every Friday to check in with me. And I went through a season of sincerely declaring that I would get a perm as soon as I had the chance. But I realized that I was seeking comfort, hoping to return to a more familiar, innocent version of myself. I knew that I was no longer that woman.

Over my years of teaching, I have come to understand what my courses mean to students. As I prepared to teach in the postracial reckoning of fall 2020, I was unsure whether I would be able to give students the "transformative," "changed my life," and "therapeutic" experiences that so many of my earlier students had reported.

My husband reminded me that all I had to do was be myself in the classroom and teach in the way I always did. His advice made me wonder, *If I were a student in my course this particular semester, what would I need the learning experience to be?* I knew that, like me, they were having difficult conversations with their inner circles, dealing with the traumas of police brutality, and rethinking their identities and overall places in the world. I imagined that they, like me, needed empathy, compassion, an expansive acknowledgment that things are not normal, an intellectual space to reckon with the summer's unprecedented fallout. I suspected that Black students, in particular, needed affirmation, sustenance, and validation.

At the start of the semester, I arranged to have the students' final papers published as articles in *Confluence*, the online journal of NYU's Gallatin School of Individualized Study, during Black History Month. This project, A Seat at Our Table, featured four to five student research papers each week on the topics Black Mothers and Boss Ladies on the Screen, Gazes on Black Hair and Beauty, Black Aesthetics and Activism, and Blackness on Film-Tropes, Trauma, and Resistance. The special journal issue was my attempt to provide students with a platform to educate a broad audience, on their terms, and in a way that would benefit their academic careers by way of having a publication credit on their résumés. This was my form of activism, a tangible action I could take in response to some of the fraught racial tensions of that turbulent summer.

During the semester, we learned of the Breonna Taylor case verdict. I recall my workday being hectic and frustrating. That evening, I lay on my sofa looking at the ceiling as I caught up with my husband, exchanging reports of COVID-related check-ins with our extended families, discussing news of Trump's threat to our democracy, and the details of the verdict. I was baffled, exhausted, outraged, but not surprised. I wondered aloud, "What kind of world are we living in? I mean, *really*, what is going on in this world?" In my silence then, tears welled in the corner of my eyes and sluiced the contours of my ears.

I realized my students had a paper due the next day. Given the state of the world, the deadline seemed preposterous. I emailed an announcement that I was extending the deadline in light of the verdict; I told them to focus on self-care rather than the paper. I figured they, too, were unable to concentrate on work that evening. I presumed they would appreciate the extension, but I was not expecting the outpouring of messages thanking me for acknowledging the psychological and emotional toll the verdict had exacted. They confided that, as Black students, sometimes the only one in a class, they did not feel comfortable asking their professors for extensions or consideration of their situations. Many said that no other professor even mentioned the Breonna Taylor tragedy. My simple gesture, which just made sense to me as an empathetic human being, meant a great deal to my students.

In November 2020, of course, there was the contentious presidential election. As Election Day approached, we were all uneasy. Caravans of Trump supporters were clogging highways and city streets. Our campus prepared for the potential of more civil unrest, including ensuring we had enough food and essentials to survive indoors for a few days, if not weeks. A couple of students confided that they had prepared bug-out bags in case they had to flee their dwellings. All these developments made us even more invested in our discussions on theories of race and political affiliation, space and place, and Black trauma.

The space and time I once had to decompress and be left to my reflections after teaching back-to-back courses was simply not there during quarantine. I would try to move about the kitchen for a late lunch or look through the window in a sort of quiet daze for as long as my children would allow, which was perhaps two minutes on a good day. My children would find me addressing myself in the bathroom mirror, as if I was speaking to my class. Once, my two-year-old son asked in all sincerity, "Mama, who are you talking to?"

There is no privacy for mamas, not even in bathrooms. I did, however, steal a little bit of private time in the shower, where I washed my hair and sorted through me.

––––––––––

I washed my hair more often during quarantine. I did it right before class, something I'd never done pre-COVID. I did not fret over drying or styling it. I just pulled the towel off my hair a few minutes before logging in to my computer to teach. It was freeing to let my fresh and clean natural crown just be. I would watch it transform on screen, from a damp and wavy look as I started to teach my (De)Tangling course to a poufy, stand-on-the-top-of-my-head partial Afro less than two hours later, when my Black Experiences course began. My hair and I were safe from the harsh elements of the outdoors, yet we were still being shaped by the world around us.

I had not realized how much Trump's presidency had made me feel like a hostage even in my own home. My hair has grayed.

On Inauguration Day in January 2021, before we saw her face emerge from the car, we saw her bouncy, free-flowing curls dancing in the wind; I knew those curls belonged to First Lady Michelle Obama. It still brings tears to my eyes; it sends joy, pride, and chills through my body to see President Barack Obama, Michelle Obama, and Vice President Kamala Harris walk through the halls of Capitol Hill. There is something about seeing Black bodies, Black women in particular, move through white spaces with authority, dignity, style, and grace that just speaks truth to power. Their silhouettes create shadows in which I and my children parade.

NATURAL'S NOT IN IT: BLACK WOMEN'S HAIR IN MAJORITY WHITE PROFESSIONAL SETTINGS

Margalynne Armstrong, JD

LOOKING BACK ON HOW I've worn my hair throughout my life is both telling and inscrutable. My preference for natural styling tells a lot about me, but so many of the reactions provoked by my hair are inscrutable because they were unvoiced, except for those chafing expressions of motherly prerogative. Unless someone *tells* me of their reaction to my hair, I am forced to infer their opinion. During most of my childhood and through almost my entire career, I have worn an Afro or some form of braided hair, with sporadic exceptions.

I never had the patience or inclination to maintain permed or pressed hair for very long, in part because the results of trying to detexturize my hair rarely satisfied.

When I was in high school and college in the 1970s, wearing my hair in an Afro seemed to be the natural choice. Civil rights laws had been enacted to protect Blacks and women from employment discrimination. Cicely Tyson had worn an Afro on the television series *East Side/West Side*, and Diana Ross, sans Supremes, sported one. Heck, even Lois Lane came out of Superman's body-molding machine as a Black woman sporting an Afro.[1] As Black women and men moved away from processed hair, no one seemed to have a problem with Afros except older Black people.

But race, gender, and class intersect in judgment of the hairstyles Black women wear to work in the United States. Even as the freedom to choose how one wants to look and the range of hairstyling choices have evolved since the 1960s, bias, assimilation, white supremacy, white dominance, and racial erasure all contribute to decouple natural Black hair from professionalism. My privilege, class, and naïveté—to the point of obliviousness—shaped my particular experiences with natural hairstyles on the job; thus, I enjoyed a certain amount of freedom.

I write from a particularly absurd position. I grew up in the 1960s and '70s sheltered from racism in one of the most racist cities in the United States. I attribute that protection to my parents, class privilege, and an idealistic world-view buttressed by a brief bloom of school desegregation between assimilated Blacks and liberal whites. The short-lived fever dream of progress created the fully integrated experimental high school I attended at the dawn of the 1970s. My adolescent belief that people were entitled to choose how they wanted to look was epitomized by the makeup-free, natural flower child Joni Mitchell on the cover of her *For the Roses* album and Diana Ross's Afro-to-the-edges on her *Surrender* album cover. Somehow, this perception of freedom extended to my understanding of Black hair in the white world, as well as to my liberation from the tyranny of cosmetics.

I grew up in one of the few integrated neighborhoods in Chicago, attending integrated elementary schools that were experiencing white flight but were not yet fully Black. As a little girl, I wore my hair in pigtails, not the silky braids of the Black girls with long "nice" hair. For Easter and class photos, my mom would press my sisters' and my hair with the hot comb and set it in curlers for a pageboy or a flip style, which is how she wore her hair to work every day, sometimes in a wig. Starting in fifth or sixth grade, I got perms, which never looked that great because my hair would break. But in eighth grade, the Afro liberated me. For high school, college, and law school, I wore short or medium-length 'fros.

One college summer, my mom cornrowed my hair before I left for a three-week wilderness program. I don't remember getting my hair cut or shaped during college, which I attended in eastern Indiana, other than once. When I spent a semester in New York City, I got an incredibly nice cut at a salon in Harlem, and Billy Dee Williams was getting his hair done in the chair across from me, so I'll always remember that haircut!

I'd begun working in my teens, primarily doing hourly, or what we'd now call gig, work, mostly desk jobs or childcare. Since the 1980s, I've worked almost exclusively in salaried or freelance positions. A waitressing job while in college was the only job I ever held that applied formal apparel guidelines (white blouse, black skirt, pantyhose, and no boots). I never had to comply with articulated hairstyling or grooming requirements. But I realize now that how I wore my hair was an issue for recruiters, employers, supervisors, judges, clients, students, colleagues, and deans. Not a one of these figures ever expressly commented that my hairstyle choice disqualified me or would disadvantage me for a role or a promotion. But the lack of explicit or expressed bias against natural hairstyles for Black women does not indicate the absence of bias.

A 2017 study confirms that Black women face bias in the workplace when wearing natural hairstyles.[2] Some companies explicitly prohibit certain natural hairstyles in the workplace, particularly braided ones, and federal courts uphold these policies. Unless a statute forbids it, employers have the right to impose hairstyling rules if such rules apply to all employees, even when Blacks, and Black women in particular, disproportionately bear the impact of these requirements. The US military at various times prohibited most natural hairstyles including "twists, dreadlocks, Afros and braids" while deployed. As a generalization, hourly wageworkers who interact with the public are most likely to be subject to appearance and hair regulations. Discrimination claims against retail fashion chains demonstrate this phenomenon. Salaried jobs in public-facing industries such as airlines have also restricted braided hair styles. But express restrictions on natural hair in high-status professions like medicine and law, and in executive corporate positions, seem uncommon. Nonetheless, only a handful of the Black women officers in corporate America photographed for the Winter 2021 DiversityWomenMedia Elite 100 wear braids or twists, and none wear locs.[3]

The Adult Working World, 1975–1979

While waitressing in Chicago during a long college break, I wore a medium-length natural. The restaurant was middlebrow, with a mostly white clientele. While there, I confronted one of the busboys, who knew me from eighth grade; he'd accused me of holding back on contributing my share of my tips to the collective pool that waitresses were required to split with the busboys. His allegation was based on the smaller amounts I contributed relative to the other waitresses. Though I was shocked and outraged to be accused of cheating, it wasn't until years later, when I read an article regarding racial disparities in tipping, that I realized I had probably been earning smaller tips than the white waitresses. A 2008 Cornell University study found that both Black and white consumers tip white restaurant servers more than they tip Black restaurant servers and that the server's appearance factors into customer satisfaction.[4]

My undergraduate school was an almost completely white midwestern liberal arts college with a student body that reinforced the 1970s' be-who-you-are ethos. I sported my Afro or headscarves, and the only time I dealt with makeup was when I participated in a modern dance performance. When the white student assigned to makeup duties for the show got to me, she threw her hands up, exclaiming that she had no idea what foundation to use on skin that wasn't white. The school was located in a part of Indiana that had both a strong Quaker and a strong Ku Klux Klan presence. Yet when I graduated in 1977 with, for the most part, white best friends, I believed that metropolitan areas of the United States were more progressive about race than they actually were.

Postgraduation, I moved to Philadelphia to live with one of my best friends, a woman of Guatemalan and German heritage. We both entered the job market with BAs in English literature. I still wore a medium-length Afro and little makeup other than lipstick and mascara. I could type, but not at a secretarial level, and was just looking for something that might allow me to use my college degree. A scientific publisher hired my friend as a proofreader. I also applied and was rejected. While writing this piece, I asked this friend what she recalled about working there. She immediately volunteered, "I do remember the Black women all straightened their hair."

After three unsuccessful months of job-searching, I left Philadelphia to live with a college quasi boyfriend, a graduate student at the University of Maryland. I looked for work in DC, at one point even registering with an employment agency. Still wearing my Afro and middle-class work clothes, I eventually found a job on the outskirts of DC on my own. I worked for a print shop where I used skills I acquired from high school and college newspaper and journal production and summers of newspaper experience acquired through nepotism. The print shop job required no dealing with the public. The only mention I recall about my appearance during this entire period was when a supervisor told me I was a little better looking than average. I took the LSAT in November, quit the print shop in December, and returned to live with my family in Chicago. I planned to apply to Georgetown Law and return to DC if admitted. A half year out of college with little to show for it, I still wore an Afro, impervious to the fact that I might have encountered discrimination because of my natural hair.

Lawyering, 1979–1986
Corporate Law Just Says No

In 1978 I began law school at the University of California, Berkeley. I entered with the advantage of having an English major and a philosophy minor, which helped me become proficient at reading formal and stilted tomes centered in the European enlightenment worldview. This prepared me for reading the law cases first-year professors assigned. My high LSAT writing score was probably a reason I was accepted at Berkeley, so I possessed writing skills useful for law school. Toward the end of first semester, I learned that I should be looking for a summer internship or clerkship. Although the law school had an on-campus interview program for law-firm jobs, its focus was not first-year students. The few law firms that interviewed first-year students on campus hired only those who received the highest semester grades or who had connections. I received no advice about how to navigate the hiring process. I had known no lawyers before law school, and had no social capital or network in California. Again, I was on my own in unfamiliar territory and did not have the savvy to seek mentors or search out more experienced Black women and ask their advice. I still sported a short Afro. In the end, I spent my first summer working at the law library and taking a bar-related class at University of California, Hastings College of the Law in San Francisco.

The on-campus interviewing program was much more robust for second- and third-year students. Second-year summer positions were tryouts for postgraduation jobs at prestigious law firms. The most successful summer externs could land an after-graduation associate position offer with their summer employers before returning to school for fall semester. During my second year, I, too, signed up for interviews. The firms that used the law placement office's process were required to see a mixture of students. The firms selected some of these students, generally students in the top 20 percent of their class or who ran the *California Law Review*. Others were students the law school placement office assigned to the firms to ensure that all students had opportunities to interview. Law firms invited the students they were interested in to callbacks at the firm offices. Callbacks were the measure of student success. In my Afro, I interviewed with about a dozen firms through placement office assignments, but received no invitations to actually interview at the firms. Of course, interviewers never mentioned my hair; doing so could have led to discrimination complaints. But I began to ponder if my hair might be holding me back. I had better than average grades, served on the *Ecology Law Quarterly* review, and worked for the law school as a torts tutor in its academic support. People working in the placement office told me that they were mystified by my lack of success. Although firms claimed they wanted to hire minorities, in passing me over, they'd rejected an academically solid Black candidate. Close to despair, I decided to experiment and try out straightened hair. Thus begins one of the most embarrassing experiences of my life, something I've never told anyone before.

Because I haven't thought about this incident in so long, it's now a recovered memory, and the details are somewhat dim. I was in junior high the last time my hair was chemically straightened; therefore, I didn't really understand what the process entailed. I didn't ask for anyone's advice or any referrals; I just set out to find a beauty parlor and get a perm. I called a salon in downtown Berkeley and made an appointment. When I showed up, the three middle-aged white ladies working in the salon all reacted to me with puzzlement. The stylist whom I'd scheduled to work on my hair told me that she had no experience working on Black hair. I did not yet understand that I should have turned around and run. I just responded, "That's OK." Naive, stupid, and sheltered, I absurdly let the white lady give me a perm. What apparently neither of us understood was that, at that time, a perm for a person with straight hair used rods and chemicals to curl the hair, while a perm for Black hair involved a relaxer to straighten it, a compound to neutralize the relaxer, and then styling. Black hair care options have increased substantially in the four decades since then, and different methods are now available.

The white stylist gave me a perm and it actually looked OK. She was really pleased and pointed out her success to the other stylists. I left wondering, *Will this make a difference in my job search?* Perhaps processed hair would signal my cultural competency with the world of white professionals so that law firms would stop worrying about me hiding a gun in my Afro, sneaking into a corporate boardroom to kill whitey. But when I got home I discovered that clumps of the perm chemicals remained in my hair at the roots, particularly near what I now know is called the *kitchen*. I had to rinse that shit out of my hair before it burned my scalp and broke my hair. After the shampoo, I no longer had a sculpted hairdo, just a shapeless mat. And that's all I can remember about that experience. I don't recall what I did to my hair over the next few days. I just recall a sense of defeat about my ability to succeed in law and a sense of shame about not knowing enough to find a Black beauty parlor and about letting a white lady touch my hair.

Through networking, I found a second-year summer job in Chicago. I worked for a small law firm headed by an attorney my father knew from local politics. In my final year of law school, I again participated in law-placement office interviews. Again, corporate law firms were uninterested in me. Had I been hired by a big law firm, I probably would have ended up hating the work, as many attorneys do, but I will always resent being rejected out of hand. In October 1980 I finally received a job offer, as an associate attorney with the Environmental Protection Agency in Washington, DC.

When you compare the work of an attorney at the EPA with that of a corporate attorney, you can understand why a government agency might have been less likely to have issues with my natural hair than a big law firm would. First, agency attorneys interact primarily with other attorneys, public officials, legislators, and regulated entities. For big law firms, the clients are often corporate or, if governmental, are higher-ups in decision-making positions.

Diversity was less likely to be a primary consideration for big law, and client skepticism about the qualifications of Black attorneys may be present if the corporate client is not diverse itself. And not many were in 1980. Second, for public agencies in DC, staffs that reflect the diversity of the public were politically valuable and made the agency appear more responsive and accountable to its constituencies. Furthermore, government entities in DC were known as good places for Black people to work. Finally, corporate America seems less welcoming to Black women with natural hair than to women who have straight hair, be it naturally straight, pressed or processed or purchased. I accepted the EPA job, but before it could start Ronald Reagan was elected president, and he appointed Anne Gorsuch to lead the agency. Gorsuch reduced the budget of the EPA by 22 percent, diminished Clean Air Act regulations, placated polluters, and visited substantial damage on environmental protections. Her son now illegitimately occupies a seat on the United States Supreme Court because the Mitch McConnell Republican Senate refused to hold hearings for President Obama's nominee Merrick Garland. I decided not to move to Washington, DC, to work for the Gorsuch EPA.

When I was back on the job market again in the San Francisco Bay Area, Reagan's recession, the worst since World War II, reared its fearsome head. I awaited bar results and looked for work when there was none. Although I learned that I passed the California bar exam in November 1981, I held only part-time jobs until spring 1982, when I was hired as an attorney for the Legal Services Corporation of Alameda County.

Legal Services Attorney

In California, Legal Aid attorneys, funded by the Legal Services Corporation, represented low-income people in civil cases, such as eviction defense and benefit denials. Most of my clients were facing eviction or had been denied unemployment benefits. The office to which I was assigned had a racially diverse clientele, but all had very low income or received social security or public benefits. My supervisor, the late great Judge Peggy Hora (prior to being elected to the bench), was somewhat reluctant to hire someone with as little experience as I had, stating, "I don't think poor people should be used to teach young lawyers how to practice." But she never had reason to regret hiring me. I still had the Afro when I was hired, but soon an Illinois farm boy who grew up to become a hairstylist marketed the Jheri curl. Comer Cottrell[5] adapted it into the Curly Kit for Black folks, and my hair set upon a new course.

I'd been working at Legal Aid for about a year when I got a Jheri curl. To maintain the curl, I had to inundate it with curl activator that rubbed off on everything. I soon reduced the amount of activator I used, but I could not lean my head on anything without leaving it smudged and greasy. Eventually I found a beautician who gave me loose naturalistic curls that I really liked. They looked plausible on me, something my hair could have been of its own accord. The 'do needed to be spritzed with a strong moisturizer, but I no longer left grease prints everywhere. For once, I was happy with my hair. My only complaint was that, living in San Francisco, I had to travel across the bay to sit in an Oakland beauty parlor for several hours on a Saturday every six or so weeks. But I always brought something to read, which is pretty telling. I was always more comfortable reading than talking to folks I didn't know well. Maybe that's how I had ended up in a white beauty parlor in Berkeley a few years earlier.

With the loose curls, I felt I looked good for a few years between ages twenty-five and thirty, and I felt comfortable going to court and representing my clients. I looked professional, my clients had confidence in me, and I represented them well. I encountered some of the common racism that Black attorneys still get in practice, such as the lawyer who greeted my white client like she was the attorney, even though the client wore jeans while I was in a suit and carried a briefcase. But I was the attorney who left the courtroom with a smirk that day because I won the motion, crushing him.

Legal Academia, 1987–Present

As much as I liked being a legal services attorney, it wore me out. The hours were erratic: if I was in a trial, I might need to prepare until one in the morning, quitting only because I had to get some sleep. I did get time off to offset extreme overtime, a perk that corporate associates did not get, but my salary was less than a third of what they made. The biggest burnout factor for me was the futility of my work in Reagan's America. Reagan tried to strike Legal Services funding from every federal budget he reviewed. Anti-poverty lawyers plagued him when he was governor of California, and as president his administration did everything it could to squelch the federally funded Legal Services Corporation. The feds cut our budget every year and increased the restrictions on whom we could serve and what kinds of services we could provide. The actual work was Sisyphean. As an attorney, I could postpone or even prevent an eviction, but if my clients' money problems were other than temporary, they'd often need the same help a few months later, when it would be less possible for me to assist them. When presented with the opportunity to work at my alma mater to direct its Academic Support Program (the same program that I'd participated in as a student and tutor when I was in law school), I jumped at it, even though it was not a better-paying job.

I was excited about working with law students of color to help them succeed in law school and pass the California bar exam on their first attempt. The previous year, I started to work a side gig as a grader for the California State Bar Examiners, a two-month, twice-per-year job. My insider's view of the bar grading process was a huge asset for my new position because Black and Latinx graduates of even the most highly rated law schools failed the exam in disproportionate numbers on their first attempt. Law professors were ineligible to grade the exams, but I did not teach or grade any classes so I could continue to gain a bar-reader's perspective.

I kept the curly perm for several more years. I wore a short tapered-cut kind of punk version when I got married in 1986 and a longer version when I was hired as a law professor at Santa Clara University the next year. In 1988, when I was ready to get pregnant, I stopped chemically processing my hair to avoid applying products that have been proven carcinogenic or that scientists found increased the risk of premature birth, low birth weight, and other pregnancy risks.[6] First I wore a teeny weeny Afro, let it grow out, and then got cornrows. Since then, I have only worn cornrows, extensions, braids, twists, and dreadlocks, except for a brief period of pressed hair brought on by my old nemesis, White-Caused Despair.

Protective Hairstyles

I started wearing long, synthetic extension braids before I got pregnant. I kept them looking neat and professional, as is expected in the workplace. After my baby daughter grew out of grabbing and pulling my extensions, she liked to roll the end of a braid between her fingers, which she called "fuzzing my curls."

Although her play wasn't great for upkeep, it was adorable to me and comforting to her. My husband liked my hair with the braids; my mother and siblings didn't. I think my birth family thought they looked ghetto. Sometimes they grumbled about "that stuff" in my hair. Once, after I started wearing dreads, my nephew told me that I looked like someone who would buy drugs on the street. My dreadlocks originally included extensions, but eventually I was able to cut them out. Now my dreads are a little past shoulder length and are still neat and professional. My mother now actually likes my hair.

I think many people, especially from other cultures, just don't understand the role hair plays in Black women's lives.
—**Solange Knowles**

At first the braids caused no problems for me at work. Everybody at the law school knew me before I'd gotten them, and the braids didn't signify anything about me except a new hairdo. My problems began when we got a new white dean who brought his own conceptions about my hairstyle to the workplace. His appointment was when my employment began to go south. Thank goodness I already had tenure and had been promoted to associate professor before he arrived. I've been frozen as an associate professor through three deans and two decades. The next two deans hadn't known me before I wore my hair natural, so I have had to contend with their preconceptions about what Afros and braided styles meant. It's hard to overcome those misconceptions, especially when a white person is unaware of having them. People never consciously think, *That hairstyle means she rejects white standards* or *She's uninterested in making white people feel comfortable about her.*

The thing is, very few white people understand Black people's hair. The ability of Black hairstyles to evoke fear in folks is mind-boggling. A white person once told me that when he was a boy in the 1960s, the close-cut haircuts of Black boys his age scared him because he could see their scalps. Even the terminology for one Black hairstyle embodies white fear: dreadlocks. This term may be derived from British soldiers' fearful reactions at the sight of Kenyan warriors.[7] Some people saw my hair as a sign of hostility to white people, culture, and society, or as unwillingness to accommodate legal-profession norms. Not unlike the law-firm interviewers of my student days, my hair signaled something about my qualifications and abilities and trustworthiness. I was the only Black professor at my school who wore braids; only three or four Black faculty members worked at the school at any given time. The men wore natural hairstyles; the other women wore processed styles or had natural hair that was not type 4C. Other Black professors at the law school were appointed to assistant or associate deanships, or left the school. Although I once inquired about serving in a decanal position, I was not selected. Of course, since the administrators treated other Black faculty differently than they treated me, they could not be accused of practicing racist exclusion.

White people need to understand that when a Black person wears a natural hairstyle, the primary purpose is not usually to signal what she or he thinks about whites or white America. My natural hairstyles have foremost been about me taking care of my body and my time. I love the term *protective hairstyles* because not chemically changing the texture of one's hair protects the hair and the whole body. It avoids unnecessary exposure to some of the dangerous substances that comprise relaxers. I returned to natural hairstyles to protect my potential children and myself. And even though I don't totally eschew dangerous hair-processing chemicals—I do dye my hair, for instance—dyeing my hair is about my vanity, insecurity, and our society's youth-worshipping culture. I admit that I did not care enough about my superiors' or students' judgment to do anything other than straighten my hair with a hot comb for a few months, at a time when I was despairing about my lack of professional success. But I came to my senses and stopped the pressing. I was not willing to return to chemical straightening, and I realized that even if I straightened my hair, haters were going to hate.

I acknowledge that wearing my hair in braids and extensions is privileged, because some employers prohibit the wearing of such hairstyles. Even though I may have been ostracized for my natural styles, once I'd attained tenure, I could not lose my job over that. This is not the case for women such as Farryn Johnson, Brittany Noble, Rachel Sakabo, Destiny Tompkins, and Chastity C. Jones. The Supreme Court of the United States declined to hear Jones's case after the Circuit Court of Appeals refused to find it illegal for her to lose her job for refusing to cut her dreadlocks. The United States needs legislation, such as a federal CROWN Act, to protect workers who wear protective hairstyles.

While my unwillingness to submit to white constructions of professionalism may have cost me materially, rarely did I care enough to conform. Those times that I had conformed were in an attempt to please or appease white people, relieving mental stress and career fallout. I got over it. My job provided enough class status for me to choose natural hairstyles, but there remains a natural-hair ceiling. Only recently is that ceiling being broken.

Works Cited

1. "Superman's Girl Friend, Lois Lane Vol 1 106," DC Comics Database, https://dc.fandom.com/wiki/Superman%27s_Girl_Friend,_Lois_Lane_Vol_1_106.

2. Minda Honey, "Black Women Speak About Natural Hair Bias in the Workplace," *Teen Vogue*, February 24, 2017, https://www.teenvogue.com/story/black-women-natural-hair-bias-discrimination.

3. Tanisha A. Sykes, "The Elite 100: A Tribute to Black Women Executives—the Change Is Here," *Diversity Woman*, February 1, 2021, https://www.diversitywoman.com/the-elite-100-a-tribute-to-black-women-executives-2.

4. Tom Jacobs, "Black Restaurant Workers Get Smaller Tips," *Pacific Standard*, September 4, 2014, updated June 14, 2017, https://psmag.com/economics/racism-black-restaurant-waiters-service-industry-servers-get-smaller-tips-90121.

5. Elaine Woo, "Comer Cottrell Dies at 82; Made Jheri Curl Available to the Masses," *Los Angeles Times*, October 8, 2014, https://www.latimes.com/local/obituaries/la-me-comer-cottrell-20141009-story.html.

6. "Big Market for Black Cosmetics, but Less-Hazardous Choices Limited," Environmental Working Group, December 6, 2016, https://www.ewg.org/research/big-market-black-cosmetics-less-hazardous-choices-limited.

7. Gabrielle Kwarteng, "Why I Don't Refer to My Hair as 'Dreadlocks,'" *Vogue*, July 16, 2020, https://www.vogue.com/article/locs-history-hair-discrimination.

PART II

THE PILGRIMAGE

PEINATE EL PELO

Carmen Bardeguez–Brown

**El que no tiene Dinga
Tiene Mandinga.**

"Carmelita ven a peinarte el pelo."
"Ya voy mami"
Uhhhhh, how I hated when mami used to comb my hair! I have curly
hair and for some people they will call it: "pelo malo."

Mami had a routine of using oils to soften the curls. There was always
a particular oil for the condition of my unmanageable hair. Mom would
put a little bit of aceite de oliva if the kinky hair was soft. If we had money

she would use coconut oil. But something was certain: I will always need
some kind of oil to soften my hair. All of those aromatic smells made me
feel like a salad plate. Like some kind of kitchen condiment.
She will only comb my hair if and only if my hair has been smeared
with oils. I wonder why she wanted to tame my lioness mane.
Mami say, that I have
"Un pelo malo pero manejable." Mom said that I was lucky
I didn't have Dad's kinky hair. I wonder what he would say about that?
In Puerto Rico there are only two kinds of hair
pelo malo or Black hair, and pelo bueno or white people's hair.
Which I don't understand because in New York, we are all Black.
But then again, what kind of hair is bad?
Is not like the hair has done anything to you. In Puerto Rico everyone
wants to have white people's hair, pelo bueno. Even if their mother is Black
or in my case, my father. Well, in here we are all equally Black. In Guayama
you will see everyone goes to the beauty salon to get their hair straightened.
But then everybody denies it. Mom already had planned for me to get a
mild relaxer but then we moved here. Moving here has brought freedom to
my hair condition. I do not know how but I was able to convince mom to
let me have my long curly, kinky hair, tranquilo.

HAIR POLITICS: AN AFRO PUERTO RICAN WOMYN'S UNTANGLED NARRATIVE

Dr. Bárbara Idalissee Abadía-Rexach

A Girl Who Was Born Black

On September 26, 1980, around 11:30 at night, in Fajardo, Puerto Rico, Olga Esther Rexach-Ayala fulfilled one of her most cherished dreams: to be the mother of a daughter. That girl was born with dark skin, brown eyes, and curly hair. Baby Bárbara Idalissee did not look like her older brothers Germán and Félix Juan. They had been born with lighter skin, light hair, and green eyes. The designated godmother, a maternal great-aunt, an Afro-descendant woman who identified as white, declined to baptize Bárbara when she saw her physical features. All her life, Bárbara has been asked if she and her brothers have the same father. They even ask why she doesn't have green eyes.

All this in Puerto Rico, a country that celebrates its *mestizaje* and denies the existence of anti-Black racism. In 2000, 80 percent of the Puerto Rican population identified as white, while 8 percent said they were Black. Ten years later, in 2010, 76 percent chose white as their only race; 12 percent chose Black. The census adheres to the same constricted categories as the United States' census does, a limitation that does not account for the breadth of the island's racial brackets. In the view of many people, Puerto Rico is seen as a white country.

I am Bárbara Idalissee, and I was born Black!

Bárbara Idalissee, six months old. *Bárbara Idalissee personal family photo*

I Grew Up Black

When I was little, my mother used to style my hair with two or three braids. My hairpins would match my clothes.

In my maternal grandmother María Virginia's (a.k.a. Prin's) eyes, my mom's way of combing my hair was superficial. My grandmother would soak her hands with pomade—I still remember the smell—and untangle my hair.

"This momma of yours always leaves you the *tostón!*" My grandmother was referring to my mother not untangling my hair correctly. My grandmother, now eighty-seven years old, refuses to show off her natural hair. She still relaxes it.

When my mom had a hysterectomy, my paternal grandmother Gilia María took care of me. She braided my hair so tight I would suffer headaches. Grandmother Gilia was a mixed-race woman who always wore her hair natural.

In an effort to resolve my complaints about the pulls and squeezes from one grandmother and the criticisms from the other, my mother chose to straighten my hair when I started first grade.

On one occasion, I contracted lice, and my mom decided to give me a boyish haircut. My Afro confused people, and they'd often ask whether I was male. I often heard slurs that my hair was like "*gazpacho 'e coco*" or "*pepita 'e jobo.*"

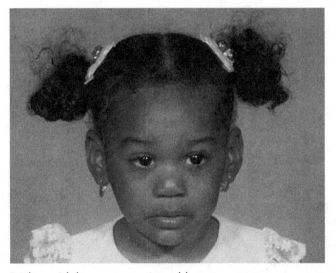

Bárbara Idalissee, two years old. *Bárbara Idalissee personal family photo*

In the Fajardo public schools where I studied, I was one of the few visibly Black people. That fact, of course, raised questions from my peers, and from me too. Today I can say that I focused on getting all As, for which I was christened "the nerd," and on having impeccable behavior to avoid harassment stemming from my skin color and "bad hair."

For over twenty uninterrupted years, I wore my hair straightened. Before I learned how to handle the blow-dryer and the flat iron, I resorted to the rollers and the hair dryer, which required hours at a stretch of me sitting in a chair until the hair was completely dry.

Black women view their hair as a problem. To enjoy black hair, such negative thinking has to be unlearned.
—**bell hooks**, author

In 1989 our family of six women and three men made our first trip to Orlando, Florida. One afternoon, after a day in the pool, my mom put rollers in all the girls' hair and also on herself. We went out to the Florida Mall like that and caused a sensation. People stared at us, surprised, and even asked whether wearing hair rollers in public was a custom in our country. I never wanted to wear rollers in public ever again.

In 2005 I was old enough to decide on my own to cut my hair, my first "big chop." My family did not take this decision well. They remarked that something must be wrong with me because "that cut makes you look like a man." When I visited Mexico, I found I left many people speechless. They were curious to know where that young, Black woman with short hair who spoke Spanish was from.

In 2006 when I moved to Texas, I got African braids for the first time. When I arrived at the humble beauty salon, I couldn't specify the precise style I wanted. My African stylist could not believe my ignorance. I had to explain to her that in Puerto Rico, I had never braided my hair with cornrows or box braids. To my stylist, it was beyond incredible to see a Black woman who was unaware of common hairstyles associated with her natural hair. I also hadn't known how painful it would be to have my hair pulled hither and yon for ten hours. On my following visits, I took painkillers before arriving at the salon. In 2008 I returned to the world of straightening.

Nowadays in Puerto Rico, the beauty industry that specializes in curly hair is growing rapidly. More and more people, particularly women of African descent, are deciding to embrace their natural hair. But racial harassment attaches and persists. Opinions abound that natural hair is unprofessional, that it needs to be "groomed." Dress codes often prohibit hairstyles associated with curly and kinky textures.

For sixteen years, I have been on a journey during which I have vacillated from straightening to braids to the big chop to texturizers. To this day, I wear my hair natural, and I confess I do not know my curl type, or how to properly care for it.

The author after the Big Chop, with braids, and with an Afro. *Bárbara Idalissee personal family photos*

So, I go on managing my rebellious/ulotrichous/curly/kinky hair with the certainty that no matter how I comb my hair or what product I apply to it,

I will always be a Black woman. The affirmation of my Blackness does not manifest itself solely through my hair. Despite all the transitions, my identification and interpellation as a Black womyn remain intact. And just as certainly, racial prejudice and discrimination remain unchanged.

Braiding Memories

From childhood, my mother was subjected to hot combs and then straightening creams to "fix" her hair. In her youth, she traveled to Chicago, Illinois, and made her first big chop. She arrived back in Puerto Rico carrying several wigs that made her feel fashionable. After later undergoing chemotherapy and losing all her hair, my mom reverted to wearing a wig.

Because of the sociocultural context in which she grew up, my mother believed our hair textures *needed* chemical products. She was also mindful of shielding me from daily racial harassment. Neither my mom nor I understood that hair was not—and is still not—the only racial marker in Puerto Rico or outside the archipelago. Straightening was correlated with cleanliness, care, and professionalism. I will never blame my mother for deciding to straighten my hair. After all, many of the memories I keep of her have to do with our hair. I treasure many of the childhood moments in which she worked with my hair. In turn, I relaxed, cut, dyed (black or with blonde tips), and combed her hair. Those were mother-daughter bonding moments that I can no longer enjoy.

When my nieces were little, I loved styling their hair. And now, they all cherish memories of those moments we spent together.

When my niece-goddaughter, Virginia Alejandra, was seventeen, she decided to show off her beautiful natural curls. Seeing her filled me with pride. A couple of months ago, my niece Daynalee, nineteen, called me on FaceTime to show me her big chop. Although they both know that I will admire whatever style they decide to wear and understand that I do not judge or demonize any woman for how she decides to style or treat her hair, it is interesting how they seek my approval when they celebrate their Blackness.

As I was reviewing this text in a Florida hospital lobby, "Brown Skin Girl" played on the radio. Meanwhile, medical staff were preparing my great-niece to be taken to the operating room. Since she was born premature and has remained in the neonatal intensive care unit (NICU), as of this writing I have not had the chance to meet her. However, in the photos my niece shares with me of her daughter in an incubator, I have noticed her head covered with hair. I had envisioned her with a bunch of curly hair, kinkier than her mother's, that I would comb while pretending she was my doll. I have thought about her fraternal twin brother's hair too. I look forward to combing their hair, enjoying their curls getting tangled on my fingers.

When my grand-niece and grand-nephew are discharged from the hospital, I will have books waiting for them, about being Black children with curly hair in a world that will insist on questioning their beauty because of their skin tone and the texture of their hair.

As my grandmother had done with my mother and as my grandmothers and my mother had done with me, I will do for my nieces. I will continue to braid memories.

Healing While Black

I live as a Black Puerto Rican womyn, and writing about my hair hurts.

Seeing photos of me from my four decades of life causes me to ponder how one survives Blackness in Puerto Rico. Embracing my natural hair has not been easy. Those of us who choose to go natural face multiple pressures that lacerate the will to wear our hair as a political and celebratory tool, as a mode of rendering Blackness visible while challenging Eurocentric beauty stereotypes.

As Black womyn, we have to gird our loins against the derogatory comments and questioning from family or partners: "Aren't you going to fix your hair?" "Are you going out like this?" "You are *esmoruzá*!" "What did you do to your hair?" Bad hair—whatever that is—must be hidden!

I cannot close without mentioning the demeaning, unwarranted screening at airports. On two occasions when I wore my Afro, security searched my hair at the Austin, Texas, airport. Why is *my* hair a threat? I do not see security scrutinizing people with other hair textures.

There are additional tolls beyond the social pressure and irreverent curiosity that causes people to reach out and touch our hair without consent: the high costs of our hair products, the often-lengthy time spent in salons. The beauty industry is a lucrative one, and for many nonwhite women, hair care is an expense for which there is not always a budget.

Photo at a 2020 exhibition at the Museum of Contemporary Art in San Juan, Puerto Rico. *Bárbara Idalissee*

It's imperative that we converse with our families, partners, and friends. We should not remain silent when they make offensive, ignorant comments. Talking about natural hair and our experiences as racialized bodies can lead us to stop criminalizing those who decide to use chemical products to straighten their hair and encourage us to start accompanying one another on our hair journeys. Talking about our hair—our different textures and curls—helps us create sororities of black womyn who can learn from each other and inspire us to wear our *marantas* proudly. Let's create spaces for hair conversations that educate, respect, heal, and celebrate.

NATURALLY: A HAIR JOURNEY TO AFRICA AND BEYOND

Kim Coleman Foote

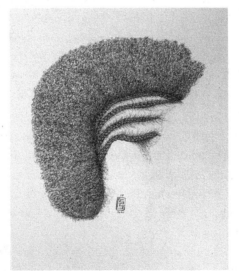

BLACK WAS NOT BEAUTIFUL IN MY HOUSEHOLD. It was the 1980s, and Afros were as passé as bell-bottoms and platform shoes. The Jheri curl was all the rage, at least until the wet-sofa-back scenes in *Coming to America*. My parents snickered at people with dark brown skin—the color of my brother's—and my brother and I followed suit. We believed that my friend's mother, who blackened her Santas with a Magic Marker, was unhinged.

I grew up learning that Black was anything *but* beautiful. Black was strong (and bottling up your unpleasant feelings). Black was proud (of said strength, if not your appearance). Black was smart and determined (three times as much as white folks). And ultimately, Black was being ashamed of most things that shackled you to Africa (a nose too wide and flat, lips too cushiony, a butt that exceeded badonkadonk dimensions, and of course, nappy hair).

The main images I saw of Africa, in addition to Eddie Murphy's Zamunda, were the bling-slinging pharaohs of ancient Egypt and the emaciated refugees who appeared on the nightly news, those wretches too weak to brush the flies from their eyes. In other words, the main representations I ever saw of Africa were a comedic version that made me laugh, an illustrious preslavery past that filled me with pride, and a contemporary "authentic" version that made me cringe.

Among my peers in the predominantly Black town of East Orange, New Jersey, a classmate suspected of being African was labeled "booty scratcher," à la the sick and starving people on TV. Boys whom girls designated as "cute" had light skin and hazel eyes. Gray or blue, even better. The most popular girl in my class was half Puerto Rican, with light skin, light eyes, and long blondish hair. My classmates orbited her on the playground one afternoon as if she were their sun, gushing that she looked like Celebration Barbie. I stood apart from them, scowling and saying, "So she pretty cuz she look white?"

In my view, *almost* white was the ideal. My complexion, while not meeting my own standard, was seen as light enough by most Black folks I met. It was the cinnamon color of the woman pictured on Ambi products. Incidentally, I used Ambi in high school, hoping to erase the black and mud-brown freckles that I felt tarnished my skin.

My hair was a different story altogether. It was not long, nor was it straight or wavy—traits that my mother designated a "good grade of hair." She never told me directly that my hair merited a bad grade, even during all those times she wrestled a comb through my naps. But according to her standard, I knew my hair deserved a D. More like an F.

I never really noticed my hair, though, until I was eleven or twelve. We had moved to the predominantly Italian town of Belleville, and my new white friend, Maria, asked me why I never wore my hair down. Maria favored pony-tails like I did, but her thick black hair looked like a cascading fountain compared to my more aptly termed pigtails. I fumbled for a response, thinking, *But it doesn't go down!* The only times it had—sort of—was when my mother or a beautician straightened it for special occasions, like my yearly dance recitals.

Maria's comment aroused something in me. I suddenly felt the urge to fit in with my peers, perhaps because I was in the minority in Belleville. Of my school's two sixth-grade classes, which together comprised about fifty children, only four of us were Black. I already stood out for being soft-spoken and smart, even antagonizing my racist teacher, so why not try to look like the majority—as much as I could, at least? And the usual method of straightening my hair—the straightening comb—wouldn't suffice. The straightening comb had been a nuisance, with accidental burns to my ears and scalp, regardless of the Vaseline my stylist applied for protection. Rainy days became my enemy, and my styles would last a week or two at best before napping up.

Begging my mother for a perm got me nowhere. She declared it was too grown-up, too permanent (hence the name). So I suffered another few years of the straightening comb and scorched skin so my hair could flow like a white girl's.

Not that the perm was worth the hype once my mother finally allowed me to get one in high school. My stylist, meeting my eyes in the mirror, called it a virgin perm. She ran her fingers through my straight strands, asking, "It feels lighter, doesn't it?" I nodded, grinning. I shook my head like they did in the movies, and my hair swished around my face. It wasn't weighted down with the grease used for straightening, grease that both protected the strands from the comb's heat and provided extra sheen.

There was just one caveat, my stylist added: hair not permed often enough would split, eventually down to the roots. That would mean a sixty-dollar salon visit once monthly, which was unthinkable to my working-class, old-school parents. If they couldn't afford it, I couldn't have it. Name-brand clothing and sneakers? Forget about it. Regular perms by a beautician? No way, not when my mother could buy a DIY perm kit to touch up my nappy roots at home. And even then, she purchased the kits only every few months.

Luckily, my stylist's omen about my hair splitting never came true. But the ingredients in those DIY kits were never strong enough for my thick hair, so I had to live with despicable puffy roots. Soon, though, I found the perfect solution for my hair at a family holiday dinner. One of my older cousins' hair seemed to have expanded overnight, becoming as full and long as Oprah's, only curly. As my mother and I gaped at it, my cousin chuckled, telling us the hair was fake. Extensions, she called it, demonstrating how she braided synthetic hair into her own. My memory flashed back to elementary school in East Orange, when one of my classmates showed up one day with her hair inexplicably a foot longer. Now it made perfect sense.

When my cousin offered to braid my hair and my mother approved, I was ecstatic. My cousin transformed my hair, which had never grown past my chin, into a full, shoulder-length mane. And how pretty it was! Boys at my high school seemed to think so too, even some of the white ones.

In high school, I'd felt even more in the minority than I had in the sixth grade. Out of eight hundred students, the Black students numbered fewer than thirty. The handful of Black boys had mostly ignored me, with my oversized nerdy glasses that took up half my face. My new hair made their eyes linger, and I felt giddy from the acknowledgment. A few years later in college, the same thing happened when I abandoned my glasses for contact lenses: the few Black guys on campus gawked as if noticing me for the first time, as if I were a new student.

Black women been styling their natural hair for thousands of years but when we got to America it suddenly became unmanageable.

—**Zellie Imani**, writer, educator, and organizer

Hair extensions are now known as a protective style for a reason. As my cousin continued to braid my hair over the next few months, my hair grew the longest it had ever been, including at the back of my head, where it used to break off at a half inch. My hair soon swept my shoulders, making my mother's eyes flash with appreciation.

Then, during a visit to a new beauty parlor for my high school graduation, a perm left too long, perhaps, caused those long, lush strands to come out in clumps. As the stylist met my infuriated expression in her mirror, she claimed that my hair had been damaged well before her treatment, that my ends had been overdue for a trim. She proceeded to hack until my hair was ear-length, my newfound beauty literally going down the drain.

One of the most important questions for my prospective colleges—academically rigorous, predominantly white, and some of the best in the country, according to *US News & World Report*—was "Where's the nearest Black hair salon?" Swarthmore College, my ultimate choice, was located in a Quaker town in Pennsylvania. It was just a half hour from Philly, where I could find plenty of salons, and a train to the city stopped right on campus. Before I could choose a salon, though, one of my classmates volunteered to touch up my hair with a dreaded DIY perm kit. But by using the perm as well as a hair dryer and curling irons, she smoothed my rebellious roots and coaxed my hair into silky strands.

I continued to glorify straight hair even as I formed a budding friendship with a Black classmate who embraced the beauty in African things, the first person my age I'd met who did that. She inspired me to weave a cowry shell or two into my strands and to wrap African-print fabric around my head. She also nudged me to stop perming, as she herself had done in high school, but the buck stopped there. She had close-cropped ringlets, which I thought of as curls and definitely not naps, and I grew up considering curls as "good hair." Despite the short length of my friend's hair, I saw it as pretty, and it could grow much faster, much longer, than mine. If I were to cut my hair and not like it—and that seemed probable, because it would probably look like a boy's—God knew how long it would take for it to grow back to a decent length.

Meanwhile, other Black girls in college who professed "going natural" had long hair, which they twisted into ropes that looked like extensions. Others promoted cornrows, a style that felt novel to them since they hadn't grown up wearing it. I'd worn cornrows throughout childhood and considered them for little girls, and I didn't think my hair was thick or long enough to twist properly.

T'Keyah Crystal Keymáh's book *Natural Woman/Natural Hair*[1] would do for me what my naturalista classmates could not. I arrived at the campus dining hall one day to find the Black female students passing that book around as if it were the Bible. I glanced over their shoulders, and what I read piqued my curiosity, enough to add myself to their borrowing queue. By the time the book ended up in my hands weeks later, its cover was creased, with the occasional greasy fingerprint on the inside pages.

The book showcased an array of cute styles beyond twists and cornrows. It also provided direction on how to transition from permed hair without cutting everything off—a.k.a. the big chop: I could just twist my hair as it was. I didn't have to worry, the author declared, about split roots; that was a common myth among beauticians, designed to frighten clients into getting perms regularly and spending more money. What *did* cause hair damage was improper moisturizing and combing.

My mother, through no fault of her own, used to comb my hair from the roots to the ends, as opposed to the recommended ends to roots. That was likely the reason my hair kept breaking off at the back. That hair, I would learn as my self-twisted hair grew without the aid of extensions, was some of the finest, straightest, and weakest on my scalp. Soon, my frizzy roots started resembling the ropes of my classmates, and I was astounded to find that I liked them more than my straight ends, which hung thin and limp.

One day at the start of junior year, I found myself before a bathroom mirror, scissors in hand. I kept snipping until the last of my permed strands littered the sink, and I was shocked to see my unpermed roots transformed further. My head was full of inch-long clumps of spiraled curls, formerly known as naps. They were teeny, the width of an ink-pen spring—nowhere near the size of my naturalista friend's. But for the first time, I thought of my natural hair as beautiful.

College transformed more than just my conception of my hair. It did a number on my very faulty and very limited awareness of Africa as well. During sophomore year, Swarthmore had a new Black dean, a warm and jovial man who declared himself an Afrocentrist. When he learned I'd taken French since the eighth grade and planned to study abroad in France, he suggested Africa instead. "They don't speak French in Africa," I scoffed, thinking it was another one of his jokes. Curiously, I'd read Ousmane Sembène's 1960 novel, *Les bouts de bois de Dieu* (published in English as *God's Bits of Wood*), about a railroad strike in Mali and Senegal, in my freshman French class. Maybe I thought it had been translated from English. Even if the dean was somehow telling the truth, I *had* to go to France, especially after seeing Parisian landmarks in all my high school language textbooks. When I enrolled in a sociology class about Africa later that year, I realized my ignorance. I learned that France had colonized several African countries, making French one of the most widely spoken European languages on the continent.

Every three weeks, our class watched feature-length movies and documentaries by African filmmakers. I'd had no clue that African cinema existed. Gaston Kaboré's *Zan Boko* became one of my all-time favorite films. Set in Burkina Faso, the story explored one of our class's major themes: tradition versus modernity. The movies weren't the astronomically budgeted Hollywood films that had fed my moviegoing diet prior to college. The production values were rough, with subtitles. Many of the performers were clearly not professional actors; their mannerisms seemed exaggerated, and their dialogue felt wooden, even as they spoke in foreign languages. Yet, those movies astounded me because they forced me to think deeply about important matters such as colonialism, culture clashes, political corruption, and African value systems. African cinema also provided me a glimpse of an Africa beyond the 1980s TV clips and *National Geographic*. I learned that some aspects I'd seen in mainstream media did still exist, such as barefoot people living in mud-brick homes with no electricity or running water, hunting and gathering for their dinner. I came to understand, however, that Africa was also full of cities with tall buildings, paved roads teeming with Mercedes-Benzes and scooters, radios blaring synthesizers and electric guitars, dapper men in suits and ties, and stylish women strutting in colorful dresses and heels and sporting wigs, extensions, and perms.

I realized that I'd grown up knowing a microcosm of Africa, just as people in many parts of the world learn only a microcosm of the United States. Had those people relied on mainstream media to educate them about my country, they might easily believe that most African Americans are criminals and carry guns and that most of us live in drug- and crime-ridden ghettos. Those African films made me wonder what else I might have missed about Africa, but I still wasn't thinking of spending a semester there.

Haile Gerima's *Sankofa* would change my perspective later that year, when the film screened on campus for one of Swarthmore's movie nights. I had no idea what the movie was about, but its official poster had intrigued me since high school, when I'd first discovered it. But the night of the screening, I was swamped with homework and decided at the last minute not to go. My naturalista friend showed up at my dorm room and dragged me to the campus cinema, ignoring my protests. On-screen, as a man painted in white beat a drum during the grainy opening shots, I fidgeted, hoping the next two hours would be worth skipping a few hundred pages of reading.

Early in the film, the protagonist, Mona, a Black model with permed hair, descended the dark corridor of a castle on a tropical African beach. She stumbled into a dungeon where she encountered grim-faced African men, chained to one other. White men brandishing torches seized her, ripped off her clothes, and branded her. As her screams echoed throughout the theater, I gripped the arms of my seat, sensing tension among the packed audience. We then followed Mona's journey back in time and witnessed her harrowing ordeal as a slave, which ended with her rebirth out of the castle dungeons as a woman of wisdom, enlightened with her history. As the credits rolled, the theater was full of sniffles, and students, including me, were removing our glasses to wipe our eyes. I felt crushed; but like Mona, I burned from the knowledge of the injustices my African ancestors suffered, as well as the travesty of many descendants like me having forgotten them. The castle she'd entered also fascinated me.

When I applied to study abroad that next fall semester, I didn't choose France. I opted instead for a program in Mali through the School for International Training (SIT). I was enticed by the opportunity to continue my French studies while learning a local language, Bambara. The program also included a month of independent anthropological fieldwork, and I proposed investigating local songs to compare with African American work songs. When I received a phone call from SIT's program coordinator, I braced myself for the admissions decision, but she was just checking in, she said, to recommend an alternate option. She thought the Crossroads of the African Diaspora program in Ghana would suit me better, as it focused on the trans-Atlantic slave trade and could therefore offer better resources for my research. I wouldn't be able to study French, but I'd have the opportunity to learn a local Ghanaian language.

I was confused; the only Ghana program I'd seen in SIT's catalog focused on arts and culture. As much as I was a proponent of the arts, I didn't want my experience in Africa to be just about playing drums and singing and dancing. Flipping frantically through the catalog, I found the diaspora program on the reverse page for the arts program. I wasn't sure how I'd overlooked it, because the promotional picture was that slave castle from *Sankofa*. Heart racing, I implored the program coordinator to switch my application.

One of the things I found most shocking about Ghana was the number of women sporting permed hair and weaves. I had anticipated this phenomenon in the cities, considering the African movies I'd watched in my sociology class, but these styles were popular even in the Ghanaian villages I visited. As I grew more and more disappointed observing women's hairstyles, I had to remind myself what my sociology class had taught me: Africa wasn't stuck in some mythical time before my ancestors were captured and enslaved. I was also learning in my Ghana lectures that African people had been adopting European influences for centuries.

Braided hair extensions were especially popular in Ghana, and the cost was appealing to us American students on tight budgets. My Black classmates and I rushed to get our hair braided during our first week in the country, since the price for styling was six times less than it was at home. We felt heart-warmed when our stylists smiled and told us they were offering us the "welcome home, my sister" discount. Only later did I learn that they'd swindled us, charging us prices that were above the average.

I would eventually find an incredible beautician, the homestay sister of one of my classmates, who was honest with her prices. When I wasn't in the mood for box braids or cornrows, she would bind my hair with waxed black thread. A seemingly endless array of these futuristic-looking styles was available, often advertised on salons' hand-painted signs. My favorite involved cascading rows of loops. As my hair grew longer, my beautician created a new style on me: trifold loops checkering my scalp. The one style I avoided screamed "picaninny"—that not-quite-human-looking child in advertisements of old, with the grinning mouth as wide as the watermelon it ate, wearing braids sticking straight up. Compounding this, I felt troubled that the pidgin English variant of *picaninny* survives in Anglophone Africa as *pikin*, which means "child."

The first time I wore my hair without extensions or thread in Ghana, I became starkly aware of how local women perceived natural hair. I was about to leave my homestay family's house in urban Cape Coast for a date, and I wore my hair in an Afro. My homestay mother, who was in the living room, paused in her ironing to ogle me. I hesitated, thinking she might comment on my leggings. My program advised female students to wear long skirts, but pants were popular among university students our age. My homestay mother was staring not at my legs, though, but at my head. She told me my hairstyle looked like a witch's. I left the house feeling shaken, though the interaction felt familiar. I recalled my own mother casting uneasy glances at my African-print head wraps, saying, "You going outside like that?" In other words, looking like a slave. Because when else had Black women worn head wraps in public?

The question Ghanaian women would ask most often upon meeting me with my natural hair was "Why don't you perm your hair?" It was typically followed by "Do you go to church?" The questions deeply saddened me. It had taken me so long to appreciate my African roots, and there I was, trying to explain that I hadn't come to the *muthaland* to put the creamy crack back into my hair, or to worship Christianity beneath the gaze of the blond-haired, blue-eyed Jesus depicted everywhere.

When I visited Ghana for the second time, two years later on a Fulbright fellowship, I felt I'd figured out the perfect response to the hair question in such a devoutly Christian society: "This is how God created me." I stopped using it after the first smug try, when my interrogator looked like she either wanted to punch me or finger her own stringy strands and weep.

———

In Ghana, I'd hoped to find the acceptance I experienced in what seemed a most unlikely place: the Dominican Republic. When I visited the country the summer before my Ghana college semester, I was pretty uninformed about the country's history, but I knew to expect permed hair. I traveled there to visit my Dominican college roommate, who used perm kits for her hair, which was longer than mine with less kinky roots. Her mother permed too, along with her aunties and cousins and seemingly most of the women I'd observed when visiting their majority-Dominican neighborhood in Manhattan. During the two weeks I spent in Santo Domingo, I was not very surprised to encounter just one woman wearing natural hair—a short Afro, which made me want to give her the Black Power salute.

I was shocked, though, that Dominicans considered me one of them, with my half-permed twists. Before arriving on the island, I felt sure people would see me as African American, as an outsider. My roommate and her family shared my skin tone, but they never mentioned any African heritage. I presumed their color came from the indigenous Taino background my roommate always mentioned. Other Dominicans I'd met before the trip were quite pale, with silky, wavy hair. Upon exiting the airport in Santo Domingo, then, I was stunned to see so many people of my complexion. Only later did I discover that while many Dominicans do indeed have African ancestry, they deny it while idolizing their Spanish and Indigenous blood. It was as mind-boggling to me as those African Americans I'd met who were lighter than me and who denied any white ancestry.

People in Santo Domingo looked into my brown face, so much like their own, and accused me of fibbing when I told them I spoke little Spanish. Some laughingly called me *mentirosa*—liar. Others' reactions bordered on anger, one man going so far as to say I should be proud of where I came from. *I am proud of my roots—my African roots*, I thought, feeling awkward. Another time, at a fast-food restaurant, one of the employees told me something incomprehensible in Spanish, and I gave her a blank stare. When my roommate explained that I couldn't hear her, the woman asked, looking genuinely stumped, "Is she deaf?"

In Ghana, I was never an insider, and it hurt. Africa was the source of Black people and Black pride—the origin of not only English-speaking Black people in the Americas but also the multitude of Spanish- and Portuguese- and French- and Dutch-speaking descendants of African slaves, stretching from Canada to South America—*including* the Dominican Republic. But the parasitic root of modernity had long since squelched many traditions in Ghana, including beauty standards. Ghanaians both admired my skin color and despised me for it, telling me that I was "nice and fair" and that I should stay out of the sun so I wouldn't get too dark. Avoid the sun—a habit my family had followed during my growing-up years, a practice I'd abandoned after learning to appreciate my ancestry. When I called myself Black, Ghanaians regarded me as if I was a dimwit. I later learned it was because their *black* is solely a color, not a racial signifier. A color that my skin wasn't nor would ever be, no matter how long I remained outdoors.

Ghana's sun turned my complexion a coppery brown, which Ghanaians called red. Most often, though, they referred to me as *oburonyi*—stranger—and "white woman." And my hair, which I had finally learned to love? Ghanaians, like many folks back home, saw it as ugly.

But times change. My mother long ago stopped perming and dyeing her hair. I like to think I was the catalyst for that move, as my naturalista college friend had been for me. My mother cropped her hair too, and her ringlets, bigger than mine but not as big as my friend's, drew more compliments than ever. She also wore head wraps when she visited me during my Fulbright year in Ghana—her first time in Africa.

In the United States in general, natural hair has bypassed the stage of the fad it seemed to be in the 1960s and '70s. Black women of all ages and walks of life now embrace it. Far more entertainers are going natural than when I did my big chop in the 1990s. At that time, Macy Gray seemed the only reference point for strangers who remarked on my hair. There is now a plethora of books about natural hair care, not to mention blogs, instructional videos, festivals, a classification system for curl types, and an explosion of hair-care products. Even Santo Domingo now has several natural hair salons; in 2014 Miss Rizos became the first.

And in Ghana, the children I met during my semester abroad in 1999 are now adults. My little Cape Coast homestay sister, who recently found me on LinkedIn, was aghast when I shared her mother's comment about my Afro. Her social media profiles, as well as those of many Ghanaian millennials, show them flashing not only bone-straight weaves but artsy natural styles. The Ghanaian web series *An African City*, which debuted in 2014, reveals the beginnings of the change. Dubbed Accra's version of *Sex and the City*, it follows the love lives of women mostly of Ghanaian and Nigerian heritage, most of whom grew up in the United States and Europe. In one episode, during which the main character, Nana Yaa, who resembles Lauryn Hill—shaggy 'fro and all—visited a hair salon, I knew what to expect, even if she didn't. The stylist said politely, "Sorry, madame, but we do not style natural hair." Then, after a pause, "Miss, why don't you perm your hair?" In another episode, Nana Yaa's mother begged her to straighten her hair so she could look respectable for their family's television appearances, but Nana Yaa remained resolute.

The web series's characters represent a subsection of Ghanaian society: upper-class, foreign-educated feminists with Western perspectives on dating, marriage, and careers. Nana Yaa and her returnee friends are Afropolitans, embracing a modernity inspired not only by Europe and the United States and their own traditions but also by African slave descendants like me, who rediscovered and redefined beauty standards for ourselves. Yet, magazine and newspaper articles from the past few years attest to a natural-hair trend in Ghana. Many salons that offered only perms have had to close.

Although my natural-hair journey started years ago, I continue to look forward to the future Black-beauty landscape. I do hope, however, that we aren't headed for yet another culture war. I saw the potential beginnings of one as early as 2001, when I came across a heated debate on a Black women's hair listserv. Some of the commentators shamed Black women who adopted unpermed styles just because they were in vogue. I could understand their concerns; surely, those folks in the 1960s and '70s who truly believed Black was beautiful lamented as they watched Black people revert en masse to straight styles and the Jheri curl in the '80s. *But at least,* I thought, *more women are now trying out natural hair, and for some of them, the change might be more than skin deep.*

The posts also criticized Black women who called their hair natural while using hot combs, blow-dryers, and braid-outs to straighten or lengthen it. Those comments gave me pause because I myself sometimes braided my hair while wet and let it air-dry to stretch out my curl pattern. I enjoyed experimenting with different looks, and straighter hair was required for certain styles I liked. The squabbling on the listserv made me realize that I didn't view my unpermed hair as a political statement. It was just hair—incredibly versatile hair with the capacity to transform from tightly coiled to straight without the use of harmful chemicals or heat. Because, while I no longer saw straightness as superior to curls, I didn't view straight hair as the new bad.

The online debate also made me consider Black women who are born with naturally straight hair. In the United States, black isn't just a skin color as in Ghana; those of us who call ourselves Black have a wide range of skin colors and hair textures. The listserv participants didn't take that diversity into account. I can't even imagine how they would have judged someone like Rachel Dolezal. Regardless of her true race, Dolezal felt obliged to take on an imitative appearance to look Black, just as some women with more African features have done with their bleached skin, color contact lenses, and straightened hair to look "prettier" (i.e., white).

Of course, we live in a society where appearances matter, even if we learn as children not to judge the proverbial book by its cover. Perhaps one day we'll hold people more accountable for their actions and for the thoughts *inside* their heads—as opposed to what they choose to display *on* them.

Work Cited

1. T'Keyah Keymáh, *Natural Woman/Natural Hair: A Hair Journey: Hairstyles and Hairstories from the Front with Simple, Step-by-Step Instructions on Taking Care of Your Natural Hair* (self-pub., T'Keyah Crystal Keymáh, 2002).

ANOTHER LAYER OF OUR FREEDOM

Lyndsey Ellis, MFA

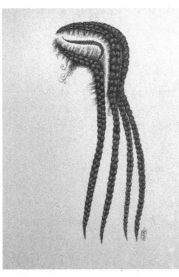

CHIMAMANDA NGOZI ADICHIE ONCE SAID, "It's not your job to be likable. It's your job to be yourself. Someone will like you anyway."

I thought I'd learned to understand what Adichie meant. Sixth grade left me second-guessing my worth as a person. Yes, I was Black and supposed to be proud of it, according to my mother and the rest of my immediate family. But at school, I often wondered if I was the right *kind* of Black because of the natural grade of my hair.

Coarse. Thick. Nappy. Stiff in the wind. Slave hair, as I once heard it called.

Nothing like the girls with a designated table in the cafeteria corner. The ones who donned their mamas' add-a-bead necklaces and were rumored to have Native American blood. The girls who got away with letting boys dunk them in the neighborhood swimming pool headfirst because, what was the worst that could happen? Their tresses would turn stringy and spongy. They'd grimace and complain about having to slick them into a wet, silky, and neat ponytail.

Black kids at my school were harshly critiqued and categorized, even and especially within our inner circles. In terms of hair, I learned very quickly that there was no in-between. You were either a Halle Berry or a Whoopi Goldberg. A Vanessa Williams or a Tracy Chapman. A Naomi Campbell or a Grace Jones. A Denise Huxtable or a Vanessa Huxtable. Yeah, Lady of Rage was cute and catchy with her "Afro Puffs" anthem, but everyone knew TLC's Chili was who you *really* aspired to be like.

It started off as just plain curiosity and a few compliments here and there, but then all of a sudden five different hands were reaching toward my hair and petting it. . . . I felt so uncomfortable. There was zero regard for my personal space or the fact that you can't go around petting strangers on the head like a puppy. It was so disrespectful.
—**Bianca Alexa**, model and blogger

I remember my then best friend and me spending hours getting ready to go to our favorite skating rink on Friday nights. We'd primp in front of the mirror and take turns smoothing down our sides with pre-con gel to see who could have the best-looking baby hair. If I didn't get a perm to tame my sides every other month, I would grow what was called a *kitchen*: matted hair coiling together at the edges. Some of the schoolgirls knew we were still using the pressing comb and teased us about it often.

Back then, like most kids at school, I couldn't articulate why we thought straight and long seemed better. It just was. Fine hair seemed less intimidating, less defiant than kinky, short hair. One classmate who dared to be different and had it somewhat figured out wore her hair in cornrows that never passed her earlobes all the way through middle school. She had smooth skin that was so dark, the boys nicknamed her Rwanda. It was their way of saying she resembled the Africans they saw on television. The connection between good hair and light skin versus bad hair and dark skin was another attitude I didn't quite know how to articulate. But I knew the viewpoint existed.

One day, I overheard a hall monitor ask the girl in cornrows, "Don't you need to look a little more presentable?" The monitor was a white parent of twin boys in my class. Although strict with her own sons, she was typically nice to their classmates, spoiling us with home-baked treats at holiday parties.

I don't recall waiting to see how the cornrows girl responded. It was recess time, and all I could think about was playing another round of kickball in the brief time we had before the bell summoned us back to class. But I did wonder why the hall monitor would care enough to ask such a question.

To a child who clearly wasn't hers to teach *or* to raise.

Why did it matter to her if a Black child chose to wear her hair in its chemical-free, natural state? How did appearing more presentable look for a sixth grader who hadn't approached puberty yet? And what benefits, if any, did the girl have to gain by conforming to this hall monitor's notion of *presentable*? Did this kid in cornrows need to prepare for her first date, or would she be interviewing for a job anytime soon? And even if she were, whose right was it to define what hairstyle was appropriate for those kinds of personal decisions?

My dormant disgust over the hall monitor's comment pricked me, even as I continued getting perms at the salon through my teens and early twenties. I knew how I was supposed to feel: nice, good, clean, and employable. However, this didn't stop the self-loathing I felt churning inside. The feeling that I was toning down who I was because that scared people who didn't have the slightest clue about what Black pride actually entailed. The idea that I was submitting to someone else's standard of beauty and worthiness in order to be part of a system that still dismissed my humanity in subtle and direct ways.

I couldn't win. And, deep down, I knew it.

The obsession with hair is still deeply ingrained in the American Psyche.
—**Gabrielle Gurley**, from "Black Is Beautiful, but Hair Is Still Political," *The American Prospect*[1]

Until 2017 I thought few things were worse than Black self-hatred and white disrespect of natural hair. My participation in a writing workshop at a Northern California conference proved me wrong.

By that time, I was sure I had been radicalized and made to see the error of my ways when it came to my hair. I was seven years in with dreadlocks, the longest I'd ever gone with natural hair. I wore them as my crown and glory. Everywhere I went, the personal royalty that grew on my scalp was with me, growing healthy and chemical-free. "Take me as I am, or leave me be," is what I said without having to part my lips. My locs—heavy and long—did the speaking for me.

But I didn't factor in the idea that white obsession with Black hair could go another way. The opposite of repulsion was an unhealthy attraction. Gross curiosity could be as damaging as constant disapproval.

On the second day of my workshop, a white attendee who also happened to be one of my housemates at the conference asked if she could touch my hair. As if that wasn't inappropriate enough, she took one of my locs in her hand while she was asking me the question.

At once, I experienced every emotion one could imagine. I was floored, horrified, deeply embarrassed. Waves of anger ran hot under my skin as if someone had plugged my body into a charged socket and lit me up like a lava lamp. "*Excuse* you," I said, as I snatched back my hair.

The woman apologized and tried to laugh it off. An awkward silence then fell over the all-white group of attendees. No one could look me in the eye. Another attendee threw out a compliment of the story I'd planned to have workshopped. It wasn't even my day to be critiqued—it was hers.

For the rest of the conference, I avoided the woman who'd violated me. It was no easy feat since, as housemates, our dorm held daily check-ins and we socialized with each other, particularly in the evening. But I kept my distance, understanding that she had committed one of the ultimate offenses. I wrote lengthy, honest details on the feedback form that attendees completed on the conference's final day. Sure, I'd heard about this kind of thing happening from conversations with other Black folks in various circles and through hearsay and movies. Solange Knowles had just released a song addressing the issue. This problematic behavior among white people continues to be publicized, and still, many aren't getting, or accepting, the message.

It's no wonder Black and Brown people's self-esteem remains fragile, constantly swinging on an internal pendulum that wavers between self-hate and a fixation on others' standards. Either we're invisible or we're hypervisible. Hair shouldn't define any person, nor should it be seen as an extension of someone's spirit in need of taming.

It's time to truly be seen and accepted and appreciated. One way to make this possible is by changing the way we view hair and its connection to diversity and ethnicity.

I don't think India.Arie could've said it any better than she did in her song "I Am Not My Hair." For Black women, hair is who we are, but it's not all we are. And until Black women like me can claim our power and individuality through our natural tresses without the interference of white reproach or obsession, there will always be another layer of our freedom for which we must fight.

Work Cited

1. Gabrielle Gurley, "Black Is Beautiful, but Hair Is Still Political," *American Prospect*, May 26, 2017, https://prospect.org/education/black-beautiful-hair-still-political.

'FRO FATIGUE AND OTHER 4C WOES

Dr. Adrienne Danyelle Oliver

THE H&M STORE'S FALL 2019 ad-campaign debacle clearly points to a need for the organization to consult somebody's Black mama before it ever puts together another ad featuring a Black child. In January 2018 the company came under fire for its COOLEST MONKEY IN THE JUNGLE sweatshirt advertisement featuring a young Black boy.[1] Just shy of two years later, once again H&M garnered backlash, this time for the way a Black girl's hair was styled (or not styled, in this instance).[2] With recovery from the last scandal still in diapers, the company was back to crawling itself out of an insensitivity fiasco. As Black

Twitter and social media flurried with commentary, I had some time to think about the attention given to my own tresses. In my forty-plus years, I've spent countless hours thinking of how to style my hair and how certain styles would be received.

In her now classic 1990 essay, writer and activist Audre Lorde asks the question "Is Your Hair Still Political?"[3] Obviously, it hella is. This H&M advertisement sparked a polarizing debate in the Black community. On one hand, some believed that we should leave that Black child alone. The other kids were caught in their natural, uncombed, fresh-off-the-playground, innocent, flyaway hair state. Why shouldn't she? We must unpack four key elements:

- The ever-evolving definition and regard for the concept of natural hair in the Black community
- The history that makes the difference in her appearance so tone-deaf
- The overlooked reality that Blackness isn't a monolith
- The problem with advertisements perpetuating racism toward dark-skinned peoples

Shall we begin?

The Ever-Evolving Definition and Regard for the Natural-Hair Concept

Before I begin any exploration of the history of how Black hair has been regarded in this country, I must establish how I define *natural Black hair*. To be clear, natural hair is hair not subjected to a relaxer or perm. A relaxer is a creamy mixture of really strong chemicals that can actually burn the scalp if applied incorrectly. A Black perm is quite different from a white one. A Black perm is *the* means for straightening tightly curled hair. It's an upgrade from the hot comb's press-and-curl styling because a girl or a woman can get her nappy head wet without it frizzing up. Thus, it is the superlative way for a Black child's hair to be as close to manageability (read *whiteness*) as possible. I could say more about the Black perm, its psychological effects on Black beauty acculturation, and the weave epidemic that plagues us today. Alas, we ain't got space for all of that. However, I will confide in the reader that the impact of the Black perm aesthetic surfaces again and again in my own natural hair journey.

Now that we have a clear understanding of where I'm coming from when talking about natural hair, we can dig into the nitty-gritty.

The History That Makes the Difference in Her Appearance So Tone-Deaf

Though we're making great strides, in some professional arenas we are still coming to terms with accepting Black women's natural hair. By *we*, I mean predominant American society. This America is not making the acceptance of varying hair dialects an easy process. In fact, discrimination toward Black women's hair goes back as far as Louisiana's eighteenth century, when the Tignon Laws of 1786 were in effect. Tignon laws forced Black women to cover their "exotic" hair because it "incited lust in White men."[4] A Louisiana governor passed a law for Black women to cover their hair, but folks were not ready for our creative wrap styling. You know how we do. Even though we've come a long way since then, the hair bias is still so strong that recently states have had to pass laws to prevent discrimination against Black natural hair. In 2019 California became the first state to pass the CROWN Act (Create a Respectful and Open Workplace for Natural Hair), a bill that then senator Holly J. Mitchell, a Democrat from Los Angeles, wrote, "making it illegal to discriminate against natural hair and protective styles like braids, locs, twists and knots."[5]

Blackness Isn't a Monolith

When I finally decided on my own grown-ass time *not* to relax my hair, it was a controversy, a sin, and a shame to many in my circle. When I first got the natural bug, my longtime hairstylist discouraged it. "You'll never get a job," she said. As a recent college graduate in 2000, I was petrified to hear this. The prospect of the job search being any harder than it already was with my one-page, creatively arranged résumé was daunting. I was scared so shitless that it wasn't until 2005 that I decided to finally make the BC: the big chop. Between 2000 and 2005, I made so many hair turns and shifts that BC was a fitting term for the moment I cut my relaxed hair off to one inch's worth of new growth. Before that moment, I had worn my hair in many styles, going from a long wrap to a short pixie cut, from black to dyed blonde.

Adrienne's hair journey through the years *Adrienne D. Oliver*

The AD—the after death of the Relaxer Me—had evolved. Because my hair was so short, I had tiny twists that I didn't like when I first started growing them. When I was a teenager, my favorite movie to hate was *Hellraiser*, and, to my eyes, I looked like the main antagonist, Pinhead. This regard for my newly twisted hair was no doubt rooted in the judgment of my pre-BC self, who associated heavenly hair with long flowing tresses. I visited my stylist every two weeks, getting my single-strand twists redone until they outgrew the Pinhead phase. When my hair got too long for single-strand twists, I graduated to two-strand twists. I missed the single-strand twists with their straw-sized Shirley Temple look. Still, the two-strand twists grew on me because I could take them out and wear a wavy 'fro.

I felt uncomfortable with being natural for the first time when I entered a 9-to-5 office. . . . I was a month in at my new work home and decided to take out my sleek bob. The receptionist who has a history of making underhanded racist jokes asked me: "If I had a long night?" This was after I entered the building with my freshly-washed and twisted natural hairstyle. This question was followed by my black female co-worker who shyly asked me when I was going to get my hair done.
—**Mellisa Scarlett**, quoted on Beauty Made Easy

Adrienne transitioning from Afro to dreadlocks. Stylist *Charmaine Marshall*

Then, I discovered *Curly Nikki*, the primordial natural-hair blog of the era, and learned the ABCs of hair texture.[6] I was delighted with myself when I figured out how to determine my hair type and discovered that I was 4C. I had the kinkiest hair type, with 4 being the last number in the four-rung "hairarchy." I soon discovered more about what I already knew—that neither Blackness nor Black hair shows up the same on all Black women.

Advertising Perpetuates Racism Toward Dark-Skinned Peoples

At this point, it's useful to reconsider the advertisement that prompted my reflection. The ad was always about *way* more than capturing a carefree childhood. The beautiful young model has dark brown skin. Americans imagine dark-skinned people as creatures of the wild. In a not-too-distant past, caricatures such as the picaninny and Little Black Sambo were popular forms of American entertainment, alongside minstrel shows. So it falls in line with this programming to see dark-skinned people as deserving less care. The picaninny caricature, popular in the nineteenth and early twentieth centuries, was a child-shaped human with animalistic movement and dark, frizzy hair reminiscent of fur.[7] Yes, our hair does get frizzy, but that doesn't mean we don't comb it. Similar to the unkempt Caucasian who wakes up in the morning and gets ready for her day, we comb. And even after we've been playing on the playground all day, our hair looks combed. The differences with regard to presentation are racist because they ignore the deeply rooted perversity of Blackness in the American imagination, thereby perpetuating its harmful legacy. Rarely has any caricature of a Black child not had flyaway hair.

Granted, in this "Topsy" illustration, the girl's hair is not flying away to the extent often portrayed. But it is still important to acknowledge the history of such depictions and its fundamental role in why the ad triggered some of us. I'm not denying that our hair *does* stick up sometimes; it is gloriously malleable. What I am arguing is that because we have *only* been portrayed this way, it is a harmful stereotype. Our hair can lie down on our heads.

In African culture, the head was regarded as the seat of the soul and treated with intricate care. Historian Victoria Sherrow says that "young girls wear braids or other designs, and . . . learn styling techniques at an early age . . . various styles with a crown-like appearance . . . extremely intricate . . . require[ing] hours to complete."[8]

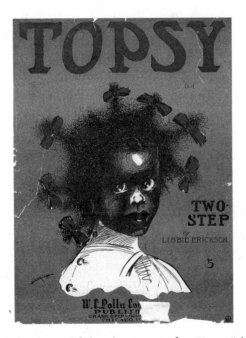

A 1903 cover of the sheet music for "Topsy" by Libbie Erickson, a ragtime two-step. *Jim Crow Racist Memorabilia Museum*

An enslaved person working from sunup to sundown had little time for the village styling technique—period. Available time notwithstanding, many customs became casualties of the slave trade, which fractured tribal villages. Thus, the picaninny imaging gravely disrespected African culture and is a cruel twisting of the knife punctured deep into the wound of a divided nation. In reality, an African child's hair was unkempt because they had been severed from their villages, stripped of their grooming rituals, oppressed, and impoverished. To suggest that the child model in the ad was simply in her natural state ignores the many dimensions of how African children—and now African American children—have been seen as untamable, animal-like creatures. Without reconciling the reality of this painful history and advocating for color-blind advertising, we will continue to see Black children brutalized by law enforcement, expelled from schools, and feared by white adults.

The racist undertones and colorism that plagues both Blacks and whites in America first surfaced during my Afro days, when I became a product junkie. I tried everything to get my kinky 4C hair to look wavy. Then I found the twist-out "cure." A proliferation of bloggers and YouTubers offered precise, detailed steps on how to get the perfect twist-out. The equation for all things pretty went like this: big tub o' product + wet hair + twisting for an hour x setting dry overnight or blow-drying = perfect twist-out. The smorgasbord of products that started appearing on the shelves in the early 2000s further complicated a not-so-simple process. The natural-hair products market felt oversaturated. It was like underground hip-hop went mainstream all over again. Just ten years earlier, I was hard-pressed to find a co-wash product on the shelf.

Knowing what co-wash even was made me feel like I was part of some insider's club that only hair bloggers knew about. It was a conditioner wash: co (drop the *nditioner*) wash! It was brilliant. The product lost its light for me, though, when other naturals would ask me, "How often do you co-wash?" The right answer was "I only have to co-wash once per week," which you'd say with curls bouncing and defined.

It became clear to me that the co-wash frequency indicated how "good" your hair was. If you were only co-washing once per week, it was because your hair had that naturally buoyant curly quality that required less water to keep.

Here we are, all grown up and past emancipation, reverting back to the house Negro versus the field Negro. The question of the co-wash and curl buoyancy was always about race and what you were mixed with to give you that "good hair" look. It was where the term *good hair* came from for most Black folks: being mixed with a white man's blood and having looser curls because of it.

By the time I decided to lock my hair, I'd had enough. I'd had enough of playing the co-wash game, of buying different products, of keeping up with the hair gospel according to YouTube for how to get my hair to act right. Wasn't it right enough because it existed and still grew from my head despite the dogged determination of this culture to make it feel less than?

Today, wearing locs has brought about more commitment to a hairstyle than I'd ever imagined possible for me. Up until my 2005 BC, I'd worn a relaxer for as long as I could remember. I probably got my first perm when I was six years old, because I don't remember ever getting it pressed. I grew up going to the salon once per week because I had a hairstylist in the family. Sometimes I would try a different style every week just because I could: a roller set, a wrap, Shirley Temple curls, finger waves, a bun, a flip. I almost got a Jheri curl in the 1980s when it was all the rage, but my relaxed hair made the transition harder. In hindsight I'm thankful, because I learned that the transition from the Jheri curl back into anything else was equally as challenging. Though it may sound like fun, the constant flux of my hair reduced my self-image to a fleeting phenomenon. Rather than being connected to the spiritual aspects of hair grooming so rooted in African culture, I was playing dress-up. The impact of this play was costly, as I objectified and prized Eurocentric beauty standards over the beauty of the diaspora. My constant transmutations were exhausting. And experiencing continued taunts after going natural added another dimension of complexity—subsequently leading to more exhaustion.

Transitioning from natural hair to dreadlocks was a huge step in my hair journey and is evidence of my 'fro fatigue. Dreadlocks do not represent absolute freedom by any means. And there is a whole universe of other natural-style aesthetics that I'll save for another essay. Let's just say that that my 'fro fatigue was so great that, in comparison, any other style felt easy. By the time I locked my hair in 2017, I'd developed extreme twist-out fatigue.

It was a sunny, summer day the month after I'd started my locs. I'd made plans to have brunch with a friend, a fellow naturalista who often wore her loose curls in braids. She'd agreed to pick me up so we could save the trouble of finding two parking spaces during downtown Oakland's brunch hour. When I joined her on the passenger side of her car, I handed her a tote bag full of products. "Here!" I exclaimed.

"You're giving me all of this?" she asked, her eyebrows raised in surprise.

"I told you, I am through!"

My friend peered into the bag and smiled. "Thank you!"

I was glad I could help her save some of the time and money I had spent chasing product promises. At least she could sample the products. "Yes, girl," I said, "everything you need to take care of your hair."

When my friend accepted my gift of more than one hundred dollars' worth of hair promises, I felt like a weight had been lifted off my shoulders. I was no longer going to be a slave to the illusion of the "good hair" twist-out. I was going to regain a lot of the time I'd invested in my hair over many years. I would write poetry, finish my novel, and write essays about my journey.

I dedicate the following poem to the little girl who posed for H&M. I can't help but wonder what she has to say about all of this, or what she will say one day when she is all grown up.

The author, age six, with her mother and younger sister *Adrienne D. Oliver*

School Clothes

for all the little Black girls who didn't get they hair combed at the photo shoot

Stop going there
            for validation
put it down
            the magazine
the remote
            the Facebook page
the IG handle
            the (tele)phone
omg smh the phone
            that be our cue to tele
port
                        to
            1990
I was an unstyled
chile
on the play
            ground
but   at   the end
of   the
day
love was on my edges
because
we worked
way too hard
to get this far
to travel cross these chain gangs
and hot combs
to not glory in a rattail tooth comb with some water on the tips
It's a Black thing
you know
you gots to be Black to
understand that those be
universes in dem edges

arrival at a timeline in my hairline
and
Madame C. J. Walker (Asè*) is watching
Rosa Parks (Asè) is watching
Coretta Scott King (Asè) is watching
Ella Baker (Asè) is watching
even Toni Morrison (Asè) is watching
and mama Maya Angelou (Asè) is watching
Harriet Tubman (Asè) is watching
[_____] (Asè) is watching
[_____] (Asè) is watching
[_____] (Asè) is watching
all my Black mamas are watching
and the little Black unnamed girl that looks like me
is watching
and the girl from 1990
all grown up and writing this poem
for us
is watching!
she checking for we
not like they getting a
check off we
and the mamas don't like
what they see
they see
the coon
on repeat
the mammy
the sapphire
the jezebel
they see
me

---

* *Asè*: In West African philosophy, an affirmative Yoruba word carrying multiple meanings, including "be with us" and "the power to make things happen." Often used in a libation ceremony to welcome ancestors into a ritual or space. In the blank lines of the poem, the reader inserts an ancestor's name into the space.

Works Cited

1. Liam Stack, "H&M Apologizes for 'Monkey' Image Featuring Black Child," *New York Times*, January 8, 2018, htttps://www.nytimes.com/2018/01/08/business/hm -monkey.html.

2. Shalwah Evans, "H&M Responds to Backlash Against Its Ad of a Black Girl with 'Undone' Hair," *Essence*, September 20, 2019, updated December 6, 2020, https:// www.essence.com/hair/hm-responds-to-black-hair-conversation-sparked-over-ad.

3. Audre Lorde, *I Am Your Sister: Collected and Unpublished Writings of Audre Lorde*, ed. Rudolph P. Byrd (New York: Oxford University Press, 2011).

4. Samantha Callender, "The Tignon Laws Set the Precedent for the Appropria- tion and Misconception Around Black Hair," *Essence*, February 9, 2018, updated October 24, 2020, https://www.essence.com/hair/tignon-laws-cultural-appropriation -black-natural-hair.

5. "National CROWN Day, Ending Hair Discrimination for Good," Senate Demo- crats, July 3, 2020, https://democrats.senate.ca.gov/caucus-news/national-crown -day-ending-hair-discrimination-good.

6. Nikki Walton, *CurlyNikki*, www.curlynikki.com.

7. David Pilgrim, "The Picaninny Stereotypes, Page 3," Jim Crow Museum of Racist Memorabilia, October 2000, updated 2012, https://www.ferris.edu/HTMLS/news /jimcrow/antiblack/picaninny/picaniny-stereotypes-03.htm; David Pilgrim, "The Picaninny Caricature," Jim Crow Museum of Racist Memorabilia, October 2000, updated 2012, https://www.ferris.edu/HTMLS/news/jimcrow/antiblack/picaninny /homepage.htm.

8. Victoria Sherrow, *Encyclopedia of Hair: A Cultural History*, illustr. ed. (Santa Barbara, CA: Greenwood Press, 2006).

PART III

INTIMATE ENCOUNTERS

SOLSTICE IN SOLIDIFIED SUGAR

Dr. Raina León

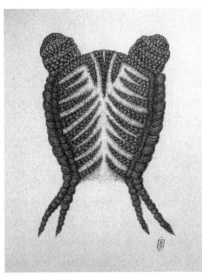

Lying lips are abomination to the Lord: but they that deal truly are
His delight.

        —Andrea Chung's art installation, *Proverbs 12:22*

she is two girls overlapping in time, la negra (o la india depending on the
voice) y la blanca. there is a girl who weeps in this story. there is a girl who
watches Shirley Temple dance while she sits on her father's lap and laughs.
one girl, an innocent memory; the other laughs, too, and doesn't know fear
and shame come next. she grows into a woman no one believes.

what do we believe? what hides in the image reflected from the glass: behind a white girl dancing with Bojangles in black and white, in front a girl in the lap of her father.

there is a black girl who will try to kill a black boy, because he is a light-skinned boy and the vessel for colorism and racism and white supremacy and patriarchy, but she doesn't have the names for that. she will try to kill her sweet little brother, who reminds her, in her womanhood, of her own son's shy tenderness many times, how she could have squelched it. she wants to be free, because she knows she already is.

i am the girl who knew joy and knives. i am not the weeping girl with testimonies.

---

what does titi have to teach me?

    her body is the sacrifice:

        the lessons to fight for a black feminist liberation written in
    what she could not live herself,
    the rules different and so she lived within them.

            black and ever not.

there is a picture of her wedding, still a girl herself, in a puffy white princess dress. my grandmother, with her cropped red hair, stands at her right hand; my grandfather, smooth and brown, his hair slicked back in a black wave, at her left. they do not smile, but their eyes do. they give away their daughter to a boricua with a French last name. a cake beside them in the photograph, layered and sweet. smoothed white fondant rolled and laid by my grandfather's black hands.

---

before my husband and i board a plane to attend our co-ed baby shower, i tell him that much of my family will come, including titi. i tell him that she is bound to say some locura; his job is to be the wall and keep me away from it. he says, "i don't know what you are talking about. she's always been nice to me." "you are white." the pronouncement is simple to say. what i don't say is that this is how i know i am supposed to feel i have become successful to her gaze: i am educated, i married a white man (a European no less), and i am pregnant with a boy.

on the plane, i wish i could have a shot of rum. i long for it.

my son kicks within me any time he hears music enter his pulsing water world.

————————

at the shower, titi talks about feminism in the new world, how proud she is of me for my education and that i travel, how in her day they never would have had a co-ed baby shower.

first, i think this is what i have always wanted: finally, to be seen.

second, i think she must be on drugs.

next, that maybe her daughter or granddaughter have had the honest conversation with her in ways i never could. feminist anything so new in the mouth i have studied my whole life.

she tells me that the women of our family have never had trouble giving birth. this news is what i also crave—don't all prospective mothers, to know that their labors will be smooth—and so i feel seen in this way; i breathe easy. i welcome that my husband does not need to be a wall. perhaps my whole seeing of her has been wrong. my whole life wrong.

menu

arroz con gandules

asopao de pollo

ensalada

perfectly sliced aguacate

we line up. i hear her say to her daughter, "aren't you going to serve your husband?"

this is what my mother was told to do when my parents first partnered, nearly 50 years before. i imagine her afro tall around the pressed and stressed. the women waited on the men and ate when the men were done. the scraps. my mother only did that once, the first time she met my grandmother, out of love for the woman who birthed her man, who loved him first. after that, my grandmother served him, because my mother wouldn't.

it's nearly 50 years later. titi's daughter has herself been married nearly
25 years. she responds, "he can serve himself."
i see my cousin in a feminist stance at the frontlines of mothering. a kind of
country.

---

at the shower, another titi, this one Gladys, makes me café con leche, the
color of the inside of my wrist and sweetened nearly to caramel.
her love, magnificent, intimate, warm, a bounty.
titi Gladys is not titi.

---

papi tells me what titi Connie tells him: one hundred brushes of my hair
each night will make it smooth, change its texture to his slick. he buys
me coconut pomade to moisten me down and i brush and i brush and
i brush. and i am still so frizzed in the morning, my mother says i look
like a witch.

titi Connie is not titi.

---

when i was a child and started school, it was titi who would pick me up
from the bus. i remember the walk to her house. we would pass the plastic-
covered couches en la sala and sit at the table in an all-white kitchen. a
snack. homework. a nap in the stale and sterile room of my older cousin
away at college, her nearly-graduating brother i rarely saw in the next
room, while titi watched her soap operas in hers. always pristine and still,
everything in its place. there were pictures of my cousin all around, her face
that of a sweetened angel. i have always admired her, the girl titi adored and
treasured.
eventually, my mother would come to pick me up, and so a day ended. i
remember being bored and internally riotous at the regularity of routine.

i had no brother or cousins to play with like at my grandmother's house, no television to watch, no dogs to tease. i never saw her backyard. i had to be careful. i walked lightly. even when i slept, i slept small and contained. i never moved too much.

---

she and tío are my brother's godparents. when we were children, they would come to pick him up, leaving me behind. he went to watch the fights on television or out to dinner. he went many places with them that i don't know. they were involved, showing him generosity and care. i remember once they bought him these white Hess trucks scripted over in green. tío said, "if you don't open them, someday they'll be worth something" to my brother, a child. to be worth something, one should not play.

my brother played. he was still worth something.

i was bitter and poisoned as uncooked yautía.

i remember only these gifts from titi: a keychain from Puerto Rico (an island to which i belonged, but to which i had never been); a t-shirt, also from Puerto Rico; and a white cabbage patch doll in a white tennis skirt (though i am not white and have never played tennis). all of these were worth something: wrapped up in an identity true and desired.

still i was always left behind.

---

i am the madrina of two little girls. i never leave their siblings behind. i claim them as my godchildren, too, though we have not been consecrated in that way. this is a generosity.

one of them calls me titi. she once tried to call me by my first name, asserting an authority in naming, and i said to her definitively, "i am titi Raina or titi. you don't call me by my first name." i will always be titi. this, too, is a generosity.

"you need to start wearing makeup." a little lipstick and blush, but not like a puta, she tells me, after she picks my brother and me up from school and walks us home. she always stays for an hour or so, watching her soap operas. the soap-opera women are perfectly coiffed. i know i am supposed to be like them, and none of them look like me.
i am 11 years old.
i do not know what a puta is. i just know i am not supposed to be one. between titi's visitation and my mother's arrival home, we have a few hours alone.
we are told not to answer the phone or the door.
that's when i nearly kill my brother.
he is a boy, never told to make himself up, how not to be a puta. he is a boy, never told who or what to be.

---

titi is not my only titi. the first and only time i met my titi Ada in Puerto Rico—really my great-aunt—after time spent in the living room to share stories, she walked us to a room, the entire space an altar to San Lazaro, orisha of healing in Catholic robes. to say his real name is to invite judgment and destruction. titi Ada told a story of how, when she was dying, she prayed to San Lazaro to heal her body and in exchange, she would honor him. he did.
in the story i tell now, San Lazaro did heal her body, but he took his praise and her mind. in dementia what she remembered as all her past slipped away to astral, it was to worship him. this she knew until she died. what i know is that she was beautiful and lovely and loved me even at first sight. i belonged in her heart and home.
what we remember. who we forget. i never forget titi. the name is a box of films i once lived.

---

i ask titi to teach me Spanish once when i am in elementary school. she teaches me la mano, los dedos. the hand and the fingers. these are the only words.

---

i wear makeup only for performance.

---

i am boricua of an old stereotype, who dances and dances with fists and can dance until the knife makes you bleed. i learned these things very young. in the times between titi and mami, i tried to kill my brother with a knife for no reason. a jagged nail, once. i can't remember the others. he was faster than me and strong, would always run and hold his door against my weight, until i slid the knife below. for years, he slept on his back, his arms primed above him as if in a push-up, ever ready to rush to push at the door. i did that.
he was a sweet little boy, now a loyal and brilliant man. he represented what i did not have the language to fight. i had time and fists and access to kitchen knives.
when i told my mother this story in college while my brother laughed in confirmation, she said, "Raina, i would have gotten you help."
what help could she have given me, the root of my desire to kill not about my brother but about colorism and internalized racism made manifest in family interactions and patriarchy and its demands in the mouths and actions of those i loved most.
i am an academic; i can theorize it now.
my brother and i, forged in steel, we are very close. we often laugh inappropriately about death, violence, and survival. there was a story in which my father breaks out two axes from his locker when he was a security guard on a college campus . . . and the one about a stabbing at a party and the one . . . don't worry. i don't have a knife collection anymore. i have theories.

---

at a black student union meeting in college, my friends talk about colorism within the black community. i talk of the great heaviness and added persecution i feel being dark-skinned. in the mirror of my friends' eyes, i see that, to them, i am not dark-skinned, that they do not understand how i can feel so ostracized and attacked within my own family.
i am the only afro boricua in the room.

---

i used to read *Latina* magazine as a teen, and the girls never looked like me. i bought hair magazines, too, and my uncle made fun of me for reading about rice water washes and how to style this way or that. when braids were in, i did them, too, and placed beads at the end to make a drum that thrummed against my face. I capped the edges with foil. when braids weren't in, i mastered the chignon, rolling my long hair, securing it with pins and a hair tie. i was always flattening, tying back, making small. *qué linda*, i was to titi, like this.

when i am 12, i have my first perm, like all the black girls in my dance class. i go to aunt Lynn's sister's salon, because that's where everyone goes. the air smells like press and curl, burning hair and the occasional softness of an ear sizzling into scar. the first time, i say, *it's burning, it's burning*, and they say *this is what beauty is* as they laugh, all the black women around me know that the timer hasn't gone off, so i'm not done. i remember how when i went to dance class my hair felt lifeless, oily and flat, how straight it hung, and limp. i was someone's perfect daughter, windless and quiet. the second time was my last. i didn't want to carry my dead magic from my head anymore, so i grew it out, wisps curling into straight irons, burned to pull them thin.

but in college i was big, washed my hair and let it dry tangled and wild and called it free, not breakage, not no care. i wrapped my hair in sarongs and learned a dozen different ways to make my head as bright as a flight of parrots. i learned to laugh without hiding behind my hands or swallowing the sound in my throat.

---

at Thanksgiving one year, at my grandmother's table, mami with her family
and my papi, brother and me with the boricua side, titi gives me advice.
i had just talked about applying to graduate school, how i was thinking of
schools in New York. "you need to go to Miami. marry a nice cuban. there's
too much black in the family. all these León men marry black women." my
mother is black. i am black. in Cuba, they had one of the biggest forced
migrations of enslaved Africans, so they certainly black. and in Puerto Rico,
i know from doing genealogical research and tracing race, generations and
generations of our ancestors are black, de color, negro. yes. we blackity
black black. and Taino and Spanish and walking survivors of colonization
and oppression, resistance just in being.
i remember putting down the knife and moving to a separate room. i have
never challenged her. always accepted a violence. out of respect for an elder,
i suffered disrespect. my brother and i shifted our eyes to papi. he ate his
chicken, sucking the bone. he hadn't heard anything out of turn.
when we told mami what titi had said, there was a war of silence against my
father for days.
i have become obsessed with genealogy. i discover, in scanned Puerto Rican
church records of baptisms, marriages, and deaths, who were the mothers
and fathers of whom and who their parents were. find the right record
and i leap two generations back. my obsession leaks into dawn hours. i
thank the God of the Church of Latter-Day Saints for missionaries, the
imperialists of faith, whose drive for the names of all to be written in the
Book of Mormon so as to find heavenly bliss, has led to a bounty of records
no hurricane can erase.
i trace names. places. race.
we have always been black. indigenous. black.

"cleave to your husband, the Bible says."
when my grandmother was dead, she bequeathed her clothes to charity.
she wanted those with nothing to receive the gifts her body no longer
needed. another aunt prepared her clothes for giving, placing them
with care on hangers. titi's husband arrived to the house, i learned, and

began taking them off the hangers and stuffing them into bags. my aunt responded about my grandmother's wishes, and he replied, "what do you care? Juanita's dead." a cruel pronouncement, the confirmation again that her mother was dead broke my aunt to weeping. he continued stuffing his bags to sell her clothes at a flea market. they could be worth something. a wish was worth nothing. when censured, titi said, "cleave to your husband." punto.

---

cleave means to hold close. it also means to split or sever, especially along a natural line or grain.

---

she says, "you are the real family." i must be in my mid-20s then. my grandmother has just come to our house to pray. she had a dream and so engaged in a visitation to the homes of all her children. we take out rosaries that we have not handled in years and certainly not at home. we do what she says and gather in the living room for a shared prayer, five decades of the rosary, and then my grandmother offers her blessings in Spanish to each person gathered: papi, mami, my brother, and me. titi has come with her and sits close, her knees nearly meeting my grandmother's. a triangle shape of bodies. she translates each blessing my grandmother offers. for some reason, we talk about my half-siblings, born before and after my parents' marriage, children i did not know about until i was 15 (my older brother and sister) and 21 (my younger brother and sister—the 80s were a wild, tumultuous time for my father). we are in my living room, and titi says after the blessings have ended, the last on the family as a whole, "but you are the real family. you are the real children." this is a translator's addition. my brother does not speak Spanish well enough to know my grandmother does not say this.

perhaps this is supposed to be another generosity from titi; it is a schism, one which is generationally familiar. did she find comfort in this for herself? my grandfather had two children outside of his marriage, too. his father before him did the same, many times. did she once say to the mirror, "i am the real daughter, the real oldest," as if to give herself more validity and authority, a greater love, though his first daughter is older than she, and her brother, born after, given more credence in the family, as the first son, the namesake. boys go into the world and lead. for girls of a certain time, the world is home and anything outside is madness.

---

for hundreds of years, my family's world was bounded by small communities in Puerto Rico (cayey, aguas buenas, santurce/cangrejos, rio piedras, trujillo alto). look at enough scans of church records and you can go back, on one branch or another, to the 1800s, sometimes even before. it's when the priests were tracking the baptisms of enslaved peoples, their baptisms a way to prevent them from buying their own freedom since a saved soul was worth more, that my people disappear. i wouldn't have been able to identify them assuredly anyway. most of those baptized received the names Joseph and Maria.

Joseph and Maria in exile, carried there by a ravenous ship instead of the docile donkey. backs split in cane.

I'm a big woman. I need big hair.
—**Aretha Franklin**

---

in blackness, we persist even in the resistance to water; in whiteness we toxify.

from archival records i learn that in 1946 my grandmother climbed into the belly of a ship, the marine tiger, with titi who was only 10 months old at the time. she went out into the world, a world in which she would be seen as white and her husband as black. their marriage still illegal then.

i am an academic, looking back on ships.

---

as i write this at a farm called smoke, my son is 11 months old.
the farm is about an hour north of Seattle. i am here to teach a workshop,
but i find myself living in sense and memory. i think about art at San
Francisco's Museum of the African Diaspora, far from here while in this
ozone-electric place. a piece in which memories seem to be pressed into
sugar that looks like glass panes made of amber. over time, even in the
chill of the museum, inevitably the sugar melts, revealing beds, Bible pages,
scores, rice, patterns erased from moment to moment. blackness encased
in the sugar that enslaves, how it melts away and reveals the freedom and
resilience that was always there.
i am there and here. i see my life through a melting lens.
smoke rises and dances with spirit.
am i pressed into caramelized sugar, a broken window pane in a house
melting away?
what are the names of the birds that chirp from the hidden boughs beyond
the reach of rustic buildings? robins, wrens, woodpeckers, others. i give over
my vision.
smoke rises and dances with spirit. this air is a performance in grief, as in,
performance, this is how grief carries itself out, even in the air and earth. is
my grandmother there, dead now five years? what other ancestors of kith
and kin? i look up again and see coils of rope.
yesterday it must have been them riding a slow wind, a puff of pollen
among so many i saw, and maybe so many of the collected dead. i thought
then, *a solstice snow.*
solstice opens the gates, right?

---

i have been thinking on Oshun recently. how often others focus on the
stories of her beauty, her sensual sway like river water, her laugh like a
tinkling bell. still, her words can burn and her laugh can fill a room at the
most inappropriate of times. she is over-the-top and devoted. recently,
a babalao reminded me that Oshun reminds us of self-sacrifice. there
are pataki that describe her transformation into a bird, who in her rise
to the sun, burns to black, and in her sacrifice saves the world. over and

over, Oshun demonstrates her love at the cost of her body, her mind, her children. she saves the world; she is beauty in form and action.
and so, with the distance of time, i ask myself, how do i conjure Oshun? how do i learn? i think it must come from titi. is memory the dance of mourning and love that survives long enough to bloom?

---

there is a moment that i never forget. i am at my grandmother's house in the Philadelphia projects. there is the scent of arroz con gandules in the air as there always seems to be in a boricua house. there are women. titi, my mother, my grandmother. i have this feeling that my grandfather is there, too, but his form is a shadow at vision's edge. merengue plays, and titi says to me, "do you know how to dance merengue? it's just like walking. one. two." and she rises from a patterned couch to dance and then her arms reach down to hold me. though i cannot yet walk, i dance, her hands keep me in balance. this was her first generosity.

---

at my grandmother's wake, titi watches me as i watch her. we perform as grief puppets. grief wears us in its theater.
childhood trauma and uncertainty always squelches emotional profundity in me. though earlier in the day, i had been hours in a fetal position, shaking a bed and a room with weeping, to see me in that moment—it was if i was watching myself on television—you would have thought that a wake was an entirely mundane place and time. i laughed and made jokes, gossiped with family members, and embraced so many gathered. as in my grandmother's hospital room, nearly 30 people always around her, moving in shifts, we boricua roll deep. her body in the casket, there are hundreds of us, buzzing. the matriarch dead. titi should be the next.
i move with lightness at the wake; it could not possibly be a shattering.
i perform that i have it together. she performs at the casket, kneels with her hands perfectly clasped, her mother's body in front of her. both of us pristine. lying. both of us.

---

at the funeral of my grandmother, she arrives at the church, just a few
blocks from my grandmother's last home. my brother is there, my male
cousins. they wait for the hearse to arrive so that they can carry a body
wrapped in steel.

my other aunt, my father, and uncles gather at the house just those few
blocks away to ride in a limousine the funeral parlor has provided. when titi
learns, she calls over and tells them to wait. she goes to the house. she, too,
must be wrapped in black steel.

my brother and i grumble, she said that she wouldn't give a dime to this
funeral, but she wants to ride in a limousine. her smile when she realized
she could ride. i remember that as she rushed off, the rare treat that
momentarily erases despair.

---

when i saw my grandmother for the last time, i broke into heavy weeping.
i had to be nearly carried away by my brother, my left hand pried from the
casket's rim.

at the repass, titi said, "i was wondering when you were going to break. you
were holding it together so long. you have to let it out."

i felt bitter at my breaking. i felt bitter that she had seen it, that she was
right.

later she said to me and my sister that we have to keep the family together,
that this is what our grandmother would have wanted. but how do you
stitch a shard?

---

at the novena, while helping my cousins and one of my aunts prepare the
repass for after the prayers and song, she comes up behind me, grabs my ass
with both hands, lifts it up and shakes. "reinita, you look good with a little
weight." she compliments its size and roundness and then she moves on to
do something else. my bodily violation nothing. my worth and sovereignty

nothing. there is a knife in my hand and suddenly there is someone in front
of me, who can see my mind empty, how my hand grips so quickly. i don't
know who it was who was brave and stepped between us. i only remember
that there was a body. that is enough for sense. it is my grandmother's
novena. the first day. all of the elders take their seats. i sit on the stairs
with my older sister, who is not supposed to be real, woman born out of
wedlock, born outside of a priest's damned blessing. we sing and pray from
a prayer sheet. it crunches. is that the sugar or some other poison? i am
surprised that i know most of the words and melodies from a time i can't
clearly remember, when my grandmother's voice would rise until mine
joined her in Spanish.

later, titi reminds me how we used to rest, my brother and me on either
side of my grandmother when we were very little. and in her story, i
remember the rose powder smell as i nestled under her arm, and she read
me the Bible. this is a generosity, so i forgive titi the violation of my body.

———————

how quickly we forgive when trauma teaches: to not forgive is to eat your
own body.

———————

i remember how when i was a girl, i would look at the strands of my hair
in the light, track the red highlights holding on there and say, i belong
to her, the her being my grandmother whose long strawberry blonde
hair once fell all the way down her back, nearly to her knees. when my
grandfather died, she cut it off and wore black for seven years. está de
luto they said with pride of her, the perfect widow, her mourning a public
display beyond the housecoats and aprons she wore at home. what will
i wear to mourn the lessons i bury from her? the curls of my hair rise,
twine within the curls of my children. we are trees growing elemental in
our own magic.

———————

"for someone you don't like, you talk a lot about your aunt," my husband says once.
until he did, i had not thought about it. it's true; i've been thinking about why for years.

---

when i was confirmed, i took the name Esther, completing the homage to my mother's mother, Queen Ester, in my name. i asked titi to be my sponsor. first, it was because it was convenient. she only lived a few blocks away and already attended our church. no need for the bureaucracy of Catholic paperwork. no need for a letter of upstanding status in the church; she attended the mid-morning Sunday mass, nearly always in the same pew, either a few rows back in the right wing or a few rows back from the priest on the nave's right. perhaps this was always about being "to the right" of the altar, if not at the right hand of the Father or father priest presiding.
looking back now, i realize i also wanted her to love me, to show love to me in a way that wasn't barbed with expectations for my behavior as a woman, as boricua, as black or not black at all. i wanted her to love me as an extension of pure faith. i wanted an amazing grace. i wanted her to love me in the way i needed to be loved: for some aspect of me that was authentic to me, my wants, my needs.
in the ceremony, i do remember her being proud, her face made rosy under the lights. the archbishop himself was there to proclaim me confirmed in Christ, remade in a new authority in the church with a name I'd chosen for myself. titi's hand rested on my right shoulder as we reaffirmed baptismal vows, the ones made on my behalf by parents and godparents. this time, my sponsor would say them with me. my voice with hers with God and Spirit. i remember feeling hollow, eager for an awe that never came. i knew, even then, that the way she showed love would never be what i wanted or imagined.
if i could teach my younger self, i would say to study the ways that she shows love already; that's what i do often now.
as a mother, i look back on another woman who offered me mothering in her own way, who taught me how to be in how i learned to resist. i had to determine my own truth, not follow her or any other without compass.

---

is this world a madness? i am in the world, of the world, outside the world that was given, creating worlds and that, too, is a gift of resistance. feminist through the sacrifice of the body. i cut my hair to delight in the heights of its coil. anti-blackness and patriarchy are vipers within my own blood; i have to check them often. how they enchant with their syrupy attractions. has titi always been walking Oshun in yellowed and ripped clothes? am i the child that was lost? i feel myself worshipping memory, stuck in a sugar-tar that never really melts away. what is freedom? is there a peek of it in this history? in this want?

PELO LISO Y PELO MALO: MY MOTHER AND ME

MK Chavez

A FAMILY TRIP TO THE ZOO, or so I thought. There is a picture of the three of us, my mother, my father, and me standing at the observation point of Twin Peaks. Behind us, the San Francisco cityscape and the bright blue sky. The fog is rolling in, and I look cold. My eyes are holding back tears.

My mother and I are wearing matching outfits. The memory lives in my body: sadness at the deceit; there had never been any intention of going to the zoo on that day. A more significant betrayal lived between us every day.

I remember the feel of the cold air hitting the back of my neck. Days before all my unruly hair had been cut off.

Matching outfits for my mother and me remained a theme throughout my childhood and an apt metaphor for my father's desires. He had wanted me to be more like my mother who was light-skinned and had long, straight hair. "She is perfect," my grandmother would say. It wasn't just my father who thought of my mother as perfection. Other family members and neighbors commented on her hair and appearance. *Maybe when you grow up you can be more like your mother* were words that followed me most of my childhood.

The morning ritual in my home was my mother brushing my hair and me crying. My sweet mother was unlike her reputation when she was dealing with my hair. By the end, she was always angry, and my head was always sore. She tried to tame my hair by creating tight braids, but she wasn't good at it. By the end of the day, my braids unraveled and looked wild. I would return home to meet her look of disappointment.

I've heard the term *pelo malo* my whole life. That's why I decided to go natural. I decided to stop letting other people define what good hair is. Hearing that term, it made me not like my natural hair. So I decided every week, Saturday or Sundays, go straight to the salon and do my hair. I could not see a curl in my hair. If I did, I would freak out, because in my culture, it's not what good hair is.
—**Jodelis Díaz**, in Remezcla

One day my mother, waiting for me after school, said we were going somewhere special. "It's a surprise," she said. We lived in San Francisco's Mission District, where the scent of cilantro filled the air and hearing Spanish was as common as it was in my home. This was the part of the Latinx neighborhood where we went to see *Cantiflas, La India María,* and other Spanish films at the Tower Theater.

One Sunday afternoon some time before this day, the whole family went to see *Angelitos Negros,* a movie starring Pedro Infante. In the film, José Carlos meets Ana Luisa; they fall in love and get married. Somehow, José Carlos doesn't realize that his wife is racist before they marry. She doesn't like that José Carlos plays music with mulattos, and she treats Mercé, the Black nanny who has cared for her all her life, with disdain. José Carlos tries to convince his wife not to be racist. The film's climax comes when a horrified Ana Luisa gives birth to a Black daughter, and she refuses to accept the baby. In the end, we learn that Ana Luisa's true mother was Mercé, the Black nanny. On the way home that night, I asked my grandmother if I was like Ana Luisa's daughter, and with a sharp look, she responded, "We are not Black."

On this particular day when my mother promised the surprise, she parked her bronze Nova on 23rd and Valencia. When we got out of the car, my hopes were high because the Mission is a hive of *panaderías*, burrito shops, and places to buy Virgin Mary statues and candles. I secretly hoped that we were going to Dianda's, an Italian bakery where my birthday cakes came from each year. We walked down the street to a beauty salon. My mother stopped and looked down at me and said, "I just can't do it anymore. I can't keep brushing your hair."

Dianda's Italian Bakery was magical: tiny fruit-shaped marzipan candies and cakes with ballerinas floating on the white icing. My father loved Dianda's because he said it wasn't owned by cockroaches, making it an excellent place to buy my birthday cakes. My father never told me exactly who the cockroaches were, but I knew they likely looked like me. Sometimes he would stare at me and ask why I was so dark. "Why is her hair like that?" he would ask. I was never sure who he was asking, and no one ever responded, not my mother, not my grandmother. The questioning happened later in the evening after he had watched television for a couple of hours, and after empty beer cans had collected around his pleather recliner.

We watched *Star Trek* together, and I thought of it as our father-daughter show. While watching the "Whom Gods Destroy" episode, I noticed my father smiling as a green woman danced onto the screen. It was a rare occasion to see him with a smile. I asked if he thought she was beautiful, and he said yes. I decided to paint myself green and searched the house for green paint, but the only green thing I could find was his Speed Stick deodorant. I did my best to cover myself with it and hoped that he would notice, even though I was not as green as the Star Trek dancing woman.

I was sitting at my father's feet when there was panic on the bridge. Captain Kirk was in charge, and Uhura hailed all frequencies. It was exciting, and it made me forget for a moment that my skin was itchy and that my father hadn't noticed that I was green, and then my father said, "I don't understand why they have to ruin the show with that *negra*."

My father had not been happy with my haircut. He said my hair was like a *negra*'s. He didn't like that my tight curls looked tighter, perhaps like a very short version of Uhura's hairstyle.

The next day at school, I wore a hoodie over my head. A teacher tried to be kind or cruel, I don't know which, and had me stand in front of the room. She pulled my hood down and said to the other kids, "Doesn't her haircut look nice?"

SELF-CARE AND SANCTUARY IN BLACK WOMEN'S SALONS

Dr. Sherry Johnson

I'VE BEEN THINKING ABOUT the relationship between hair care and the development of cultural meaning. Hair care is a significant part of Black identity, regardless of where in the African diaspora one resides. Unbeknownst to many onlookers, salient understandings of the self occur in the salon. While there are many aspects of the salon—from walking in the door to the group discussions that occur within—I want to talk, here, about shampooing hair. The act of someone washing my hair—what I call a praxis of laying on of hands[1]—has helped me to cope with quotidian stresses of life and with deep traumas. Washing hair as a praxis of cultural meaning-making began for me long before I ever stepped into a salon, as a little girl kneeling on a chair, head bowed over the kitchen sink as my mother caressed my head with one hand while gauging the temperature of the water with the other.

The Development of Being in Quiet

There was always an air of anticipation on hair-washing days. The production? Pull out your hair,[2] get the towel, bring the chair. When everything was set in place, I'd kneel on the chair and bow over the kitchen sink. I remember the cool of the sink's rim against my arms as I leaned over and held my head still. Mummy would work the comb through my hair—ends to scalp, ends to scalp, over and over again. Then, the warm water, the cool shampoo on my scalp, the sudsy sound of the thickening lather in her hands. I squeezed my eyes tight against the shampoo's burn. (Later, I'd learn that holding the tail of the towel over my eyes mitigated this pain.) The scent of the conditioner was its own treat. No matter how strongly my hair's musk revealed the sweat-filled days of playing kick the can or jungle gym tag or bike riding underneath the hot summer sun, the conditioner's sweet coconut-oil scent signified renewal, a clean slate: a fresh me. I loved getting my hair washed.

My natural hair is an exquisite crown.
—**Stephanie Lahart**, multigenre author and Exquisite Black Queen

After the conditioner, the brush and the hair oil. I would meet Mummy in the living room, where I would sit on two cushions on the floor between her legs. Mummy, sitting on the couch, would part my hair with the comb, tracing the edge of the comb in the part again and again until the line was perfect. She'd then take a big glob of green Dax Pomade and place it on the back of her hand. With just the right amount on her finger, she would glide that finger down the part. I always marveled at what my hair could do. It shrank after a wash, yet still my mother would stretch it out into neat plaits, the ends of which would brush my neck. My hair was magic.

Mummy gave nonverbal directions. Turn your head? She would gently tug the hair on the side she wanted me to turn toward. Bow forward? She would push the top of my head forward and down. I didn't say much; I'd often hold her feet, which she'd loosed from her house slippers. My fingers knew the curve of each of Mummy's toes. Tiny, dark spots the size of a pinhead were at her hair follicles, her fair skin smooth even when dry. Sitting there at her feet, her hands on my head, we presented a tableau of mother and daughter, of healing and humility.

Rituals of hair washing are a part of a legacy Black women pass on from one generation to the next. Here, we sat in a living room in Toronto, Canada, yet this praxis of memory in which Mummy enveloped me came from multiple generations of Black women from Jamaica.

Tresses and Meaning-Making
Confronted with a marriage ceremony or a game of football, for example, an observer from a culture where these did not exist could present an objective description of the actions which took place, but he would be unable to grasp their meaning and so would not be treating them as social or cultural phenomena. The actions are meaningful only with respect to a set of institutional conventions.
—**Jonathan Culler**[3]

Although hair washing was the reason we sat there, we didn't talk about that. In fact, we didn't talk much at all, as I remember it. The only conversation might be between Mummy and the TV program to which she responded aloud: a laugh, a kiss-teeth, a "watch deh!" Or she could be talking to a girlfriend, phone cradled between shoulder and ear. It's telling that no memorable conversations come to me now. As a woman and mother today who finds comfort in my own company, even in the midst of people, I understand that for Mummy, washing my hair was a routine task of paradox: a chore, though nevertheless one during which she could commune and spend time with herself, watching TV, talking to friends on the phone. As she sat and worked, neither Daddy nor my siblings would bother her.

She could simply *be*. While I, too, would *be* in these moments, I was not invited to *be* with her. As with the pastor who lays hands on a new convert in the baptismal pool, the action is that of bringing one into community, of blessing, of rehabilitation. My job was to be still, to listen, and to learn: hair care brings healing.

Ms. Nemecek was the first teacher with whom I really connected, though I liked all the others fine enough. But Ms. Nemecek was special. And my classmates agreed. We pooled our money to buy her a birthday present. My classmate Shannon and I were in charge of this task. On the way to the mall, my dad picked Shannon up so we could buy the gift. Even then, I realized the large owl statue we chose was ugly, but we wanted something big enough to communicate how much we loved Ms. Nemecek, and the owl stood on a huge pedestal. Daddy brought the statue to school for the big reveal. We asked Ms. Nemecek to leave the room; one classmate sat outside with her while Daddy, Shannon, and I set things up. When she returned, she seemed thrilled with our gift. I'm sure Ms. Nemecek knew her fourth-grade class loved her, but I longed to show her that *I* loved her.

One morning, after everyone at home had already gone to work and school, I remembered—belatedly—that my class had a field trip that day. Lunch was not an issue; we always packed those the night before. Clothes weren't an issue either; I had everything I needed, and there was always something clean. Still, *my hair*—it was not in a "field trip" style. And Linda, our Italian neighbor in middle school, would arrive at my home any minute to meet me for the walk to school. I called Mummy at work. I hated to disrupt her from whatever nursing duties she was doing at the hospital, but I was worried. When she answered the phone, I explained my plight.

"Oh no! OK, just brush up the front. It will still look nice."

Brush up the front? I thought. Mummy's suggestion, along with the amusement in her tone, let me know she didn't see the matter in the same urgent light as I did.

"OK," I mumbled through a pushed-up mouth, indicating my displeasure. In every Jamaican household—at least, in every one that I had been in—were clothes for every occasion: house clothes, church clothes, play clothes. For my mother to catch me playing outside, say, in my good church socks, the white, cotton, crocheted knee-highs, was tantamount to blasphemy. At the least, I'd get a slap on the legs and be told, "Get inside and take off those socks!" At the most, Mummy could embarrass me in front of my playmates as she showed up with a "Get inside!" pointing her finger in the direction of the house. "I tell you, *don't dress and judge!*"[4] Similarly, showing up to some special place in clothes that did not reflect the seriousness of the situation was a problem. I could hear my mother's disgust as she talked on the phone while doing my hair: "You mean to tell me she couldn't put something better on her little girl for church? My God!" Just as there were rules with dress, so too were there rules for appropriate hairstyles for every occasion. And, going on a field trip required a style other than my everyday, normal plaits—not quite church style, but not my school style either. I should have at *least* one "bubble" somewhere in my hair (this is the way we pronounced hair *bauble*) or a couple of hair clips. What if pictures of us ended up in a year-end slideshow or something? I could hear my Aunt Imogene: "You mean Sherry couldn't make her hair look a little better than that? My goodness!" I hung up with Mummy, and the idea came to me: Ms. Nemecek. She could do my hair! I'd ask her before we boarded the field-trip bus. In my mind, the problem was solved. I gathered my things and was ready to go when Linda knocked.

With my comb, brush, and clips in tow, I put my request to Ms. Nemecek when I got to school. I can't remember what story her face told; even when our mouths say the right things, our faces often reveal how we really feel. What I *do* remember is that before we left, she took me out in the hallway, where we sat on the bench along the wall where we hung our coats. She put a bubble in my hair. Her hands weren't as strong as my mom's or my aunt's or my sister's; clearly, combing a Black little girl's hair was not something she'd done before. Perhaps the lack of confidence I felt in her weak grip was actually discomfort, both hers and mine. *Maybe my asking was a mistake*, I thought. Two things, though: Ms. Nemecek's face didn't disclose anything untoward and my ambivalence about whether my request had been the right thing to do waned. For a few minutes I had Ms. Nemecek to myself, all her attention just on me. In the hallway's quiet, as I handed her the brush, I was communicating to her: I trust that you care for me.

An outsider observing the process of washing my hair and then combing it would not be able to understand the magnitude of the moment unless there was something akin in their own culture. Ms. Nemecek was Czechoslovakian. And, although Canada proudly touted multiculturalism as a part of its national identity, each culture mainly showcased its pride on World

Food Day. On this day, at school and at work, everyone shared some dish from their native culture. I might have brought a box of Michidean's beef patties, warmed in the cafeteria oven, and then quartered to share. Filipino Fruit Salad never lasted long; it was everyone's favorite, regardless of one's place of origin. Still, this practice of sharing food was often devoid of the deeper cultural meaning of preparing the food. No one shared how the dish returned them to a humid, late afternoon, forearms resting on a plastic place mat at a dinner table by the window through which they watched the sun slip to sleep. Rather, the lukewarm foods simply remained in a dish behind a folded cue card with the word JAMAICA written on it. But I don't remember sharing anything really meaningful, certainly nothing akin to the meaning of allowing someone to put their hands in my hair. That sort of sharing with *everyone* would have revealed too much.

As I look back today, I realize that on those days of sitting on cushions between my mother's legs, I learned to associate doing hair with a demonstration of love. And, when the opportunity arose for me to communicate how I—apart from all the other adoring students—felt about my favorite teacher, I took it. Hands in my hair—even a white woman's hands—meant something altogether more than what an outside observer could see. When I was nine years old, it had not yet seeped in that my hair was anything about which to be ashamed. Instead, as my teacher stood behind me in the quiet of a school hallway, my hair became a medium for affection, and, of course, an opportunity to have my hair styled appropriately for a school field trip! I'm not sure that Ms. Nemecek understood the magnitude of what transpired that morning. But I'm not sure that it matters.

Tresses, Trauma, and Healing

Once I'd become a woman—many years past the prepubescent years when I sat at my mother's feet—I regularly made my way to Salon Paradise to see my stylist, Del. One week when I arrived for my visit, something had changed.

"Your hair is breaking in places that don't make sense," Del told me. She parted my hair and scratched my scalp before she leaned me back in the washbowl.

"Really?" I answered. "I've noticed a lot comes out when I comb it too. So weird."

"OK, hush." She saw the worry on my face. "We'll do a treatment today."

"OK," I said.

For the next couple of visits, Del and I had reprised some version of this conversation. In one, she held up a lock of my hair and let it fall as I looked on in the mirror.

"It's just dead. No body. This is not your hair."

"I don't know, Del. I don't know what's going on," I said.

"Don't worry. Lemme give it a good trim, and we'll see."

I *was* worried; I had other things on my mind, not my hair. And talking to Del was therapeutic in a way it couldn't be with my best friends, because Del *knew* what I was talking about. Her mother had passed away a few years before from Alzheimer's disease; I was dealing with Mummy's early onset of the same. One memory I shared with Del was how Mummy called me one Monday morning and wondered why I wasn't getting ready to go to church.

"You just left church a couple days ago, and you're ready to go back already, Mummy?" I asked. "It's Monday."

"Monday?! You're joking!" she whispered with a laugh.

The laughter Del and I shared at the memory mirrored the laughter Mummy and I shared that long-ago morning. Part of Mummy's mirth was at her mistake, the other part was because she planned to pretend she was going somewhere that required Sabbath wear just so Brother B., my stepfather, wouldn't know the mistake she'd made. I laughed because the woman that raised me remained; Mummy was still incorrigible. Although we laughed about her out-of-order days, the alarm I'd sounded years before with family and friends had become a screaming white noise. Mummy's displays of forgetfulness jarred me, and I couldn't accept her go-to explanation: "I'm just tired. I need to sleep." That's when I decided to pack up my apartment, put everything in storage, and return to my old bedroom at Mummy's. Whatever ailed her, it'd be better if I was home with her. Del agreed, although she warned me it was going to be a crazy-hard situation.

I soon realized what Del meant. Watching my mother mentally deteriorate was formidable. After realizing I couldn't work without Mummy knocking on my room door every ten minutes to ask if I was busy, forgetting that she'd asked me that question only a few minutes before, I worked at the local library each day. Returning to that house was hell. *Hell.* Forget about waking at night to find Mummy peering at me in the dark. Forget about the animated conversations she muttered to herself. Forget her persistent preoccupation with knives. Forget the shrill yelling and screaming for reasons that made sense only to her. Forget the fear that bloomed in me with every forgotten pot left boiling on the stove, filling the house with smoke. I experienced a particular torment in seeing the vacant look in her eyes, in watching her get dressed as she casually drew her stockings up over her already socked feet, in the way she searched my eyes for affirmation that she'd done some simple act right. She'd forgotten me, her sequencing was out of order, her womanist confidence had turned to childlike uncertainty.

Every day when I left the library, I stopped at the plaza by the house to smoke a cigarette. I needed it. I needed it before returning home to either an upset Mummy or an absent Mummy—figuratively, physically, or both. In her lucid moments, Mummy insisted she was fine, that she needed to head out to give a Bible study somewhere, only to get lost. While Toronto's Ministry of Transportation could revoke her driver's license, they couldn't take her bus pass. At times I would hold my breath in appeal to the darkness that fell: please let her appear, safe.

That year, my hair got shorter and shorter. It kept breaking, and Del kept trimming. She must have realized my hair unmasked the trauma my disposition concealed, yet we never talked about that. We talked about her kids, about my love life, about treatments. We'd share stories about the funny things her mum did in her illness, and I'd share mine, and we'd laugh. There were times, though, when I tried to tell some episode, but in the middle of it the words would disappear. I'd simply sit in her chair, in silence, my puzzled reflection looking back at me from the mirror in her styling station, and then the tears followed.

"Mmm," Del would say.

Smoothly, she would put her curling iron on the stove, reach for and pass me a tissue, return behind my chair, rub my arm in silence, and wait. When I'd lower my hands from my eyes, holding the soggy tissue, she'd pick up the iron and return to my hair.

"I don't know, Del. I can't—"

"I know," she'd reply.

I suspect the relationship one has with their stylist differs for everyone. For me, critical to any meaningful relationship is the ability to simply *be* in one another's presence. If Del felt like talking, great; but silence together was equally meaningful. For in the silence in which Del massaged my scalp and washed my hair, she renewed my spirit. After her laying on of hands I could return to care for a mother who was swiftly slipping away.

All quiet isn't comforting, though. When the congregation's silence greets the pastor's word, he stutters, forgetting what he was about to say. Or, when my mother was angry about something or another, we found no solace in the refrigerator's hum. Regardless of comfort or the lack thereof, silence resounds— not just with soundlessness, but with meaning. In the salon, I can just *be* for an hour or two while Black women spend time on me. From the kitchen sink to the salon, the praxis of laying on hands is healing. It is the praxis of self-love—a radical idea in a society that refuses to see Black women's joy, or their trauma. Others may not understand the meaning of no-talk quiet, nor of the salon. Still, salons are powerful places where Black women minister one to another. At the wash station, the sink's edge cups my neck, the water drowns out surrounding chitchat, Del's fingers massage my scalp, and I am baptized anew. Returned to myself, I find answers; I find peace. Sometimes, when I close my eyes, I am kneeling on a chair, my head bowed over the kitchen sink, holding the towel's tail over my eyes. I feel my mother's hands on my head, and I hear her humming, "Nearer, my God, to Thee, nearer to Thee."

Works Cited and Notes

1. *Encyclopaedia Britannica*, s.v. "Imposition of Hands," accessed July 30, 2021, https://www.britannica.com/topic/imposition-of-hands. Imposition of hands is a religious practice in which a religious authority places their hands on a congregant's or new believer's head and prays for or blesses the individual. Laying on of hands is an old practice found in both the Hebrew and Christian Bibles and in several religious practices in both Judaism and Christianity. "The New Testament . . . indicates that the imposition of hands conveyed a blessing and was a means of healing," according to the *Encyclopaedia Britannica*.

2. Throughout this essay, I use common phrases from a Jamaican patois, the meanings of which do not always translate effectively into standard American English. In this instance, to "pull out" one's hair does not mean to tear it from the scalp; rather, it means to undo the plaits, or to remove the clips, in preparation for shampooing.

3. Jonathan Culler, "The Linguistic Foundation," in *Literary Theory: An Anthology*, Blackwell Anthologies, ed. Julie Rivkin and Michael Ryan, 3rd ed. (Oxford: Wiley-Blackwell, 2017), 134.

4. Later I learned that what sounded like "dress and judge" was "dress and *drudge*." Meaning, don't mix up the clothes in which you get dressy and the clothes in which you do drudgery—which included anything other than going someplace fancy or important. The only time I could mix them is when something unfixable happened to a dress; then, it would be moved into the drudge category.

MY LOCS, HER LOCS: OUR PERSONAL JOURNEY

Sulma Arzu-Brown

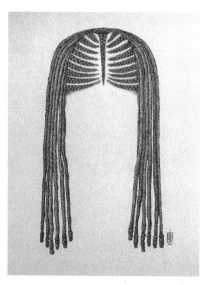

MY DAUGHTER, BELLA-VICTORIA, cut off one of her long locs because she is ready to transition out.

I, however, am not ready for this transition. I am afraid.

The questions in my mind are, Is she really ready for a very short Afro? Is she ready to face the non-Black girls whose hair will continue to blow in the wind? Is she ready to face off against societal beauty standards with patience and with love for her own wonderful beauty? Will she later ask me to chemically straighten her Afro?

I am the author of the No Pelo Malo book series. Bella-Victoria inspired my very first title, *Pelo Malo No Existe* (published in English as *Bad Hair Does Not Exist*). I wrote this book when her caregiver used the colloquial *pelo malo* term to describe my daughter's tight curls. For this book, I partnered with an illustrator who created beautiful depictions showcasing Black girls' and women's diversity, with all different types of hair. The book reverberates with the timeless message that *all* hair is good. My goal was for Bella-Victoria and Suleni, her older sister, to see their beauty reflected back to them in my books, and to arm other parents who wanted tools to empower their own children. My daughters often joined me in my book talks, as allies and advocates. I watched them blossom into powerful young women. But in this world where social filters wage war against all aspects of Black women's natural beauty, I am still afraid for Bella-Victoria.

Bella-Victoria has always been tender-headed. To this day she still detests wash day. Unlike my experiences with Suleni, wash day has never been a bonding experience with Bella-Victoria. As gentle as I tried to be, wash day was torture for her. I endeavored to make the process as comfortable as possible for her, and I know she tried hard to tolerate the pain.

Ultimately, I made the decision to loc my own hair and decided to take her along for the journey. I knew that convincing her to loc her hair would not be easy, so I offered the proposal to her in appealing terms: "You like long hair, don't you? Well, locs are one way that hair can grow to its maximum potential." Or, "We wouldn't need to wash your hair as often during the time it would take our hair to loc." I had set the bait, and Bella-Victoria took the hook, agreeing to accompany me to the salon to begin the locking process.

On the day that we arrived at the salon, our stylist took Bella-Victoria first. I watched the stylist put two-strand twists into my daughter's hair. I wondered, *Is this the style in which one begins to loc their hair?* However, after the stylist completed my own hair, my style looked very different from my daughter's. When I questioned the stylist about the discrepancy, she said, "The two-strand twists will buy Bella some time to think about the direction she wants to go in before she fully commits to locking."

Natural hair often makes a bold statement. Our crowns help to define our royalty. If you go out in public and see a black woman rocking a twist out or fancy updo, nine times out of ten her hair is screaming confidence. Natural hair is just another feature that makes black women beautiful.
—**Kamica Price**, public relations specialist

So here we are, almost three years since that salon visit, and my daughter, during her most formative years, wants out of her natural style. Now, during a time when the world is after my daughter's self-esteem, her mind, and her soul, when our Black community, bodies, and our hair are under attack. At a time like this, my daughter wants her locs out. Am I losing a fighter? A brilliant warrior and ally?

As mothers, we are forced to confront our fears so that our children know that fear can be overcome. We confront our insecurities so our children may understand that they can rise above. As a mom, I will don the armor of love, patience, and courage. I hold fast to the words of my Almighty God who says, "What God has blessed, no man can curse." Bella-Victoria's name means "beautiful victory." Suleni's name means "daughter of the mother" in my native Garifuna tongue. I realize my girls are gifts from God, and I am ever so grateful that He gave them to me. I will acknowledge and respect their personal journeys—in hair or otherwise—in the same way in which they've always supported my own journeys.

I say, lock hands and lock hearts. It's the only way to win.

MY CURLS, MY CROWN

Dr. Priscilla Ferreira

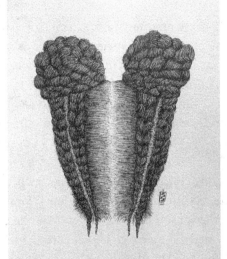

Meu cabelo é meu firmamento (My hair is my firmament)
É meu céu inteiro (It's my entire sky)
Protege meus pensamentos (It protects my thoughts)
Para com eles todo cuidado (To my hair: all of my love and care)
                    —"Tempo Fértil," Renato Pessoa

MY LITTLE KINDERGARTNER SELF hated the cold water dripping on my forehead in those early mornings when my dad would lean my head back in the sink to wash my hair, then brush it, before school. When my mom left early in the morning to go to work, my father took care of my little 'fro and my fear of bullying.

I am not sure how my dad could live up to the task of caring for a little Black girl without himself having had parents to teach him how to show love for delicate things like curls. I just remember that while I cried in anticipation and fear of the hostile, exclusively white environment that was my preschool, my father's fingers gently caressed my scalp with Neutrox conditioner. As he untangled my curls, he hoped to untangle my courage from my fear and sadness. He rinsed my hair and massaged my self-esteem while assuring me that my 'fro would look gorgeous. I couldn't help but cry in existential discomfort. He dried my hair with a towel, then shook it carefully in the towel, saying, "*Vai ficar um Blackie bem bonito, minha fia.*" (It's going to look amazing, your little 'fro, baby.")

I protested hard, every morning. I feared and hated, every morning.

I went off to school, angry and anxious. At their first opportunity, white kiddos would greet me at my classroom door: "*Cabelo de Bombril! Cabelo de Bombril!* (Brillo pad! Brillo pad!)" *Cabelo de bombril* is how schoolchildren harass Black girls, implying that their hair is as hard and unpleasant to touch as a steel scouring pad. When I came home crying, letting my dad know that once again classmates had called me a Brillo pad, I am sure that my reports pinched his heart. But his gentle touch on my hair every morning was his way to disavow the abrading violence of the belief that my hair was ever unpleasant. When he recited his morning mantras—"Your 'fro is gorgeous"—he was teaching me my first lessons of how one wakes up in the morning to fiercely, but gently, prepare oneself for a rough world, having love as self-defense. He showered me with love and shielded me with affirmation.

Despite my parents' dedication to helping me craft and uphold my self-esteem, and their aesthetic militancy notwithstanding, I tied my hair back every day until the age of fourteen. All messages I received other than my parents' were that my hair was too ugly to deserve any respectable attention, too undisciplined to be let free, too targeted to be exposed. It seemed easier to twist my hair, abdicating my right to be fully myself, then tie it back real tight, corralling myself with a subjugating knot.

I was one of two Black girls in a majority-white private school in Mato Grosso do Sul, a state in the Brazilian Midwest. The other Black girl was the daughter of my Portuguese teacher, Tía Clarinda. Tía Clarinda was the only Black teacher (or professor) I have had in my entire life. One day she asked if I would like to get my hair braided. I refused. But the ancestral *insurgente* in me knew better and, still uncertain of my feelings, I walked to Tia's house one day. Her sister braided my hair. I felt both ecstatic and anxious in anticipation of what others might think.

If you're familiar with the dynamic of a Hispanic household, you know that straight hair is good hair and wavy, curly, or kinky hair is "pelo malo," or bad hair. ... Textured hair has yet to be accepted as "normal." "*Eso es la moda ahora*," or "that's the style now" is everyone's favorite line when asked why my hair is so big and curly. My hair is not a fashion statement; it is a part of me in the most literal and figurative way possible.
—**Janibell Roseanne**, Afro Caribeña digital creator

Deep inside, my ancestors celebrated those braids. The ancestors have always been about rescuing each second of our lives that white supremacy steals from us. My braided hair saved me two hours in the shower every morning fighting against my curls, battling them with a brush in an attempt to tame my curls into a straitjacket of white aesthetic. But no matter how many hours I had spent in this time-sapping endeavor, it was of no use. While drowned in conditioner and tied down, my hair "behaved," as a white neighbor used to say. But as my stylist Doña Iansã air-dried it with her windy messages of confidence, my curls rebelled and stood up in 'fro. From the time Tía Clarinda's sister braided my hair, I spent four years wearing my hair in braids. When it was time to undo the tresses, I would rebraid them myself on the same day. My confidence was still not ready to fly along with my natural hair's free takeoff to the high and round contours of my 'fro queendom.

I have never used chemicals to straighten my hair. But that did not spare it from Brazilian society's racist toxicity. I was eighteen years old before I found myself looking in the mirror and thinking, *Envious fuckers! My hair is so beautiful! I have been fooled! Fucking envious liars!* When I threw my self-recognition against the mirror of white supremacy, shards of white lies shattered all over the room. I replaced that broken reflection with the veritable mirror of Doña Oxum.[1] *That* mirror reflected the outlines of Black golden curls that matched the outline of my free existence.

Some years later, I visited Gorée Island, Senegal, for an International Institute on Human Rights for young women activists of African descent. When I'd arrived, I was so happy to return to the Motherland. There were about seventy of us from fifty African countries and across the diaspora. My hope was to connect with sisters from the continent. I knew Gorée Island witnessed the largest recorded shipments of enslaved Africans destined for the Middle Passage. At the institute, some women wanted to talk about racism, racial inequality, and pan-Africanism. However, African sisters from the continent insisted that their issues and concerns were not about racism but globalization. Discussions were heated, and divergence became stark.

Afro Brazilian activists were very vocal. We had a conflict with the organizer, who insulted us, telling us, "You white Westerners come here to tell us what Blackness is all about. Pan-Africanism isn't but a handful of African Americans coming to Africa to do their little festivals and shop for fabric and handcrafts."

The mean-spirited statement was meant to disconnect and to hurt. The disappointment cut so deep because, as a young Pan-Africanist, I still carried an internal yearning for connection with, and avowal from, African sisters. That night, nine of the young women from both the continent and the African diaspora sat down side by side, our legs hanging down a cliff at the edge of the island overlooking the Atlantic Ocean. We spoke in nine different accents. We had nine shades of skin color, nine unique and proudly fashioned hairstyles, and innumerable experiences of being both women and descendants of Africans. We watched the sunset and looked at the horizon. We talked about the ocean, the ship, the crossing, and the distress on both shores of the Black Atlantic. At that moment, I realized I did not need anyone, not even the darkest-skinned African sister, to tell me who I was: Black, not Black enough, white, not white enough, Brown, Red, or whatever other melanin metrics people might adopt. I determined that no one would define my negritude but me.

The next day, I shaved my hair completely. Then, I returned to the cliff, beside the Door of No Return at the edge of the island, and I threw my hair and my trauma, my self-doubt, the bullying, and the wounds into the ocean. I asked Doña Iemanjá,[2] the goddess of the sea, to take away all the gratuitous trauma inflicted against my hair, head, and mind. I felt that Doña received my hair as an offering of trust and a confirmation that I'd heard her guidance. I, her child, had returned not only to the departure shore but also to the firm ground of self-determination. I was finally prepared to receive the gentle touch of the healing salty water upon my head and accept unconditional self-love with confidence, the way my father had modeled during my childhood. My hair was gone, but my mind was present to accept the gentle rinsing out of the violence at last. Self-love, self-affirmation, self-defense, after all, were not about hair, but about Orí, the temple of the divine at the crown of our heads.[3] I no longer needed external markers to affirm my Blackness, my sense of belonging as an Afro Brazilian woman, activist, educator. It was not in my hair, but in my head, my heart, my spirit that *herstories* of resilience, beauty, strategy, care, confidence, and love were entangled.

Not all Black women have been lucky enough to find the mirror of Doña Oxum,[3] through which they can see their Black Power surrounding their third eye in the silhouette of a perfectly round Afro, shaped high like a crown. Not all Black women can look back at their experience with their natural hair and remember the softness of their father's best intentions of helping them feel, see, and embrace their natural beauty, power, and boldness. Not all of us have experienced our parents' morning rituals of venerating the magnificence of Black girls' curls, and the divinity of their Orí crown, of their queendom.

I am proud to be part of a generation of young Afro Brazilian women who have emancipated our natural hair. As if guided by fugitive routes mapped on our heads by our ancestors, we have found the path of self-love and self-affirmation. I have seen how my liberation has influenced my younger generation of cousins, friends, students, and goddaughters, and that moves me to tears.

Iemanjá has waved away my curls. She sluiced away the traumas that had intoxicated its textures and poured upon my Orí a salty riddle to share with my sisters: have you found the mirror, the waves, the Secret?

Works Cited and Notes

1. Cláudia Cerqueira do Rosario, "The Ladies of the Water: Iemanjá, Oxum, Oiá and a Living Faith," *Wagadu* 3 (Spring 2006): 142–153.

2. Cerqueira do Rosario, "Ladies of Water," 142–153.

3. *Orí*, literally meaning "head," refers to one's spiritual intuition and destiny. One with a balanced character obtains an alignment with one's *orí* or divine self. It is also believed that *orí* should be worshiped like orisha. When things are not going right, *orí* should be consulted. And to make things right, *orí* should be appeased because whatever one becomes or whatever happens in one's life is as destined by *orí*. For more information, see Baba Ifa Karade, *The Handbook of Yoruba Religious Concepts*, rev. ed. (Newburyport, MA: Weiser Books, 2020).

PART IV

THE UNSHACKLED CHRONICLES

YO SOY PARTE DOMINICANA, YO SOY BLACK, YO SOY MISMA!

Tyrice Brown, MA

YO SOY PARTE DOMINICANA.

That's the line my *tía* taught me before my first trip to the Dominican Republic. I knew the basic essential Spanish phrases that most Americans were taught in school: how to ask for *el baño*, how to say I was hungry or thirsty. And of course, I knew what *coño* meant. I could dance *bachata* to Aventura songs, reciting each line with the passion of any thirteen-year-old girl. In the States where the island's descendants sometimes traded their tongues for the socioeconomic perks of assimilation, these small details were enough for me to fit in. I could easily merge into Dominican spaces. Never before had anyone asked me to quantify my genes. I had just been Adoni Garcia's daughter, but going back to my father's home country required something more complex from me: an explanation of my identity. My aunt needed to teach me how to flesh out which part of me was authentic. She knew I could not merely blend. I had to exist as Dominican—even if only *parte*.

Yo soy parte

Not entirely of this place
or this culture
but half.

My heritage was running through my veins. It showed up in the way my skin caught the sun, that rich orange island undertone that browned without blistering. It was carved into my face, lips, nose, and eyes, all present in the people of La Romana. On mute, without language, I saw myself in them, not just 50 percent of me, but my mother's African culture. Though not always recognized as coming from the continent, the diaspora was etched into Dominicans, their rituals and food, their muscles and movements.

Learning how to say "*Yo soy parte Dominicana*" and including that whenever I was introduced to someone new bruised me in a way that I couldn't express back then. I just knew I wanted to go home, where 100 percent of me was valid. It wasn't until one early summer morning in the DR, when I sat down in that tiny salon chair, that I realized why it ached to only be half.

My aunt had given me and my cousins money to get a blowout. I had never had an official Dominican blowout before. My maternal *abuela* had laid a hot comb to my hair for special occasions such as Easter or Christmas, and I had recently started getting relaxers every six to eight months to loosen my curls. But the majority of the time, I wore my hair in long braids or ponytails.

My mom would make sure I wore cornrows when visiting *that* side of my family. "They don't know how to take care of your hair over there," she'd warn me. "Don't take these braids out and be running around with your hair all over your head."

Unlike my cousins who wore their hair loose or wet and curly—their edges easily lying in smooth waves across their foreheads—I had to keep mine tied up or else risk days of detangling when I returned home, because my Dominican family had not correctly managed my multitextured hair. So needless to say, I was excited, but scared, to get a blowout. Could the lady get my hair bone straight like my cousins'?

I think I've heard the term *pelo malo* all my life. In DR, it's since like you're five years old, they're already telling your mom, "*Oh, esa niña con ese 'pelo malo.'* You have to start either relaxing her hair or taking her to the salon every weekend." . . . I tried not to pay too much attention to that phrase, *pelo malo*. But when it came from my family, it really hurt me, because it's like wow, it's something that is mine. And they're blaming me for that.
—**Corianny Rosario**, in Remezcla

I woke up that morning, dressed, took a quick bite of toast and eggs, and walked with my cousins down to the salon. I was to go first because my hair was the hardest. Everyone else had gotten blowouts so often that their hair had been trained. Even though their hair still curled up when washed, it was easier to lay flat.

The stylist began to speak to me in Spanish.

"Lo siento, yo soy parte Dominicana pero no hablo Española." I gave it my best accent, and she nodded, speaking what broken *inglés* she knew. The cold water was shocking but refreshing, and after the fourth wash, she lifted my head from the rim of the sink's basin to detangle my naps. She pulled and yanked, sucking her teeth with every stretch of the comb. "Aye dios mío, gurl!" she proclaimed. I began to shrink, my full Blackness on display—nigga naps and all pulled right out of my scalp. She pulled huge clumps of hair from the wide-tooth comb, throwing them into the sink with disgust. Then she'd start again yanking my head this way and that until my neck became sore and small tears puddled in my eyes.

Yo soy parte Dominicana, I thought as I closed my eyes trying to imagine the results. Straight flowing hair was just a few moments away. If I could bear the pain long enough, I would look like the girls on the salon's posters. I would feel like the sexy women who danced salsa and merengue with their men, undulating their bodies, their hair following in their wake.

The stylist said something to my cousins in Spanish.

"She wants to know if you want a perm." My cousin translated the words nonchalantly as she thumbed through a magazine. I shook my head no, and the stylist hissed her disapproval under her breath. Finally, I made it under the blow-dryer, where the setting was turned all the way up and the smell of my heating scalp began to fill the room. The stylist wrapped sections of my hair around a circular brush, and with the strength of many women, she pulled my wet hair through the bristles until it was dry and straight. As if the heat from the blow-dryer wasn't enough, she cranked the flat iron to 375 degrees and ran the plates down my hair. The smell of burning hair replaced the scent of my burning scalp. She blew at the pieces to cool them before they hit my bare back, and then it was over. In a gestured motion, she asked me which side I wanted my part on, and I replied by sweeping my tamed hair to the right side. She ran the flat iron over the hair in the front and handed me the mirror as she wiped the sweat from her brow. I looked at myself; my face was red from the warming day and the salon's heat. "Qué linda!" she said, gently sliding my hair over my shoulders, so it lay on my growing chest. I smiled and thanked her, getting out of the seat as my cousin, already washed by the prep girl, slid herself into the chair.

I spent the rest of that trip trying not to sweat out my blowout, taking all measures to maintain the resemblance of beauty. Once we got to the resort in Santo Domingo, though, all the girls, myself included, had had enough. We cannonballed into the pool and let the water revert our hair back to its original state. My curls were not as defined as before, and a few straight pieces lay lifeless where my root curls met heat-damaged ends.

Black at the roots. Dominican at the tips. *Yo soy parte Dominicana.*

Whether it be straight from Africa or rooted in the diaspora's combined cultures, the richness of my identity has always shown up in my hair. My hair is overwhelming to those who require simple boxes to check.

Are you Dominican? Are you Black? Are you mixed?

Yo soy auténtica, Yo soy misma!

I am thirty-one now and have spent all of my twenties rocking my natural hair. I have shaved my head twice, worn braids, tried locs, dyed my hair, worn weaves, even patronized Dominican stylists in DC, where I live now. Though politer about it, they still griped about my thick naps, sometimes asking me if I want a perm, just like the hairdresser years ago. But I am not that young girl anymore. I have grown up to find Afrocentric communities that normalize what is natural and appreciate the excessive volume and complex features of Blackness.

Unfortunately, I cannot say the same for the workplace. I find that corporate America still adheres to straight, undefined, "safe" looks. I learned this when I worked as a flight attendant. I was reprimanded for my hair being too big. I can still see the words *hair* and *excessive volume* highlighted on the page. The bright yellow highlighter ink burned my eyes as I read it. I remember thinking, *Am I reading this correctly? Does this piece of paper say that my natural hair is taking up too much space?* Never had I heard *excessive* and *volume* coupled together as a negative connotation for hair.

Excessive: more than is necessary, normal, or desirable; immoderate.

Volume: the amount of space that a substance or object occupies.

"Policy states," the white male duty desk manager kept repeating and pointing to the line on the page that mentioned my excessive volume. "It is policy, and policy states that your hair is too big, falling under the category of excessive volume." He pointed at the rules and regulations sheet he had printed out. "You can keep this sheet for your records," he said, handing me the highlighted paper. I carried it in my free hand while pulling my rolla board out of the Flight Attendant Lounge. It was before 6:00 AM in Atlanta—the sun hadn't even announced the day—and here I was being told that my natural hair was too much. As I approached the stairs that led up to the terminals, I paused, wondering what to do next. I knew I hadn't said or done enough to defend myself. I really couldn't even remember what I actually *had* said. My lack of response was a product of shock. When the duty desk manager had approached me, I'd been taking my first sip of black coffee. I was focused on the departures board, checking whether the gate for my flight had changed. Fresh out of training, I was "new to the line," in the industry's parlance. I was still adhering to every guideline I had learned during my in-flight training: "After the preflight briefing, be sure to check the board and ensure that the gate for your flight has not changed." My flight instructor had never mentioned my hair being wrong, and neither had the executive team when they attended my training cohort's graduation ceremony. Yet here was the duty manager, asking me to pull my hair back before passengers began to board the plane because it was noncompliant. I stood at the step long enough to relive the scene. An older white woman with years of seniority and a hard-teased bob had passed us. She'd waved at the manager, her blue dress altered well above the knee, and her cleavage waving too. This was classic diva senior mama behavior; they did as they pleased without reprimand. Instead, it was I, the young Black girl, following all the rules except the Eurocentric ones, who was punished. As my tears welled up, I wanted to yell.

I would never be able to stand up for my culture if I was sobbing. My words would be lost, and the manager would pity me without learning the lesson I needed to impart. I wanted to be bold, articulate, wielding feminist terms I'd learned in college to tell him a piece of my mind. I pivoted to head back, but I found myself rooted to the spot where I stood. Years of suppressed anger bubbled up, and I was a snot-nosed mess. I sprinted up the steps and into the terminal's bathroom, where I called a Black friend who held a leadership role in the airline. It was early, and her yawn let me know that she had been fast asleep. However, as soon as she sensed the urgency in my voice, she was alert. I rushed her, crying and explaining in a hushed yell so as not alarm the passengers using the stalls next to mine. She did not tell me to calm down. She did not interrupt. She waited. She listened. When I had heaved out my final words, she spoke. "I'll handle this. Don't put your hair up!"

I exited the bathroom stall and took a good look at myself in the mirror behind the sinks. *Keep your hair big and your head up!* I pep-talked myself. I straightened both my uniform and my spine and walked onto the plane with the hair God had given me.

When I reached my layover city, I learned that my friend had called the duty station to complain. Then she had called my direct supervisor to voice how insensitive and racist the "excessive volume" comment was. Before the day ended, the reprimand had been taken off my official record and relegated to an informal write-up. But the duty desk manager carried his grudge to his boss. He had a problem with my friend calling him out—by inference—as racist. What my friend had actually done was call his actions socially and racially insensitive. But all he heard was a suggestion that he was racist. He rebuked this notion, claiming his homosexuality as a racism pass. After all, how could one marginalized group have the ability to mistreat another? My friend wound up having more issues stemming from my incident than I had. She was called into one meeting after another, our friendship on trial as colleagues expressed curiosity about why she cared enough to go to bat for a rookie.

A year later, she sat in the salon with me as I shaved my head for the first time. After four years of going natural, I'd received a bad chemical relaxer job that had caused so much damage I had to chop it off.

"What do you think they'll say about this look?" I asked her. "They can't say it's too big, that's for sure!"

She laughed.

"Was it worth it? Having them tear through your personal life, trying to find out why you were sticking up for me and my hair?"

"We Black women are worth a million wars, and for you, I'd fight again and again," she said, taking my hand as a clump of hair fell over our fists.

Dedicated to all the rays of sunshine that pass through my life in the form of women

POWER STRUGGLE

Jasmine Hawkins, MA

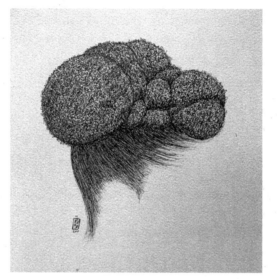

COMEDIAN PAUL MOONEY said it best in Chris Rock's *Good Hair* documentary: "If your hair is relaxed, white people are relaxed. If your hair is nappy, they aren't happy."[1] This thinking is the reason many Black girls grow up with wash-day stories laced with the pain of altering unacceptable natural coils. We've internalized outside perceptions and woven them into the fabric of our identities. Our hair, like our lives, has always been dissected, policed, and in need of taming, leaving us with skewed views of ourselves, our beauty, and our value.

In sixth grade, my inquisitive blonde teacher called me to the front of the class. The school was predominately white and Christian. I was one of a handful of Black students, though prior to this particular day, that hadn't mattered much.

As I walked toward the front of the room, my freshly braided curls, which mother had done the night before, dangled well past my shoulders and bounced with each step. I stood next to my teacher facing all the students as she pinched one of my curls between her thumb and pointer finger and asked, "Is this real?"

In that moment, my teacher and I were physically next to each other but existed worlds apart. What could I say? Answering "no" would acknowledge that I was flawed, in need of enhancements to help me blend in. Clearly, I wasn't blending.

I lied. "Yes."

"This *is* your hair? It seemed much shorter yesterday."

"Yes, it is." I spread a story around the school about me having a product called Hair Grow-Fast. Admission to weave would be conceding to every stereotype and perception regarding Black hair. I was not going to be the bald-headed Black girl.

I'm not sure whether it was my teacher's audacity or the question itself that offended me most. Apparently, this teacher felt comfortable dissecting me. I was the subject of the day's lesson, without my approval. I still can't explain what public inquiry does to a girl. Suddenly, parts of you are no longer solely yours. My hair was something to defend. I had to lie about it, contain it, justify it; I could do anything but wear it because someone always had something to say.

When I say Black hair is political, I prefer to borrow writer and activist Mazuba Haanyama's definition from her essay "Untangling the Knots: Understanding the Hair Politics of Black Women (Revisited)."[2] She states, "Conversations about Black women's hair are necessarily political. By political I mean involving both power struggle and negotiations." My sixth-grade experience was a power struggle and negotiation. My teacher used her authority to dissect me, and I had to sacrifice the truth to maintain some semblance of dignity. This exchange was one of my first lessons in survival: compromise and perform. It was a microcosm of the much larger issue of which Haanyama was speaking.

In many ways, starting with our hair, society asks us to perform identities for the comfort of those around us, specifically for the comfort of those in power. Our performance is—too often—an expectation of conforming to rules and standards that uphold an exclusionary norm. The result is that daily decisions about our appearance shift from personal preferences and self-edifying expressions to public breeding grounds for pushback, scrutiny, and critique.

When I decided to loc my hair in May 2019, it was a personal decision, much like a decision anyone else makes to color, cut, or style hair. I found locs to be more fitting for my active lifestyle. However, in making that choice, I subjected myself to an even greater power struggle than the one I experienced in sixth grade. I placed myself in the box with Chastity Jones, a young Alabama woman who interviewed for a job and received an offer, *with* the condition that she cut her locs.[3] When Jones inquired why she needed to cut her hair, the human resources manager informed her, "They tend to get messy. Not that yours are, but . . . you know."

What exactly do we know?

We know that Jones's job offer was rescinded because she refused to comply. We know that locs are, historically, worn by people of the African diaspora. We know that by hiding behind a race-neutral grooming policy that requires a "business professional image" where "excessive hairstyles and unusual colors are unacceptable," we are, however covertly, saying that the acceptable image is one that demands that Black women negotiate and conform.

That is what we know.

Sadly, Jones's story progressed through a six-year court battle, ending in a 2016 ruling that upheld the dreadlocks ban—prohibiting dreadlocks like the ones I wear today—in the workplace. The court's stance was that while hairstyles are "culturally associated with race," they are not "immutable physical characteristics." In other words, as Black people, we have the ability to alter our hair and conform.

One of my earliest hair memories is conforming, a baptism into Black womanhood commonly known as wash day. I would bend down into gushing faucet water and rise up with a shriveled bush. The tangled dripping mass emerging from the sink was never acknowledged as beautiful. With conditioner trickling down my forehead, I stared in the mirror and told myself, *No one can see me like this.* The process to make me "presentable" took hours.

If you ask any Black woman about the infamous wash day, you're likely to hear a story about sitting in the kitchen with an older Black woman and a hot comb. The goal was to look as far from natural as humanly possible because that is truly what was meant by "getting your hair done." The shriveled bush from our baptism needed to be stretched and tamed because "good hair" was viewed as long and flowing. Our shrinkage—hair that coils tightly in its natural state—had to be dried, fried, and laid to the side.

The hot comb was the most dreadful part of wash day. As if blow-drying my bush wasn't stressful enough with all the tugging, tangles, and heat, my mother also had to press it out. She'd always take the heated comb fresh from the stove and set it on a folded paper towel to cool. Starting with the shortest peasy strands in the back of my head, she would pick up the comb, blow on it, and rake through my hair. I sat cringing internally, because doing so outwardly meant getting burned. This was the process of looking pretty: squirming in the kitchen, fearing the sizzling straightening comb, and waiting for the torture to end. As far as I knew, there were no other options. My hair was unmanageable, and, *No one could see me like this.* My Blackness had to be contained.

Don't remove the kinks from your hair. Remove them from your brain.
—Marcus Garvey

As a young girl, the only images of Black hair in its natural form that I saw on television were women on plantations, working the field, or fighting for freedom. Whenever I saw my natural hair in the mirror, I saw those women. I felt I, too, belonged on a plantation working in a field. My hair was fighting for freedom. It was short, untamed, and a sign of inferior status.

Spoken or unspoken, our mothers pressed out more than hair. They burned into our minds a new understanding of self. We were only good enough to be accepted *if* we made adjustments. I didn't understand the impact of these internalizations until my college years, when I made the commitment to see myself as beautiful. I started wearing my hair in its natural form. Even if I didn't feel attractive, I trained my brain to equate my textured hair with beauty.

The truth is that in my American story, I rarely get to see myself through my own eyes. I'm compelled to view myself from the perspective of others. W. E. B. Du Bois called this dilemma *double-consciousness.* In his popular book *The Souls of Black Folk,*[4] Du Bois says, "It is a peculiar sensation, this double-consciousness, this sense of always looking at one's self through the eyes of others. . . . One ever feels his two-ness,—an American, a Negro . . . two thoughts . . . two warring ideals in one dark body." When I think of the fight to see my hair as normal, acceptable, and attractive, I think of these words: an internal warring. What appears to be a simple mutable characteristic to the outside world is really the extension of a deeply rooted societal tension. Our hair is not our own. It is another part of us that is subject to policing.

Audre Lorde captured this conflict in her 1990 essay "Is Your Hair Still Political?" She states, "The obsession with African American hair is deeply ingrained in the American psyche."[5] This statement remains true today. As a society, we have internalized misconceptions and passed them down through generations. For Black people, these internalizations can create a self-hate no person should ever have to endure. We should never look in the mirror thinking something is wrong with the way God made us. We shouldn't have to compromise parts of ourselves to blend in or fit anyone else's norm. Our differences are not a subject for public critique. Our hair is personal.

As a sacred, uniquely beautiful part of the African diasporic experience, our hair is an entry point into our world. In America, it represents centuries of fighting to be seen as human rather than other, to exist without policing, and to live without conforming. Our hair, like our lives, makes others uncomfortable, and that is a burden we have carried for too long. It is not our job to make others feel comfortable.

It *is* our job, however, to control the narrative. We do this with representation, by proudly wearing our kinky, curly, coily, puffy hair in professional and educational spaces. The more we see pro athletes like Serena and Venus Williams or celebrities like Viola Davis boldly rocking their braids and Afros on TV screens, the more confident we become, knowing we can do the same. We can be ourselves and still be beautiful. We can be ourselves and still be employed. We can be ourselves and still be successful.

At this point in my life, I choose to wear my hair in ways that will give my future daughter the freedom to see, love, and accept her natural coils. I haven't quite figured out how I will teach her to navigate teachers like the one I had in sixth grade or how to counter unfair laws, but if Paul Mooney was right about the nappiness and relaxation of our hair, I will make sure my daughter knows that she will make some white people very unhappy. Regardless, that will never be a reason to conform.

Our hair is an entry point into our world, and we will continue to rock it just as we please.

Works Cited

1. Jeff Stilson, dir., *Good Hair* (New York: HBO Films, 2009).

2. Mazuba Haanyama, "Untangling the Knots: Understanding the Hair Politics of Black Women (Revisited)," *The Feminist Wire* (blog), April 9, 2013, https://thefeministwire.com/2013/04/untangling-the-knots-understanding-the-hair-politics-of-black-women-revisited.

3. Nadra Nittle, "It's Still Legal to Ban Dreadlocks in the Workplace," *Racked* (blog), May 18, 2018, https://www.racked.com/2018/5/18/17366610/dreadlocks-ban-supreme-court-case-chastity-jones.

4. W. E. B. Du Bois, *The Souls of Black Folk* (New York: G&D Media, 2019).

5. Audre Lorde, *I Am Your Sister: Collected and Unpublished Writings of Audre Lorde,* ed. Rudolph P. Byrd, Johnnetta Betsch Cole, and Beverly Guy-Sheftall (Oxford: Oxford University Press, 2011).

IN THE KITCHEN

Jewelle Gomez, MS

WHEN I WAS A girl, the back of your head was known as the *kitchen*. I don't know why. There, at the tender nape, my hair's natural texture seemed to fight for its life. And there, naps that every colored parent taught us to hate sprang to life, curling tightly around themselves into small individual beads, defying the curses of mothers and beauticians, defying chemicals and hot combs. It was decades before I believed that those coiled naps were not an insult to beauty but a natural part of it. Between then and now I've saved snapshot memories of the many colored girls who suffered and survived the same assaults on the kitchen as I had.

"How her mother let her leave the house like that?" The early 1960s, South End of Boston. The eyes of neighborhood mothers spoke more loudly than any words they dared to speak. The young woman with the short Afro walked down Tremont Street as if she were strolling the bank of the Niger River. Every time I saw her in our mixed, working-class neighborhood, my gaze turned to the spectacle of openly displayed naps coiffed into a modest, yet regal, crown.

Conk, 'do, process, permanent, relaxer were code words for "I am ugly unless I look like white people." And this young woman was the first person I ever saw who sported a dramatic alternative. All I knew about her was her name: Gilda. To me at age twelve, she seemed a visitor from another galaxy, one where little girls didn't have to be tortured in a "beauty" parlor every two weeks. She was an antidote to every self-hating remark I'd heard from kids and adults in my neighborhood, on my television, and in my head.

Deep inside, even then, I held the secret knowledge that I would grow up to be a lover of women. Without ever having heard a word spoken, I also understood that I would be scorned, just as Gilda was, if the neighbors learned my secret. Without her knowledge, that young woman walking serenely, defiantly through my neighborhood was leading me toward my own liberation from the tyranny of straight hair and the deep love of my natural self. And how *did* her mother let her leave the house like that?

———

At sixteen I'm standing in my stepmother Henrietta's kitchen, clutching the hot curling iron and trying to do her hair. One of her shiny curls clings to the smoking rod in my hand. I tug firmly as she's taught me to do. The curl pulls away from her head—completely! It is a burnt thing on the iron leaving an empty space in my stepmother's going-to-work hairdo. I gulp in terror; she laughs, grabs the iron and the scissors and takes over, snipping her way out of my embarrassment.

———

Even though I loved singer Jackie Wilson, I couldn't date boys who straightened their hair. Once, I slow-danced in a church basement with a neighborhood guy, recoiling when my hand touched his stiff, slick hair. His hair felt as if it'd been preserved in formaldehyde. I was even more out of step, since all the girls seemed to love it. I wondered then if that really confirmed my identity as a lesbian.

I have several photographs of my no-cookie-baking grandmother, Lydia, at the beach. A glamorous, charming, and sexual woman, she refused to forget what it was like to be young. At the drop of a straw hat, she and her friends would pack themselves off to Revere Beach, risking the perils that might befall any person of color travelling through Boston's Irish and Italian outposts for a few rays of sun. And every summer she'd take the three-hour drive through the WASP enclaves of Cape Cod to stay with gay friends living in Provincetown. In one photograph we're standing together, arms crossed, me imitating her. She gazes directly into the camera. Her hair is blowing, and she's unconcerned about it—not a natural bearing for a woman of color at the beach in the 1950s or 1960s. No scarf is binding her hair, nor is a cautious hand trying to subdue it.

But as I look at the photo, I can remember how I felt: the roots of my soft, fuzzy hair were pulled tight, locked into braids meant to keep my naps from showing. My grandmother, with her closer link to our Ioway and Wampanoag ancestors, had "good" hair. I did not.

When I was a teenager, before leaving for church dances, I would comb my straightened hairdo to the left side, where I fluffed the luminous curls around my ear. The right side was pulled taut across my head, held by bobby pins and combs. So, when I slow-danced with boys I had one side, at least, that would defy humidity and remain a refuge of the curl cascade I'd constructed at home.

I don't know what came over me, or maybe I do.

It was 1968. The Black Panther Party was serving free breakfasts in Oakland, California, and carrying guns in public just like John Wayne did.

Martin Luther King Jr. had been murdered the past spring.

Africa had become more than just a punch line for comedians' jokes.

I now knew that my adolescent neighborhood hero, Gilda, was not a total anomaly. There had actually *been* African queens. So while my great-grandmother—who was also my guardian—traveled to a convention, I visited the Beau Brummel Tonsorial Emporium in Roxbury, where a handsome brother named Dasal Banks cut off my straightened hair. Dasal wore a vibrant dashiki and the confidence of a young prince. He wielded his clippers like a sword.

The moment I saw my new self in the mirror, a frisson of recognition and fear ripped through me. When my great-grandmother came home, she squinted at me with glaucoma-clouded eyes and asked what I'd done to my hair.

"Nothing," I said, with all the confidence at the disposal of a lying nineteen-year-old.

My great-grandmother harrumphed but said no more. Her eyesight really wasn't *that* poor. Nor was her understanding of how history moves on.

We, the "Angelas," never prearranged meetings. We'd simply find ourselves sitting at the same table in the university cafeteria or on a bench in our college's urban quadrangle. Our hero, Angela Davis, was a fugitive, wanted by the FBI, suspected of taking part in an attempted prison break of Black revolutionaries that had left people dead. She was Bonnie without Clyde, but with a mission instead. We shared stories of what it felt like to know that some people, occasionally the police, suspected you were Angela Davis. While we knew her as a political hero, they saw only America's Most Wanted. A couple of women had even been taken into custody and treated to the casual brutality of unwarranted imprisonment until the police could verify their identities. Sitting together on campus, we were both proud and terrified. None of us really looked much alike. It was the hair. The sight of a halo of unrestrained, kinky hair on fair-skinned women scared folks so badly they couldn't see anything else. But, we saw each other.

On her mantelpiece, my mother kept a framed collection of family portraits going back to my great-great-grandmother. I'd visited my mother annually since I was a child and eventually noticed that my photos stopped appearing around 1967, just before my visit to Beau Brummel. I was never sure whether she stopped adding new pictures after that because I no longer straightened my hair, or because it's when she learned I was lesbian.

To celebrate my birthday in September 1976, I went to the Booth Theatre on Broadway to see Ntozake Shange's choreopoem, *For Colored Girls Who Have Considered Suicide / When the Rainbow Is Enuf.* I sat mesmerized, even though I'd seen the performance a dozen times at off-Broadway theaters. I'd come this time just for the delirious joy of seeing a full cast of colored women with their natural hair on a Broadway stage. Most of my friends who accompanied me wore naturals or dreadlocks. And the audience was generously sprinkled with other colored lesbians sporting various natural hairstyles, smiling and greeting each other in public like I'd never seen before. In contrast, the many black stars in the audience, such as Diana Ross, had hair so *done* it was as if the culturally conscious breakthroughs of the 1960s had never happened. And those stars with male partners sat as stiffly as their processed hair, trying to reveal nothing of their deepest feelings that arose from a play about their liberation.

In the 1970s my then lover, Sandy, lighting designer and reggae aficionado, started locking her hair after hanging out with Rastafarians in New York City's Washington Square Park. The ganja-smoking religious sect required members' hair be covered—both men and the few women. Thick and black, Sandy's hair locked quickly, soon becoming an amazing and glorious mane. But whenever she left the house, I was frightened. It was 1978, and Rastas would scream, "Fashion dread!" and "Lesbo!" at women as they passed. Their uncovered locs made them targets for both verbal and physical violence.

Without a plan, I started locking my hair in 1981. I had been home for two weeks with illness, and during that time I began twisting. Because my hair was so soft it took those two weeks for my hair to begin holding—just as I recovered from my illness and began job-hunting. I went to all my interviews wearing scarves and Nigerian *geles*, which I'd chosen to match my outfits. I tried for a cosmopolitan look halfway between Nation of Islam and *Essence* magazine. But still, I was nervous. Months passed before I had locs that were more than sprouts sticking out all over my head. In my new job in the Dean's Office at New York City's Hunter College, I wore a scarf for almost a year until my locs dropped; that is, until they had their own life and direction.

When I came in to work one day without a scarf, a senior secretary, Edith, a mature Jewish woman and my supervisor, commented, "I haven't seen your hair before! It's gorgeous." She sounded as much like Barbra Streisand as I could have wanted. After that I didn't care what anyone else said.

In the fiction I've written in the past forty years, I find many places where women of color are combing each other's hair. In my novel, the main character, Gilda, is an escaped slave who remembers the feel of her mother's brush in her hair, and it evokes many other forgotten comforts. Later when she combs others' hair, they are usually laughing and telling stories. That particular activity is a natural focus for me. I write about what interests me: women. Women together. Hair preparation, even when it's torturous, is the time when women, lesbian or not, are totally involved with each other. We can show care for each other that is specific to an imposed social trauma. We touch each other and display unadorned and unashamed pleasure.

Or, we can pass on self-hatred.

In the last picture of my stepmother, Henrietta, at age eighty-three, her pure white, natural hair forms an aureole. She'd given up the hot comb as soon as she'd retired from her job as a cook. In the photo, she's flanked by a young niece, Catherine, and Catherine's fourteen-year-old daughter Atia, both of whom have pressed their hair into obedient, patent-leather helmets framing their chestnut faces. How did their mother let them leave the house with their hair like that?

I've wondered whether the myth of Medusa, with her hair of snakes and her lethal gaze, is simply the embodiment of people's fear of colored women's hair. In the 1980s when I tied my dreads up in bright cloth, allowing them to point in random directions, people stared—and not with the pleasure of my supervisor, Edith.

The first time a woman touched my dreadlocks playfully, sensually, I was startled. All my life I'd seen women's hair as a symbol, as a fetish that obscured whatever our true feelings might be. I've spent years trying to discard the image that others had grafted on to me. Although hair is only part of it, my ability to denounce an image—one that had begun with others' distaste for how I look and how I love—was critical to building my own image. I let go of cultural constructions that high school photographs, glossy women's magazines, advice columns, and swimming caps represented. It was not a free fall into a void but an ascent, hand over hand through braids, plaits, locs, and naps.

Since I was a little girl, they used to say—and me, myself, I used to say—"pelo malo." So to me, it was like normal until I started discovering there was nothing wrong with my hair. ... I began to transition to natural hair. ... Still to this day, sometimes I go to the hair salon and get my hair straightened and they'll say, "Asi es que te ves bonita." But I realized, that's my culture, especially the older people, that's the mentality that they have. I'm not going to change their minds. So I just pay no mind to them.

—**Brisa Cruz**

When she touched my locks, when we sweated together, I wasn't worried they'd "go back" or some other natural disaster. Like my body, my hair was finally my own. In the four decades since then, my locs have been short, long, wavy from braiding, and bobby-pinned into tiny curlicue question marks. Courtesy of Lady Clairol, they've been blonde, red, and auburn. And then— this time courtesy of Mother Nature—salt and pepper. I haven't cursed rainy weather since 1968.

The pressure that unrelieved images of Black, silky-haired movie stars, middle-class professionals, and singers in popular media—both white and Black—creates is as seductive today as it was forty years ago or one hundred and forty years ago. From Beyoncé's fierce mane to Condoleezza Rice's conservative sheen, the hair says it all. Cultural pressure means our hair can seduce women away from themselves, and away from one another.

But that influence isn't as deadly as it has been in the past. Now that so many others don't conform to that Eurocentric beauty standard, it's possible for young women to feel like they have an array of options available to them, from the bald beauty of Lena Waithe or the fictional Wakanda's Dora Milaje to the natural-curls profusion of Tracee Ellis Ross, to Regina King's braided cornrow patterns to Ava DuVernay's lengthy braids.

Now, my hair is all white. I've returned to that simple, close-cut natural that first intrigued me in the South End of Boston. I'd never thought I'd live to see movie stars and notables like Toni Morrison, Whoopi Goldberg, or Alfre Woodard on public stages wearing naturals and dreadlocks, but there they are! Hot combs and chemicals still sizzle throughout the Black community, but Gilda is no longer alone. Some Black women wear natural waves, others tight curls, others locs. Still others sport extensions or wraps or African knots. And some wear it differently every week. That's what's new for this current generation. Yes, some schools still send Black kids home for wearing braids or dreadlocks, but now their parents stand up for them and challenge the racist system. For them and for me, the naps are freeing. The kitchen is no longer a place of shame.

I followed the image of a young woman strolling the street because it was more compelling than anything else I was being force-fed. And she turned out to be me.

BEAUTY IS PAIN:
A HAIRSTORY

Kelechi Ubozoh

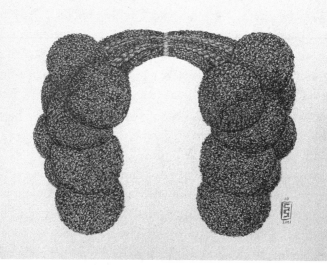

Chapter 1: Hot Comb with a Side of Charred Ear

"You're not too ugly," she said. That was high praise coming from my child-hood playmate, Camilla. We were playing in her Care Bears–themed room. Thick, long, wavy hair framed her creamy complexion. Although we were both Black, her daddy was Italian, mine Nigerian.

Even when she *didn't* listen to her mother's advice about avoiding direct sunlight, Camilla sometimes passed for white. She always passed the brown-paper-bag test, an unfortunate part of our collective Black American history.

If your skin was darker than a brown paper bag, you would be excluded from jobs, fraternities, sororities, and the Black elite. This is a test I would never pass.

Camilla studied my hair and face. "I know how to make you prettier," she said. I eagerly awaited what she could do with this sad canvas. She took my hand, and we went downstairs to the basement. Camilla's father was a traveling costume designer, hairdresser, and makeup artist for New York City's theater district. He stored hundreds of wigs and glamorous clothing in the basement.

After several moments of digging, Camilla unearthed a bobbed wig, most likely from the *Dreamgirls* production, and squeezed it on my head. Then she snuck into her father's makeup vanity and pulled out a compact. She led me into the basement's bathroom, and I closed my eyes while Camilla applied the nearly white concealer and powder to my brown face.

When I opened my eyes, I was greeted by a horrifying powder-cake face. Chunks of foundation fell into the sink. I cried as Camilla laughed at the sight of the small, melted monster. I was about eight when I learned that the world thought I was ugly. My later misadventures with Camilla confirmed my suspicions. Store clerks of every race and ethnicity slipped Camilla extra lollipops, and little boys, who typically despised little girls, broke character and offered her big toothless smiles. *I* was invisible. I did not have the language to express the concepts of colorism or internalized racism, but looking back it is evident how these experiences became rooted into my psyche.

More than ever, I wanted to look like Camilla. Her life appeared perfect. It was the early 1990s, and the beautiful biracial songstress Mariah Carey was climbing to fame. Mariah was my hero; Camilla could have been her mini-me.

Being Black was hard enough, but Nigerian too? Yikes! Not only could no one seem to pronounce my name (hello, middle school microaggressions), but also the other kids would frequently shove pictures in my face of nude African tribe members à la *National Geographic,* asking me why everyone was naked and strongly suggesting I return. Even my other Black classmates expressed these sentiments.

After the cake-face makeup incident, I realized that nothing was changing this brown skin. But . . . I *could* do something about my hair.

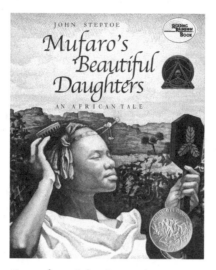

Cover from John Steptoe's
Mufaro's Beautiful Daughters.
Puffin Books.[1]

I had thick, comb-breaking Nigerian hair. Getting it done was a daily fight with my mother, entailing her chasing me around our small living room while I screamed, "No, please, don't!" The only way I would let her even touch my head was when I was seated in front of Popeye the Sailor Man, mesmerized by the power of spinach. Afterward, Mom would sprinkle my face with kisses and tell me that Black was beautiful. I'd curl up by her side and fall asleep as she told me the story of *Mufaro's Beautiful Daughters,* an African folktale akin to Cinderella. The characters looked like me, with deep golden-brown skin and cornrows. My mother tried to instill confidence and pride within me, but I received messages much louder than hers.

Trust the Universe and respect your hair.
—**Bob Marley**

I was done with braids and cornrows and worked up the courage to ask my mom if I could get my hair straightened. Mom said I was too young for chemicals, but I could have the hot comb.

Let me tell you about the hot comb. It is a Black-beauty torture device that derives its power from blinding-white heat. The hairdresser must run the searing sharp-toothed comb through thick, kinky curls and not burn you *too* badly. The more you moved, the more likely you'd have a patch of burnt skin as a souvenir. For some reason, no matter how talented the hairdresser, no one could quite find a way to not burn your ears. The top of mine were always dark and crusty after a long hot-comb session.

I am sitting in Miss Robin's salon chair with a hot comb to my head. *Sizzle. Pop. Hiss.* "You are so tender headed," Miss Robin complains. "Stop squirming!" But anyone would have a tender head the way she'd snatch up my microcurls and yank back my hair. I hold my breath and try to sit still, hoping to avoid a bad burn. *Sizzzzlle. Beauty is pain. Beauty is pain.* I whisper this mantra. It is also possible that trying to look like someone other than yourself is painful.

Chapter 2: The French Jheri Curl

Shirley Temple and Bojangles are tap-dancing across my television screen. The vibrant fifty-seven-year-old Black actor holds hands with the cutesy six-year-old Shirley and crystalizes the happy tap-dancing Negro routine. I squirm uncomfortably without knowing why. What catches my eye and interest are Shirley's golden tresses. She looks like an animated baby doll, angelic and kind. The bouncing, bold ringlets that frame her face fascinate me.

One thing becomes clear. I want—no, I *need*—Shirley Temple curls. However, at age nine, I've somehow internalized that children should be seen and not heard, and I would rather listen to, than talk with, adults. My nervous words would come out in jumbled heaps, and under no circumstances would I *ever* correct or talk back to an adult.

And this is how the great miscommunication of 1994 occurred. I'd had it with the hot comb. My scalp had become a patchy forest of tiny burns that I continued to pick at despite my mother's scolding. ("Stop scratching!") My straightened hair only lasted a day or two at best. As an elementary school kid, I found it impossible to avoid moisture. That meant no sweat, no swimming pools, no water guns, no water balloons, and definitely *no rain*. Because I hadn't figured out a way to control weather or hateful boys, my hair frequently was in a state of frizz, with, at times, a bird's-nest quality to it.

I told my mother I wanted curls that would stay bouncy no matter what. I dreamed of being dainty and feminine with satin-soft baby-doll curls.

We returned to Miss Robin's salon with a new plan. Miss Robin was one of many hairdressers at the large salon, where older Black women sat under rows of hair dryers poring over *Jet* and *Ebony* magazines. I was the youngest person there. Searching through photographs and stacks of Black-hair magazines, I pulled out pictures of women who sported styles reminiscent of Shirley Temple's bouncy curls. In silence, I showed them to Miss Robin.

"I want big curls like these," I say with my head down.

Miss Robin shoos the pictures away, seizing one word: *curl*. "What you need, honey, is a Wave Nouveau curl. It's new, it's French, and you'll be able to keep your curls fresh." Miss Robin is eager to get me in and out of the chair. I ask, quietly, whether I'll look like the pictures, but she doesn't respond. Before I can blink, I'm plopped into a swivel chair and getting my hair washed in a large black basin.

Two hours later, what I get is a Jheri curl. Popular in the 1980s, the Jheri curl is a juicy, glossy, and wet-curled hairstyle. Think Michael Jackson's *Thriller* album cover, or Samuel L. Jackson in *Pulp Fiction*. When I swivel in my chair to see myself in the mirror, I try not to cry. Moist curls hang around my face dripping onto my shirt and getting the back of my neck, the chair, and towels damp. I don't look like anyone's baby doll. More like a sad used mop.

"Don't you look pretty?" My mom and Miss Robin beam over me. I force a smile and swear that I love it.

To maintain the Wave Nouveau style, I slept with a plastic cap over my head and applied masses of curl activator, a pungent spray that really lingers; think rotten egg. I wore a large piece of cotton that wrapped around my head to keep the "juices" on my hair. If I slept in certain positions, the cold liquid oozed down my back, staining my clothes and waking me in the middle of the night. Soon my mom received angry phone calls from other mothers following sleepovers where I'd forgotten to wear my cap. My uncovered hair would leave a greasy residue, soiling pillows, blankets, and couch cushions.

Worst of all, the chemicals made my hair highly flammable, and thankfully no one was hurt during my birthday party where I leaned a little too close to the cake candles, causing a minor spark to hop onto my head. My emergency-room-educated mother quickly killed the almost-flame before anyone (besides me) could be traumatized.

At school, the boys would yell, "What's with the Jheri curl?"

"It's French, damn it!" I'd scream defiantly. At least I had my pride.

Chapter 3: The Little Chop

There is no big-chop story. I didn't one day gather all my courage, stare in the mirror at my overly processed broken hair, and say, "I'm done." I didn't take shiny sharp shears and slash the remnants of pain and oppression, of control and chemicals.

I didn't liberate my locks by any traditional means. I had a little chop. I stopped going to salons to get my hair permed. I embraced cornrows and braids and let my hair grow out of the past. One thing I appreciated more as I got older was my time. I've pondered the number of hours I've spent waiting in a chair or under a blow-dryer. I reclaimed that time by upending that painful hair narrative. Over time, my hair became long and thick. Today it is chemical-free, but it wears many masks and lives in constant fluctuation and transformation.

My first love told me he was not attracted to me when I wore braids. He liked my hair straight and thought I was prettier that way. Being young and in love makes you do things you are likely to question later. While we dated, I refused to get braids, even though I was dealing with Georgia heat and a lot of hair maintenance to keep him happy. He fed into the same garbage about Black beauty not being real and needed me to match some sort of Eurocentric standard.

I later discovered the truth: I was pretty, period. I returned to the salon for my braids, and he left.

Sometimes, my hair is strategic.

One white colleague said to me, "You look so much more *professional* with your hair like that." That colleague was referring to my change from braids to a straight-hair weave. I silently cursed him and realized the truth. I was more likely to get a return call for jobs if my hair appeared straight. During job interviews, I wore weaves and laid down my edges with gel to get my foot in the door. Once I was hired, I'd unveil my natural hair and let it breathe. I'd wear braids, cornrows, whatever style I was feeling.

I soon decided that working at a place where people would judge me and hire me based upon my appearance was reinforcing a colonized beauty measure, and was an unhealthy choice in the long run. Eventually, I quit my job.

When I wear Marley faux locs, men are far more respectful, and I receive fewer catcalls. However, assumptions follow, about what I eat (no pork, only veggies), how much I smoke (a lot) and *what* I smoke, and how radical I am (shouldn't I be organizing something?). Oftentimes, a self-proclaimed ally, a curious bystander, or someone with no home training will try to touch my hair. For the record: No, you cannot touch my hair.

My hair is a fluid choice, *my* choice. Sometimes I like wearing bouncy curls that tend to shave years off and brighten my mood. I also love wearing colorful braids that highlight my cheekbones. When I need more strength, I look to locs to charge me with power and queen-like moves. My hair is political and brings me joy. I don't assign it labels of good or bad. Black women and natural hair have a complicated history and relationship, and I'm working toward healing it—my way, and on my terms.

Work Cited and Note

1. John Steptoe, *Mufaro's Beautiful Daughters: An African Tale* (New York: Puffin Books, 2008). See also "Award Winning Children's Books," Fairy Tales and Folktales (website), n.d., https://fairy-tales-and-folktales.weebly.com/award-winning -childrens-books.html. Author John Steptoe died in 1989. In 1997 Puffin Books reissued the book with an updated cover: https://www.penguin.co.uk/books/40425 /mufaro-s-beautiful-daughters/9780140559460.html.

HAIR CHRONICLES OF AN AFRO PUERTO RICAN

Dahlma Llanos-Figueroa

1955, New York City

I was six years old and so excited. My mother and I dressed for the first important step in my new journey: the next day, we were going to get on a plane to visit my family in Puerto Rico. We had lived in New York City for four years, and I barely remembered Puerto Rico and all the people we had left behind. The trip would be the first time going back, and Mami said I was to be at my very best, which meant I had to look beautiful for all these people who were waiting for us. So, we went off, just the two of us, to the beauty parlor to do what beautiful ladies did: fix our hair. In those days, that meant we would have our hair washed, pressed straight, and then curled again, a softer curl than what the stylist had just pressed out. But I didn't know or care about the process. I just knew that I had to go to the parlor to look pretty for Mami and for everyone else. Gloria, our stylist, put a crate up on the chair so I sat high, feeling like a real lady. I felt warm and loved and grown up as I stepped down, a picture-perfect copy of my mother.

When we got home, I watched TV while Mami finished packing. My favorite commercial came on the screen: A beautiful lady was washing her long blonde hair. She had a huge smile as she joined her family. They smiled too as they surrounded her, covering her in hugs and kisses. They touched her swinging hair with obvious admiration as they all went off to have fun.

That commercial gave me an idea. I would surprise my mother by being as beautiful as I could be. I would be a Breck lady, too. Because I wanted to surprise her, I locked the bathroom door. I didn't have shampoo but I wet my hair and rubbed our bar of Palmolive all over my head, making sure to work it into a thick lather. Rinsing the suds out of my hair, I couldn't understand why it had shrunk right back to what it had been before we'd spent hours at the beauty salon. I didn't look like the Breck lady at all. Mami was banging on the bathroom door now. I was so upset; I didn't know what to do. When I finally opened the bathroom door, she was surprised all right. She was furious and even looked like she was going to cry. While I hadn't gotten the results I wanted, I couldn't understand why she was so angry at me. That night I went to bed spanked and sobbing and confused.

Lesson learned: My hair was ugly, not good enough, and I had shamed our family.

1958, Carolina, Puerto Rico

Our Bronx neighborhood had become dangerous. One day when I got home from school, a dead man was lying in a pool of blood, right in the lobby of our building. My parents shut themselves in their bedroom and talked for what seemed like forever. Not long after that day, I was on my way to rural Carolina, a town on the northern coast of Puerto Rico. My parents felt I would be safe there until they could save enough money for a down payment on a much-dreamed-of house. I was to live with my grandmother, Sofía. All my similar-age cousins were boys. So, without Mami around anymore, my two youngest aunts became my role models.

Mami's sister, Titi Betty, was glamorous and beautiful with deep brown-sugar skin, and when she laughed, her laughter filled the room. A popular and successful businesswoman, she and her family had just moved into a brand-new house in a brand-new development. A separate building in the back of her property became her new hair salon, which drew women from all over the area. Her business was making them all look beautiful, and business was good. Titi Betty had money stashed away all over the house; one day a month, she would sit for hours and polish her jewelry collection. In my eyes, she was the epitome of beauty and success.

Titi Lourdes, single and ten years younger, was also beautiful but in a very different way. Her smile was infectious, and she was the family princess. She was young, full of energy, and ready to go out and explore the world. Her honey-brown skin was flawless, and she took care of it carefully. But, to her dismay, she also had tightly coiled hair. In the island's tropical climate, keeping it relaxed was a challenge. I remember her running to wrap a bath towel around her head whenever there was unexpected company. Presentation was important to her. Like most young women her age, she was focused on finding a suitable, handsome young man to complement her. No one was ever allowed to see her natural hair. Not even me.

Lesson learned: Our natural hair was inferior. I would never find a husband and success unless I presented myself properly coiffed and perfumed at all times.

1962, New York City

At thirteen, I was finally allowed to wear my hair pressed on a regular basis, rather than just for special occasions. The trip to the salon became a rite of passage and a time for mother-daughter bonding. Mami and I had a monthly standing appointment with Gloria, where I learned to live in a woman's world of beauty, hair and nail care, and fashion standards. I was on my way to becoming less a child and more a woman, which translated into certain restrictions. Because there was neither time nor money for repeated trips to the salon, I was to do nothing that would lead to profuse sweating, as that would cause my hair to revert to its natural curl. That meant no skating, no sports, and absolutely no swimming.

One time, my mother and I were out and about when we were caught without rain gear. We stood under an awning for an hour rather than let our hair get wet in a sudden rainstorm. Thereafter, I carried a kerchief or plastic rain hat, just in case the weather changed unexpectedly.

Lesson learned: Above all else, protect your pressed hair.

1964, New York City

Miss Bacon, our gym teacher, announced at the end of one class that we would not have to change into our green gym suits the following day. All the girls in the class let out a collective "yeah!" and were excited about the news until she finished her little speech. The following morning, she would check our scalps for lice. We were to wash our hair and have it squeaky clean for the inspection.

Miss Bacon had shiny black hair that swung around her head every time she moved. She was of the I-wash-my-hair-every-morning school of beauty. That woman had no idea what it took for most Black women to do their hair in those pre-Afro days.

Every two weeks, my mother pressed my hair with a hot comb because she didn't want me putting strong chemicals in it to relax my natural curl. Miss Bacon's "just wash your hair tonight" mandate meant hours of work: washing, air-drying (no money for a hair dryer back then), pressing, and curling—not the kind of thing you asked your mother to do for you on a weekday night after a long day at work. So, I knew what Mami's answer would be to being asked to do my hair midweek.

I dreaded going to class the next day, but I went and prayed, in vain, that something might happen to delay the inspection. Miss Bacon stood at the front of the gym, a table next to her and a chair in front. She wore surgical gloves and pointed to the seat as she called each girl up. You were supposed to sit, with your back to her as she parted your hair with Popsicle sticks.

The white girls and the Hispanic girls with straight hair did fine. The teacher smiled at each of them and called up the next girl. But as each Black girl sat in front of her, Miss Bacon made a face. Some girls had chosen styles with neat parts that didn't require separating the hair into sections for inspection. But for the rest of us, it took a little more effort to part hair that had been freshly oiled and curled, hair that I knew had taken hours of work. But

Miss Bacon was not pleased. As she inspected each Black girl, her grimace became more pronounced.

When it was finally my turn, I sat down, my face burning, knowing she would find two weeks' worth of normal scalp secretions: dandruff, oil, and perspiration. I could feel the Popsicle stick on my scalp and imagined the look on her face. The sooner I could get up, the better.

I felt the first tug all the way down the back of my head to my neck.

"What's wrong with you people?" Miss Bacon's words bounced off the tiled walls and reverberated all around me. She punctuated each word with another tug at my hair. "Didn't I tell you yesterday to wash your nappy head?" Her words spilled like acid over my head and shoulders.

I sat in the chair, ears, throat, eyes burning, my dignity in pieces on the floor around me. Girls walked all around me, quietly picking up their books and clothing. Then they were all gone and I was the last person left in the world. I just couldn't move. My mouth was straw dry. Time stopped.

Almost sixty years later, I still remember every detail of that incident. I felt hurt and humiliated, but I was also seething in anger. Miss Bacon's words were meant to shame and demean. That woman's hatred and her irrational rage, conducted through each tug of my hair, told me all I needed to know about racism in our society. Luckily for me, I had been given enough positive messages at home that this assault only served to make me stronger in ways that I could not even begin to imagine at that time.

1964–1967, A Very Personal Education

The incident with Miss Bacon was a pivotal moment in my life, the beginning of a lifelong journey rejecting the lessons I had internalized about the measure of beauty in general, and of our hair in particular. My primary task was to define myself *to* myself, without the emotional and psychological pressures of my home culture or the overarching dominant American culture. Outwardly, I changed little. But over the next few years I traveled a long, circuitous, often painful journey into self-identity. It was a very personal and very private revolution of my own.

The American civil rights movement, with its mantra "Black is Beautiful," was my entrée into a different way of seeing myself. I started paying attention in my history classes and questioning everything: so-called heroic historical figures, current-events articles about "militant" thugs and "radical" ideas, and the absence of women in leadership roles, television portrayals, and literary allusions.

The library became my best friend. I lost respect for many of my teachers and clung to those who encouraged me to keep mining for truth. I started reexamining everything that had come before, cutting through the evasions, omissions, and misrepresentations that became more and more obvious to me. My mind became a surgical knife, excising everything that felt false or contrived.

I watched the news and read the papers, challenging any narratives that felt false or contrived, questioning what was presented as universal truth, rejecting every generalization and caricature. Every Puerto Rican man on the news was a mugger or an addict. All Black men were lazy or dealers. What about the brown sea of men, including my father, whom I watched making their way to the subway every morning? Every Latina on the movie screen was oversexed or subservient and passive. Every Brown or Black teenage girl was an unwed mother leeching off the system. What about all the Black nurses and caregivers who took care of the sick and elderly? What about all the women who cleaned and scoured and cooked in the homes of white families on a daily basis? What about all the girls who competed to get the scholarship that would get them into a college that they really didn't even want to attend? The papers were full of Black boys, gang members who carried guns and held up little old white women. What about my brother and friends who were just teenagers having a good time on the basketball court after school? In our school textbooks, Abraham Lincoln was viewed as a benevolent father who freed the slaves. What about the fact that he had been a slave owner himself? The Black Panthers were a bunch of radical hoodlums. What about those free-breakfast programs they started? The Young Lords were out to destroy society. What about those after-school classes they held in church basements for kids who couldn't read? We needed to send our young men to Vietnam to fight communism. What about all those burned Vietnamese children who had nothing to do with politics and had done nothing to us?

I experienced a lot of wake-up calls. There was that Puerto Rican counselor who would not accept applications for ASPIRA scholarships from Afro Latino students, because we could apply for financial aid from the United Negro College Fund. Then there was the white academic counselor refusing to send my transcripts to my college of choice because *she* felt I would be better off taking a secretarial course. She sent my records to a local community college instead. Still another advisor decided my brother was not college material and would be drafted anyway, so why bother giving him any information about other options? I thought about the counselor as we helped my brother pack for basic training and then for Vietnam.

In my deep-seated sense of outrage, I questioned why the women in my family, and many Black women in my culture as a whole, had accepted so many negative messages about their hair, in particular. None of them claimed to be white. In fact, my mother was clear about her pride in being a beautiful, proud *negra educada* who wasn't going to accept being put down by anyone. She fought racism on many levels at work, in the stores, on the street; but that didn't keep her from her standing appointment with Gloria. Her hair-care ritual remained sacrosanct.

I didn't think the women in my family would ever accept that they had internalized the insidious racism implicit in the colonialism that had held such a stranglehold on our island for hundreds of years. Standards of beauty had filtered down through the lens of European domination, and, as such, our natural beauty was never considered beautiful enough. I loved my mom and loved them all, and they loved me. But I had to find my own way, a path different from the one they traveled.

1967, New York City

It was Thanksgiving and my parents were a half hour late. I was excited about coming home from college for the first time in months. I found a relatively clean floor space near the arrival gate at the Port Authority bus terminal, dropped my knapsack, with its POWER TO THE PEOPLE and BLACK IS BEAUTIFUL stickers, on the floor, and sat cross-legged to wait. I pulled out my copy of *Down These Mean Streets* and got lost in its pages. I was almost done with this book and was planning to start *The Autobiography of Malcolm X* next.

It was 1967 and the country was in the midst of a cultural revolution. Demands for civil rights, women's lib, and Black Power, along with antiwar sentiments, rocked every campus. The Young Lords, Black Panthers, the pill, and *Roe v. Wade* were flashpoints. The Stonewall rebellion was around the corner. The country was experiencing an upheaval, a rebirth, I hoped. But within the walls of our South Bronx home, it was still 1957. My parents were still recuperating from the Korean War and World War II and even the effects of the Depression. Everything that happened in the mainland United States had filtered down to its Puerto Rico colony—only about ten years later. In the 1960s, that filtering took a little less time, but my parents were late bloomers in terms of change. I heard my mother's worried voice and looked up. "¿Donde estará esa muchacha?"

Even after decades of living in New York City, she still wasn't used to the cold. She wore her good wool coat with a fur collar, and her usual lock of stray hair escaped her knitted cap. She had dressed up just to come and pick me up. Her efforts to look her best, and the worried look on her face, warmed my heart, and I got teary-eyed. She paced up and down in front of me, heels clicking, apprehension written all over her face as she searched the crowd for her daughter.

"Mom, Mami, here, I'm right here!" I waved, got up, and opened my arms to her.

It took her a minute, but she finally focused on my face. Confusion, followed by recognition and then horror, registered. "¡Ay, Dios mío!"

I had forgotten that I had changed a bit since she had last seen me. She had proudly sent off a daughter who was her version of a college coed, complete with kilt skirts, white blouses, penny loafers, bangs, and a properly brushed head of silky hair. What stood before her now was an army-booted, fatigue-wearing radical with wire-rimmed spectacles and a thriving Afro. I probably looked like a Puerto Rican Angela Davis in her eyes.

Recognition was quickly followed by my mother's hand snaking into her handbag, retrieving her ever-present silk scarf. She tried to cover my hair right then and there.

"Tomorrow, we're going to Gloria's."

Pushing her hands away, I was hurt. "It's nice to see you too, Mom."

And that's when and how our hair wars began.

My parents, like many others, were terrified of the rapid changes taking place in society. They felt they had sent away, albeit reluctantly, a nice, middle-class Puerto Rican girl with a bright future. Who was this angry and outspoken rebel, with atrocious clothes and wild hair?

Of course, Mami was pleased to see me, and she quickly followed her initial reaction with hugs and kisses. In the days to come, there would be favorite dishes and calls to all the relatives, a celebration of my homecoming. Nevertheless, the first thing the next morning, Mami called Gloria. She had scheduled my hair appointment by the time I woke up.

I could see where my visit was going. I had missed my parents and my community. I wanted to have a good stay at home, a rest from the overwhelming homogeneity of school (twenty thousand white students, fifty minorities). So, I agreed to get my hair "fixed" just to keep the peace while I was home. But I insisted on a compromise. I wouldn't, under any circumstances, let Gloria chemically process my hair. The most I would do was get it pressed with a hot comb so that I could revert to my natural hair in two weeks when I returned to my campus life.

Who taught you to hate the color of your skin? Who taught you to hate the texture of your hair? Who taught you to hate the shape of your nose and the shape of your lips?
—**Malcolm X**, Muslim minister and human rights activist

What my parents didn't understand was that this wasn't a phase or rebellion or trendy political posturing. This transformation was the manifestation of my continuing journey of self-exploration and self-discovery. Before the era of Afro Latinx pride, I had to navigate between friends who saw me as African American and family who saw me as Puerto Rican—a Black Puerto Rican, but Puerto Rican foremost—especially in a United States that didn't want to recognize Afro Latinos at all. The concept that those two identities were sides of the same coin was alien to both racial groups. And so began my long, lonely, and often painful journey. I alienated many people, lost some friends along the way, but an unrelenting drive to find the essential *me* that superseded everyone else's expectations propelled me in my own direction. My hair and my insistence on wearing it in its natural state was the strongest outward symbol of that internal journey.

1969, SUNY Buffalo

For my college graduation, my proud parents drove eight hours and five hundred miles to attend my commencement ceremonies. My father sported his new navy suit, and Mom was stylish in her matching dress and hat. I had selected a halter-top, floor-length, imitation-kente-cloth dress, and my Afro was trimmed to perfection. But Mom stood in my dorm room as I was getting dressed, holding out a well-tailored pastel linen dress—a mini like I liked them, she said—and a synthetic wig. By then, she knew there was no way I was going to relax my hair for graduation. She gave me an ultimatum. My parents would pay for graduation photos only if I wore that carefully selected outfit, including the shoulder-length wig. My mouth dropped open.

We came to a settlement: there would be two official photographs. Older family members would receive the one of me wearing my cap over that ridiculous wig. The younger generation, my cousins and friends, would receive the other photograph of me wearing the dress I had chosen with no gown and, in a nod to academia, holding the cap rather than messing up my hair. I didn't know then that those two photos were symbolic of the two Dahlmas, the one my parents imagined they had raised and the one that was just beginning to emerge as a separate self. That wig was my last trade-off.

One of the official
graduation photographs.
Courtesy of the author

1975, New York City

My parents weren't unique in their perspective. As a young woman, I found plenty of others who were members of their ranks. One night when I was in my thirties, I got all dressed up to go dancing. It was summer, and I was nice and copper tanned. I wore a stark white, off-the-shoulder outfit to show off my sun-kissed skin and wore my hair braided into an elaborate style. I *knew* I looked good. I loved my Latin music, and live bands were all the rage, seducing me into going to the popular clubs of the day.

I was a good dancer who appreciated an equally adept partner. But I sat the whole night waiting to be asked to dance. Finally, my friend's date felt sorry for me and pulled me onto the dance floor. Once there, I thoroughly enjoyed my dance but had lingering feelings of rejection. No sooner did I return to my seat than two men held out their hands in invitation. I was so tired of being a wallflower; I got up and danced with one of them. I just wanted a body to move to the rhythm of the music with me. I was in no mood for conversation. But, no! He just had to start talking.

"You dance really well," he said.

The author in the 1970s.
Courtesy of the author

I said, "I should. I've been dancing to this music my whole life."

"Oh, you 'Rican?" His eyebrows arched as he went on to explain that he would have asked me earlier but he'd thought I was a *morena*.

I said, "I *am* a *morena*. You ain't blind, right?"

He said, "No, no, I thought you were Black."

I said, "I *am* Black."

"No, you don't understand," he said. "I thought you were *Black* Black."

I said, "I *am* Black Black."

He said, "You know what I mean." The more he tried to fix it the more he smeared it.

I said, "Yeah, damned straight. I know *just* what you mean, you racist shit." I turned and walked away, leaving him, jerk that he was, standing in the middle of the dance floor.

There it was. Racism waiting for me, all big and bad, right there in my Latin club. So no, bigotry isn't just the purview of white people. It comes in all ages, many shades. It speaks many languages and can live right in your home.

1988, New York City

I had always loved our family's vacations to the island. It was a special kind of home for me where I connected with my clan. There must have been hundreds of relatives when we all got together, and I reveled in the intimacy and shared memories of family.

I was different from my female cousins, who were focused on finding the future father of their children or who were already married and settled into an acceptable routine of wife and mother. I guess I was the wild one. We all still went shopping together or sat on the tiled porches to play jacks, a throwback to our childhood. We took time to try on makeup and practiced dancing.

Some of my male cousins hated my women's-libber notions and didn't want me contaminating their girlfriends with my feminist ideas. But one male cousin in particular embraced my thirst for going beyond the accepted, for exploring and finding new ways of living and looking at the world. We took off for the museums and galleries and theaters of San Juan and talked for hours about our dreams and passions and need for self-expression.

When I was almost forty and on one of my trips back to the island, my grandmother pulled me aside to, ostensibly, help her wash the dishes. Her house was usually packed with people, so I was glad to have her to myself for a while. I relaxed and settled into the flow of our shared task, feeling warm in the familial glow. And then she started giving me advice, as elders are wont to do. She didn't want me to end up being a spinster. I started tensing up. Besides, she wanted to see me "settled" before she passed from this earth.

My heart sank. What was she trying to say?

"Abuela, are you sick?"

"No, no, Nena, I'm fine, just fine," she reassured me.

"Thank God! I thought—"

"No, not that. But there's something else I want to talk to you about."

I went back to wiping the dish.

"Nena, I'm worried about you. You're not a teenager anymore and . . ." Her voice was taking on a familiar tone.

No, not again, not here, not from her too.

"You know, you're not getting any younger and . . . well, you need to start planning for the future."

"Abuela, it's *my* future." I tried to change the subject. "Pass me that bottle."

"Well, don't you think it's past time you found a man and gave me some great-grandchildren? What are you waiting for?"

The author in the 1980s.
Courtesy of the author

"Grandma, I can't manufacture a husband. When the time comes . . ."

"Well, let's be honest. You have to start taking care of yourself. No man is coming near you with that hair."

"What??" I knew she held these beliefs but couldn't believe she was saying those words to me, right to my face. I had to try really hard not to be disrespectful. Really hard. "You mean the hair I was born with?"

"Now, don't get mad—"

But I was already heading out the door. Why hadn't I seen that coming?

2002, New York City

The final straw came as I was preparing for my wedding. I was fifty-two years old and was finally taking that step. As is part of every anticipated wedding, there was much excitement, especially since my aunts had given up on me ever "doing the right thing." Mami and Abuela were, sadly, long gone by then, so my aunt Betty felt she had to have the mother-daughter talk with me.

She asked me about the preparations and all the details about my dress and flowers. She loved Jonathan, my fiancé, and was so happy that I was finally settling down. She got teary-eyed when she talked about how happy my mom would have been to dance at my wedding. And then, she got to the crux of her matter: "I imagine you will finally get your hair fixed up for this special day."

I was so incensed that my words just shot out, right out, without any hesitation. "Titi, there's no need for pretense. I have been living with this man for years. And I assure you he is *intimately* familiar with the texture of my hair, *all* my hair." I walked away before she could find the words to express her outrage at my disrespectful retort. Ask me no questions, and I'll tell you no lies. Even at this stage in my life, that bygone phantom was rearing its ugly head.

November 2015, San Juan, Puerto Rico

I was attending the Primer Congreso de Afrodescendencia en Puerto Rico, a symposium I never dreamed would happen. I stood on the stage at the main theater at the University of Puerto Rico and looked out on an auditorium filled with all manner of representations of Black women: different ages, various walks of life, variation of skin and hair types. I was so pleased that the vast majority of them had embraced their natural hair. Some were even dressed in African garb. I smiled, thinking about my personal hair wars. I thought about how young women were still wrestling with the standards of beauty imposed on them and redefining those standards for themselves. I loved being surrounded by people who were the living manifestation of all my years of struggle. I was an elder by then and felt so good about leaving behind a special kind of legacy.

I read from my first novel, *Daughters of the Stone*, a narrative spanning five generations of an Afro Boricua family, from West Africa to colonial Puerto Rico to the urban United States. Hair, in all its variations, is an integral part of my work and always will be. I heard my voice ring out, speaking my truth, and watched the audience nod in agreement. After my presentation, several young women, and a number of older ones, came up to tell me how much the reading meant to them. Students and professionals alike expressed their appreciation of my having put their stories on paper.

And always, with me, beside me, behind me, within me, stood all my female ancestors, even those with whom I battled for so many years. They come to me in dreams now and tell me their stories that perhaps they couldn't embrace while they were alive. Now, they offer them to me to pass on to future generations. And I will pass them on. I'll pass on the stories of endurance and jealousy and strength and rebellion and betrayal and survival and machismo and community and love. I'll pass all of it on, including the struggle to find our own authentic answers to pressing questions, and to find the legacy of beauty, our own beauty, in our own way.

New York City, March 2020

I called relatives in Puerto Rico in search of those two versions of the 1969 graduation photographs. My cousin Hector put me on speakerphone because he thought his granddaughters should hear their titi's story. There was silence on the line, as the girls listened to the account of my hair chronicles. Even though they choose to wear their hair relaxed and flowing, they know my preference and couldn't believe I had gone through all those struggles to arrive at the decision I have about my hair.

Hurricane Maria had destroyed many of our family records. The girls sifted through what was left. Two days later, one of my nieces emailed me a copy of the one graduation picture they could find, the one with the dreadful wig. The other is, unfortunately, lost to memory. But my physical presence is

The author in 2020. *Courtesy of the author*

a testament to my continued insistence on wearing my crown as a symbol of my pride in my Afro *descendencia*.

I look forward to my next trip to the island. I know my nieces will have many questions when I see them again. And I will have many stories to tell, the chronicles of an Afro Puerto Rican woman who found her way to pride in her own beauty and has never looked back.

TURNING THE LENS
RIGHTSIDE UP

Lyzette Wanzer, MFA

The most disrespected person in America is the Black woman.
The most unprotected person in America is the Black woman.
The most neglected person in America is the Black woman.

—Malcolm X

HAVE YOU CONSIDERED why so many people feel entitled to touch Black women's hair without permission, often with so little warning and with such stealth that we don't have a chance to duck? The reasons are incontrovertibly linked to our hair's assumed lack of allure and even to its lack of worth. Our hair—ever the locus of tyranny, fascination, trepidation, and fetishization—does not fulfill the paradigm of American womanhood. As the essays in this book have made clear, that exalted paradigm is the provenance of Caucasian women. That same prototype, however, is also the result of our society's failure to view Afro Latina and African American women on our own terms. Our *own* terms, not as a sorry antithesis to white presence. A further complication exists. We live in the crosshairs of intersecting experiences: first as Black, and then as women.

Unfortunately, as several of the essays in this book reveal, many of us have received messages about the undesirability of our hair from people who are closest to us. In turn, we have transmitted these same conventional messages to subsequent generations. Historical antecedents are the drivers behind these messages about our hair and other disagreeable phenotypical aspects. Those of us of a certain age remember the paper-bag test,[1] the pencil test,[2] and the doll tests.[3] They are part of a cumulative, historical angst so inherent in Black Americans' collective psyche that we perpetuate this generational trauma. Quite often, the vilest reprobation comes from our Black colleagues, friends, and families. It's important to understand that this state of affairs is not their fault. However inflammatory or smarting their criticisms—often provided under cover of "suggestions" or "advice"—these individuals typically have our best interests at heart. They are fearful we may not secure good employment or present well in an interview, or they think we'll be passed over for a promotion. Perhaps we'll even lose our jobs, be undesirable to potential partners, and embarrass family elders. The list of apprehensions is lengthy. Deep in our collective unconscious, we know that slaves who received the most favorable treatment were those whose appearance was, along the tolerance gradient, closest to our masters' in skin tone, hair texture, or, better yet, both. Light skin and straight(er) hair inoculated one from the harsher treatment and station of field slaves. Slavery bears the culpability for this caste system. During Reconstruction, light skin and straight hair continued to confer benefits of employment eligibility, commerce opportunities, and a larger slice of life. Black people

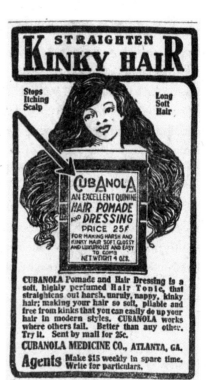

Two hair ads from the *Dallas Express*[4]

needed to position themselves to take advantage of cracks in the doors of opportunity. Our own shop and store owners equipped their businesses to assist our people. The marketing-speak in all ads was at once cautionary and reassuring: we could rectify the problems with our hair with the right process or product.

The Plough's Hair Dressing advertisement I referenced in my earlier essay appeared in a Black newspaper. Recall the language this ad used: "Have straight, soft, long hair by simply applying Plough's Hair Dressing and in a short time all your kinky, snarly, ugly, curly hair becomes soft, silky, smooth, straight, long."

The *Dallas Express,* a weekly newspaper known as "The South's Oldest and Largest Negro Newspaper," carried the two ads shown left in its March 8, 1919, issue.

Again, note the language. The Cubanola ad lays it on especially thick: "straightens out harsh, unruly, nappy, kinky hair."

The *Nashville Globe,* an African American Tennessee newspaper, advertised Herolin Pomade Hair Dressing. Here's one of the ads from a 1918 issue, promising "soft, silky, straight" hair "without snarls," making it "pleasant and easy to handle."

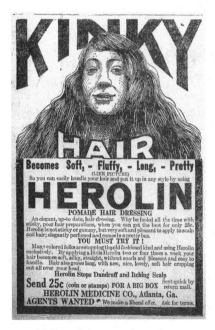

Nashville Globe Herolin Hair Pomade ad[5]

Page 8 from the January 21, 1921, issue of the *Black Dispatch,* an Oklahoma African American newspaper.[6]

I selected a random page from the *Black Dispatch*. This one page featured *seven* hair ads. The ads occupy more real estate than the news reporting does, leveling a visual, psychological assault on the reader. An air of desperation wafts from these pages. Note that these ads disparately impact, and are targeted toward, women—not men. The photos and drawings are of women. The only takeaway from the proliferation of these advertisements was that Black women's hair, in its natural state, was objectionable and, worse, repugnant, disgraceful, inferior, defective, and in need of redress or concealment. Our own Black newspapers and weeklies were teaching us this lesson! Alter the hair to resemble Caucasian hair as closely as possible, or else your best bet might be to hide it.

Today, many Black women wear scarves, bandanas, *geles,* turbans, *dukus,* and other headdresses. Sometimes to cover a bad-hair day or to cover unlaid edges but often to showcase our heritage and racial pride. YouTube is full of instructional scarf-tying videos. Wearing headdresses as adornment is a cultural reclamation. Black women have worn a variety of decorative headdresses on the African continent for centuries. Scarves conveyed important information about a woman's marital status, community, wealth, even upcoming ceremonies.

But in eighteenth-century Louisiana, scarves were a suppressive requirement for freed Black women. Governor Esteban Rodriguez Miró—a Brown person, no less—instituted the Tignon Laws in 1786, while Louisiana was still a Spanish colony. (*Tignon* derives from the French word for "cloth" or "scarf.") The governor enacted this law at the urging of nervous, insecure—and, perhaps, envious?—white women. This legislation stipulated that Creole women must wear head coverings to prevent them from "displaying excessive attention to dress in the streets of New Orleans."[7] The governor was supposedly concerned that freed slave women were too tempting for white men, and he sought to curb freed slaves' vanity. But the true reason for the laws isn't tough to decipher: they maintained current social order; that is, the scarves served as caste signifiers, relegating freedmen—and women, specifically—to the bottom rung of society.

Today, the reemergence of scarf-wearing is a powerful symbol of both resistance and celebration. And in those states and municipalities that have enacted the CROWN Act, we no longer need to hide our natural hair under coverings just because our texture differs from that of white women.

Hair is not just something to play with, it is something that is laden with messages, and it has the power to dictate how others treat you, and in turn, how you feel about yourself.
—**Cheryl Thompson**, "Black Women and Identity: What's Hair Got to Do with It?"[8]

I need to acknowledge the role that Black men play in penalizing Black women for residing at the intersection of Blackness and womanhood. Too many men engage in misogynoir[9] in American society because the colorism lens has blinded them, too. Note, for example, the number of Black male entertainers who favor light-skinned, straight-haired Black women as partners. The bulk of antiracism demonstrations revolves around violence against Black and Brown men, not violence against their female or trans counterparts. We don't often see one Black man calling out another for sustaining or even memorializing instances of misogynoir in slander, jokes, and lyrics about Black women's skin tones or the grade of their hair. Nor do we see that in platitudes about respectability politics that sideline or ignore #SayHerName victims. We don't see a lot of Black men stepping up to rep #PassTheCrown. Few African American boys sat between their mothers' legs as children, flinching while enduring a hot-comb treatment or cringing at the salon while caustic hair relaxer seared their scalps.[10] They got their hair clipped at home or at the barber's, but they rarely invested the amount of time Black girls and women did (and do) to make their hair approximate white society's definition of "presentable." Yet Black men have the same kind of natural hair that Black women do!

Please know that some Black men champion Black women in all their natural glory. You've seen some of them featured in this book's sidebars. You can hear from men on both sides of this complex equation if you search YouTube for an *Essence* video called "What Black Men Really Think About Our Hair." Listen to the supportive comments, but pay particular attention to the contradictory, contorted logic underlying some of these men's remarks. Notice how many men have bought into gender norms dictating that women's hair should be bouncy, flowing, and straight (or straight*er*). Women, from an early age, receive messages about acculturation that lead them to associate hair with beauty in a way that boys don't.

Of course, today we also contend with a flip side: increasing numbers of Black boys wearing dreadlocks, Afros, and braids to school and being criminalized for doing so. The Eurocentric norms that imbue workplaces have also taken hold in elementary and high schools. In schools, especially, boys come under fire for wearing natural hair, almost as often as girls do. What Ra'Mon Jones calls "the fight for the right to be kinky" has occurred in public schools across the nation.[11]

In 2013 Faith Christian Academy in Orlando, Florida, gave twelve-year-old Vanessa VanDyke one week to decide whether to straighten her hair or receive an expulsion. The school's dress code said in part that hair "must not be a distraction." That same year, Deborah Brown Community School in Tulsa, Oklahoma, excused Tiana Parker—a second grader!—from class because she was wearing dreadlocks. The school rules said that natural hairstyles such as Afros and dreadlocks were "unacceptable."

In 2015 an administrator at Immaculate Heart of Mary School in Belmont, California, called kindergartner Jalyn Broussard's mother and requested that she pick him up. Jalyn was wearing a fade. School personnel deemed the hairstyle "distracting."

In 2016 Isaiah Granderson, a football player at Mystic Valley Regional Charter School in Malden, Massachusetts, was slapped with a detention for showing up to school wearing an Afro. The school's appearance policy included phrases like "Students may not wear . . . hairstyles that could be distracting to other students."

In January 2020 the Barbers Hill High School in Mont Belvieu, Texas, suspended two young men, De'Andre Arnold and Kaden Bradford, for wearing locs. In this instance, the policy transected intersectionality from a different aspect: being Black (race), male (gender), *and* wearing long hair (gender again, since girls at the school were permitted to wear long hair). The school's policy read, in part, "Boys' hair will not extend below the eyebrows, below the ear lobes, or below the top of a t-shirt collar."

My worst hair experience was when I was trying to relax my hair and my grandmother did it. It went all straight and I looked like a black Bee Gee.
—**Jamie Foxx**

The number of discriminatory practices against natural hair and expressly Black hairstyles at American schools is almost interminable. I posit that, if we as a society are going to rectify these policies and course-correct the white gaze's lens so that it's the right side up, we will need a CROWN Act federally enacted at the national level, protecting both workplaces and educational institutions, right down to kindergarten. We need a moratorium on discretionary discipline with inordinate targeting of African American natural hairstyles. A Brookings Institution article sums up the plight in a scathing indictment: "Discretionary suspension based on hairstyles and dress code is another failed opportunity our public education . . . system could have leveraged to better understand its students' cultural differences. [Natural hair is] one of the last connections to a history all but washed away through the middle passage, integration, and assimilation."[12]

In the introduction to this book, I mentioned Jeffrey Thornton, the man who is suing his employer for making his job offer conditional upon his agreement to cut his dreadlocks. And while I know other Black men have faced similar discriminatory demands, newspapers and media sites over the years have brimmed with accounts of employment-related bias against Black and Afro Latina women. The bias, whether conscious or unconscious, appears stacked against us to an undue degree. Realize that this bias is not merely inconvenient or irritating; it is actually a human rights violation.

As I related in the New York City subway vignette in "Toward Decolonizing Our Roots," women who wear their hair in Afros or dreadlocks may need to traverse misreadings from people of all races, like the presumption that our politics must be militant. We may have to counter other fallacies, such as that we are devotees of specific belief systems or spiritual practices. And maybe we *do* follow such beliefs and practices, but the odds are just as good that we do not. Many Indian sadhus and yogis wear dreadlocks to signify that they've embarked on a journey of spiritual discipline.[13] They follow an ascetic, simple lifestyle. And although many Jamaicans refer to themselves as Rastafarians, true Rastafarians grow their locs in adherence to the Old Testament's Nazarite vow, which extends beyond hair to dietary and other customs.[14] There's no singular meaning to sporting dreadlocks.

In the 1960s Black activists began wearing Afros to signify civil rights struggles, the Black is Beautiful motto, and the Black Power movement. Entertainers in the 1960s and '70s, including Pam Grier, the Sylvers, Gloria Hendry,

Sly & the Family Stone, Vonetta McGee, Richard Roundtree, Diana Ross, and others wore the style during performances, movie roles, and television appearances. While this trend helped depoliticize the Afro, normalizing it as a fashionable hairstyle, the Afro has never been able to shed its laden symbolism of an earlier decade. In the current natural-hair movement, the Afro is making a burgeoning comeback. Unfortunately, too often white society still reads Afro-wearing women as militaristic or hyperpolitical, the result of beauty standards set "by groups of individuals to whom racial identity is not a central life experience."[15]

Note, however, when white women appropriate millennia-old African and African American hairstyles, our culture dons entirely different lenses: suddenly, these styles are creative, stylish, nouveau, and unique. Not militaristic, distracting, or unprofessional. White privilege rears up in full force, claiming misplaced, undue credit. Remember Bo Derek, the white actress who rose to fame in the 1979 Blake Edwards movie *"10"*? Posters immortalized her in the dream-sequence beach scene, where she is wearing cornrows adorned with beads. This scene actually played a part in plaintiff Renee Rogers's defeat in her lawsuit against American Airlines.[16] Defendants R. L. Crandall and Robert Zurlo argued that their requirement that Rogers style her hair in a bun instead of cornrows was reasonable because Black women were not the only ones who wore braids, and the style was, in fact, "popularized by a white actress [Bo Derek], in the film *'10.'*"[17] *People* magazine credited Derek with elevating braids to "a cross-cultural craze and beauty-salon bonanza."[18]

Let's set the record straight here: Derek did not, *did not,* popularize cornrows. African, African American, and Afro Latina women were wearing cornrows hundreds of years before she did. My younger sister and I and our friends grew up wearing braids with beads in our hair well before *"10"* was released. We even braided and beaded our dolls' hair! The movie did interpolate unwanted aftereffects into our lives. After the movie began showing in theaters, grown white women would approach my sister and me at the mall or in grocery stores, asking how we felt about Bo Derek's hairstyle. We were too young to know the word *appropriation*, but we most certainly understood the concept. I, for one, resented the questioning. Seeing ads and posters featuring the cornrowed Derek made me angry, but at that time I couldn't articulate why. My sister would reply to our questioners, while I just ignored them. Looking back, I cast the whole business in a preposterous light. What made these white women feel they could approach two little girls—who happened to wear braids and beads—and inquire about our political stance regarding a charged phenomenon stemming from a film we weren't even old enough to see?

Hairstyle choices are an important mode of self-expression. For blacks, and particularly for black women, such choices also reflect the search for a survival mechanism in a culture where social, political, and economic choices of racialized individuals and groups are conditioned by the extent to which their physical characteristics, both mutable and immutable, approximate those of the dominant racial group. Hair becomes a proxy for legitimacy and determines the extent to which individual blacks can crossover [*sic*] from the private world of segregation and colonization (and historically, in the case of black women, service in another's home) into the mainstream of American life.
—**Paulette M. Caldwell**[19]

Afro Latina, African American, and multiracial women, though not the sole victims of hair bias, continue to bear the brunt of hair discrimination in this country. Will we ever have a federal CROWN Act? That remains to be seen. It's difficult to comprehend why proposals for hair-bias legislation at the federal level have failed to become law, but with each state and municipality that adopts some version of such a law, we are one step closer.

Works Cited

1. The paper-bag and ruler tests were colorist barometers designed to exclude darker-skinned African Americans from attending certain events. Upper-middle-class and upper-class African American society members often wielded these markers of inculcated racism against other Black people. Aspirants' skin color had to be as light as, or lighter than, a paper bag or a ruler in order to gain admittance to private societies and clubs, exclusive parties, selective organizations, historically

Black colleges, and other privileges. These measures reached their zenith in the early 1900s but still exist in some form or other today.

2. Originating during the apartheid era in South Africa, the pencil test involved placing a pencil in a Black person's hair to see whether it fell out. If it did, the person was eligible to gain prerogatives that other Black people, whose frizzier, kinkier hair held the pencil in place, could not.

3. Psychologists Kenneth and Mamie Clark's doll study played an influential role in the 1954 *Brown v. Board of Education* Supreme Court decision. This famous study demonstrated that African American children associated white dolls with positive qualities and Black dolls with negative characteristics. The results confirmed the Clarks' thesis that educational segregation exacted an adverse toll on children. See https://zebrastrategies.com/amplifying-voices-advancing-society-mamie-kenneth -clarks-doll-studies.

4. "No More Short, Harsh and Unruly Hair" and "Straighten Kinky Hair": advertisements, *Dallas Express*, March 8, 1919.

5. The *Nashville Globe* ran from 1906 to 1960. Herolin Pomade Hair Dressing ad, *Nashville Globe,* April 26, 1918, https://www.newspapers.com/image/174646087 /?terms=herolin&match=1.

6. This Oklahoma City–based newspaper ran from 1914 to 1982.

7. Ashley Alese Edwards, "Who Decided Black Hair Is So Offensive Anyway?" *Glamour*, September 10, 2020, https://www.glamour.com/story/black-hair-offensive -timeline.

8. Cheryl Thompson, "Black Women and Identity: What's Hair Got to Do with It?" *Michigan Feminist Studies* 22, no. 1 (Fall 2008–2009), accessed January 7, 2022, https://quod.lib.umich.edu/cgi/t/text/text-idx?cc=mfsfront;c=mfs;c=mfsfront;idno =ark5583.0022.105;view=text;rgn=main;xc=1;g=mfsg.

9. Black Queer feminist Moya Bailey coined this term to capture Black women's unique discriminatory position in the crosshairs of being Black and womanidentifying. See Moya Bailey and Trudy, "On Misogynoir: Citation, Erasure, and Plagiarism," *Feminist Media Studies* 18, no. 4 (2018): 762–768, accessed January 17, 2022, https://doi.org/10.1080/14680777.2018.1447395.

10. Witness, however, the number of Black male entertainers in the early to mid-1900s who slicked their hair down with straighteners, gels, and all manner of chemicals to achieve a sleek, straight appearance. Though nearly iconic in this representation, Cab Calloway and the Nicholas Brothers were not the only stars of this era to cultivate this look.

11. Ra'Mon Jones, "What the Hair: Employment Discrimination Against Black People Based on Hairstyles," *Harvard BlackLetter Law Journal* 36 (July 2020): 27–45.

12. Howard Henderson and Jennifer Wyatt Bourgeois, "Penalizing Black Hair in the Name of Academic Success Is Undeniably Racist, Unfounded, and Against the Law," Brookings Institution, February 23, 2021, accessed January 20, 2022, https:// www.brookings.edu/blog/how-we-rise/2021/02/23/penalizing-black-hair-in-the -name-of-academic-success-is-undeniably-racist-unfounded-and-against-the-law.

13. Jeffery Bradley, "Dreadlocks and the Holy Monks of India," Dreadlocks365 (web-site), December 14, 2017, accessed January 20, 2022, https://www.dreadlocks365 .com/dreadlocks-holy-monks-india.

14. "The Spiritual Meaning of the Nazarite Vow," Divine Champions for Christ, Janu-ary 6, 2020, accessed January 20, 2022, http://divinechampionsforchrist.com/the -spiritual-meaning-of-the-nazarite-vow.

15. Barbara J. Flagg, "Fashioning a Title VII Remedy for Transparently White Subjec-tive Decisionmaking," *Yale Law Journal* 104, no. 8 (June 1995): 2035n52, quoted in Taylor Mioko Dewberry, "Title VII and African American Hair: A Clash of Cultures," *Washington University Journal of Law & Policy* 54 (2017): 348.

16. See my earlier reference to this legal case in "Toward Decolonizing Our Roots."

17. Rogers v. American Airlines, Inc., 527 F. Supp. 229 (S.D.N.Y. 1981).

18. Suzy Kalter, "In an Odd Twist, from *10*, the Beauty Biz Finds the Cornrow Is Oh, So Green," *People*, updated February 11, 1980, https://people.com/archive/in-an -odd-twist-from-10-the-beauty-biz-finds-the-cornrow-is-oh-so-green-vol-13-no-6.

19. Paulette M. Caldwell, "A Hair Piece: Perspectives on the Intersection of Race and Gender," *Duke Law Journal* 1991, no. 2 (1991): 383, https://scholarship.law.duke .edu/cgi/viewcontent.cgi?article=3147&context=dlj.

READER DISCUSSION GUIDE

Reflecting on Personal Experiences

1. What is your earliest memory of having someone touch your hair without permission—just to "see what it feels like" or because they claim they "just *had* to touch it"? Do you recall how the encounter made you feel?

2. Have you, members of your family, or any of your friends experienced any undue reaction to wearing natural hair at school, in your workplace, or in another academic, corporate, or professional setting?

3. Significant hair discrimination exists *within* African American and Afro Latina communities, often coming from family members, friends, or colleagues. What beliefs and fears prompt these attitudes within our own communities? How do you address these situations when they arise?

4. Which specific—and typically uncrsytallized—tensions associated with natural hair are responsible for inheriting social, familial, and workplace mistreatment?

5. What are some examples of *texturism* (the idea that certain natural-hair pattens are more desirable than others) or other microaggressions you've experienced from friends and family members?

6. How has situational power and privilege operated in your life to make others feel they have the right to dictate to you how to wear your hair?

7. If you began getting your hair relaxed during childhood, how old were you before you knew what your real hair looked like?

8. Has your hair ever been labeled "distracting," "disruptive," or "too much" in a school setting? How did the experience affect you? Write a two-page response, reflecting on the way you responded at that time and detailing the way you would respond if the same situation befell you today.

9. What is the CROWN Act's larger indictment concerning inclusivity and representation?

10. Here's a moment-of-truth question: Have you ever supported jokes, memes, late-night skits, or other content that propagates ridicule of, or aversion to, natural hair? How have the essays in this book altered your perspective on that content?

11. If you are biracial or multiracial, have you ever chosen a natural style such as locs, twists, or knots as a way to demonstrate or prove your ethnic ties? If so, what changes did you notice in people's attitudes and approaches to you after you changed your hair?

Reflecting on Readings

1. In her Quartz web article "The Natural Hair Movement Is Forgetting Its Radical Roots," Aamna Mohdin mentions, "The natural hair movement is about many things. It's about knowing how to style your hair and keep it healthy. But the movement is also rooted in revolutionary political ideas. It's about rejecting unattainable beauty ideals, not allowing them to demoralize us." Other than the points she lists in her quote, what other factors do you think Mohdin may be including when she says "many things"? Write an analysis using supported reasoning and citing specific textual evidence.

2. In her 1990 essay "Is Your Hair Still Political?" writer and civil rights activist Audre Lorde explains how she nearly missed out on a Caribbean vacation because a Black immigration officer in the British Virgin Islands took issue with her locs. Why do you think the obsession with African American and Afro Latina hair is so deeply ingrained in the American psyche?

3. Read "When Natural Hair Wins, Discrimination in School Loses" by Brenda Álvarez (published September 17, 2019, in the National Education Association's *NEA Today* magazine). In this article, social studies teacher Gerardo Muñoz says, "This is typical of those in power. They don't see that something is an issue because they find themselves unable to relate, and since the issue is outside of their immediate experience, they doubt its validity." Should Black students and their parents shoulder the onus of demonstrating the "validity" of their hair? If so, how would they go about doing so? If not, how do they respond to this form of oppression, without compromising their authentic selves and bodies?

4. In what ways is the process of attaining the hegemonic ideology of *pelo bueno* a violent journey for Latina women?

5. In the United States, the policing of Black hair is not new. The Black body has been a site of political struggle since the antebellum period. For proof of this, look no farther than Louisiana's eighteenth-century Tignon Laws. Governor Esteban Rodriguez Miró passed these laws, which stipulated that Creole women must wear head coverings to prevent them "from displaying excessive attention to dress in the streets of New Orleans." Read Maxine Harrison's "How the Tignon Laws Backfired" in *Era* online magazine (February 9, 2021). Discuss how today's Black women have leveraged eighteenth-century legislation meant to diminish them, turning scarf- and headdress-wearing into powerful statements that represent symbols of resistance, pride, cultural ownership, and celebration.

6. Since the period of enslavement in the Americas, diaspora people have used their bodies as canvases upon which to articulate their presence as subjects. Our natural hair—constantly in motion, searching for recognition and appreciation—is one of those canvases. Hair's connection to beauty, and its intersection with race and gender, places a particular burden on Black females whose naturally kinky hair textures are low on beauty continuums. Citing material from the essays you've read in this book, discuss current topics and trends surrounding the stigma and politics of natural hair.

7. Read "Time for Nursing to Eradicate Hair Discrimination" (*Journal of Clinical Nursing,* February 15, 2021), paying particular attention to sections 2.2 and 2.4. If you were a nurse singled out for hair racism, how would you constructively and diplomatically surface and attenuate your employer's gaslighting tactics?

8. Did you know that only nineteen states have a requirement that cosmetology schools offer training in natural hair care and styling? Brandi Daniels's "Hair Bias in the Beauty Industry" examines the discrepancies plaguing cosmetology training programs. What ideas can you posit to address the segregation issue within the beauty industry? See https://naturalhair acceptance.wordpress.com/2021/12/19/hair-bias-in-the-beauty-industry/.

9. In what ways have the essays in this book shifted or changed your thinking about the CROWN Act specifically or hair bias generally?

10. In "Hair Has Nothing to Do with Competency," Candace Laster says, "Black women have reported that 'hair isn't just hair. Our hair is our crown, and the celebration of it, as such, is deeply woven into our ancestral history.'" Explain how Black women's hair is "deeply woven" into their cultural, political, and social history since the time of slavery. See https://www.newhaven.edu/news/blog/2021/discrimination-and-hairstyles.php.

Reflecting on Attending School or Work While Black

1. Over the past several years, a number of highly publicized incidents have occurred regarding middle and high school dress codes that appear to target students of color. How do you think these schools' dress codes accentuate the majority culture's preoccupation with African American hair in general and natural hair in particular?

2. What happens when an employer's dress code or attire policy bars certain hairstyles, resulting in adverse actions against those who refuse to conform by altering their hair texture, length, or style? Many victims comply through fear of termination or of being seen as unemployable. In the Latina community, characteristics like hair are both race- and status-charged. What can employers and school administrators do to ensure they are not discriminating against natural hair?

3. Federal courts in the United States have said that, under Title VII of the 1964 Civil Rights Act, the only protected natural hairstyles are Afros. Why do you suppose Afros were singled out for protection in this act, but not braids, dreadlocks, or twists?

4. Malden's Mystic Valley Regional Charter School served up detention slips to twin sisters for wearing box braids. A twelve-year-old at Florida's Faith Christian Academy, having complained about bullying related to her Afro puffs, was told to straighten her hair or face expulsion. In San Diego a sophomore boy missed three days of school because he refused to cut his braids. He was also slapped with an "insubordination" suspension. When these children and their parents refuse to conform, school authority figures threaten their education for wearing their hair the way it grows—naturally—from their heads. Students gained strength and support from one another with the advent of the #SupportThePuff and #PickFrosNotFights hashtags. When children's natural hair breaks school rules, what

is the appropriate, effective response? What recourses are available? And how do you frame the fight for affected, hurt, and traumatized students?

5. Why has the majority culture been so invested in the criminalization of Black hairstyles? Think of the battle over natural hair as a type of proxy war. In your estimation, what serves as the proxy in that war?

6. The Civil Rights Act of 1964 prohibits employment discrimination based on race, color, national origin, religion, and gender in companies with a minimum of fifteen employees. During the 1960s and 1970s, natural hair became an expression of self-love, a rejection of the Eurocentric beauty standards that have, historically, policed Black hair and deemed it unattractive or unprofessional. In what ways did Black women of these two decades use their hair as a key medium of creative and political expression in everyday life, including at school and at work?

7. Why is it important to employ an intersectional lens when examining workplace and school inequity?

8. Hair-shaming in school settings is a source of longstanding social trauma and identity negotiation. What do schools need to write into their hygiene and dress-code policies in order to comply with either the CROWN Act or their own proposed unbiased grooming policy?

9. Why do you suppose hair bias against women of color has been permitted to exist for such a sustained time that antibias legislation was warranted in 2019?

10. Read "Hair Matters: Toward Understanding Natural Black Hair Bias in the Workplace" (https://journals.sagepub.com/doi/10.1177/1548051819848998). Write a brief essay addressing the impact of hair bias on Black women's actual and projected social identities.

Reflecting on Dialectic Topics

1. How did reading about these experiences impact you? What did you realize, or what was unburied? Describe some of the emotions that erupted for you.

2. Afro Latinas learn about good and bad hair valuations through communication from adults, peers, and males—very often, from their own family members. Hair valuations tend to elevate white beauty standards and devalue hair textures common among Afro Latinas. Many women are

challenging this *pelo malo* idea out of frustration regarding the erasure of Blackness within Latinx communities. Name some specific actions Afro Latinas can take to rise above the indoctrination, brainwashing, and internalization of the destructive *pelo malo y pelo bueno* construct.

3. White people often benefit from appropriating Black-hair culture, without incurring the same punitive measures that Black people incur when wearing these styles. How should states *without* a CROWN Act handle the instances in which this arises, especially at school and in the workplace?

4. Why do so-called race-neutral standards that apply to "everyone" in a workplace or school exert an inordinate effect on African American women and Afro Latinas?

5. What is the relationship between Afro Latinas' and African American women's natural-hair choices and the aesthetic messages that culturally specific magazines and media portray?

6. The Afro Latinx community has faced erasure in both the United States and other countries. Many Latinas don't acknowledge their Afro roots. What are the myriad ways in which Latinas are rooted in radicalized and racialized notions of beauty?

7. Natural hair figures prominently in the politics of visibility, inclusion, and exclusion within Black antiracist aesthetics. A legacy of slavery has yielded racially motivated beauty standards that work against Black women and Afro Latinas. How does the physical and cultural violence perpetuated in the quest for "beautiful" hair consequently foment a generational cycle of identity erasure? How do we teach white society that there can never be a definitive reading of Black beauty?

8. Discuss whether the CROWN Act truly aligns with American values. Look beyond the legislation's language to its possible applications.

9. What is the purpose of protective styles for Afro Latinx and African American people? Can you think of any protective styles that Caucasian people use? What is being protected in these styles?

10. What are the evolutionary and geographic rationales for the differing hair textures among different ethnicities? What role do historical climate factors play in the hair profile of women of African descent?

11. In what ways does hair bias constitute a form of not garden-variety injustice but specifically *systemic* injustice?

12. In the 1960s the Afro hairstyle came to represent the "Black is Beautiful" motto and the civil rights movement. Does the message of "I Am Not My Hair" conflict with using hair to demonstrate political beliefs and make social change?

13. In the 1980s esteemed African American activist and scholar Molefi Asante coined the term *Afrocentrism* to refer to a cultural and political movement that reflects traditional African principles. In what ways does the wearing of natural hairstyles manifest Afrocentrism?

RESOURCE GUIDE

THESE RESOURCES are more representative than exhaustive, and all were current at the time this book went to press. Always visit the resource's website for the most up-to-date information.

Additional reading
Books

African American Hair and Its Role in Advertising, Black Women's Careers, and Consumption Behavior. Sandra Radtke. GRIN Verlag GmbH, 2005.

Afros: A Celebration of Natural Hair. Michael July. Natural Light Press, 2013.

Blackberries and Redbones: Critical Articulations of Black Hair/Body Politics in Africana Communities. Regina Spellers and Kimberly R. Moffitt, eds. Hampton Press, 2010.

Bulletproof Diva: Tales of Race, Sex, and Hair. Lisa Jones. Anchor, 1997.

Can't Tell Me Nothing: The Uncomfortable Hair Truths of Black Women. Dr. Carey Yazeed. Shero Productions, 2021.

Don't Touch My Hair. Emma Dabiri. Allen Lane, 2019.

Edge Control for the Soul. Brianna Laren. Black Girl Black Books Publishing, 2020.

God, Do You Like My Fro? What My Natural Hair Has Taught Me About My Faith. Janay Brinkley. Lincross Publishing, 2017.

Hair Matters: Beauty, Power, and Black Women's Consciousness. Ingrid Banks. NYU Press, 2000.

Hair Raising: Beauty, Culture, and African American Women. Noliwe M. Rooks. Rutgers University Press, 1996.

Hair Story: Untangling the Roots of Black Hair in America. Ayana D. Byrd and Lori L. Tharps. Macmillan, 2014.

Hairlooms: The Untangled Truth About Loving Your Natural Hair and Beauty. Michele Roseman. Healthcare Communications, 2017.

Me, My Hair, And I: Twenty-Seven Women Untangle an Obsession. Elizabeth Benedict, ed. Algonquin Books, 2015.

My Beautiful Black Hair: 101 Natural Hair Stories from the Sisterhood. St. Clair Derrick-Jules. Chronicle Books, 2021.

My Hair Ain't Nappy: A Black Man's Introspection on Natural Hair. Darrius Peace. CreateSpace Independent Publishing, 2012.

Péinate: Hair Battles Between Latina Mothers & Daughters. Raquel I. Penzo. CreateSpace Independent Publishing, 2018.

The Politics of Black Women's Hair. Althea Prince. Insomniac Press, 2010.

Resistance and Empowerment in Black Women's Hair Styling. Elizabeth Johnson. Routledge, 2016.

Stolen Crown: Black Hairstories, 400 Years Later. Isis Brantley. Self-published, 2021.

Style and Status: Selling Beauty to African American Women, 1920–1975. Susannah Walker. University of Kentucky Press, 2007.

Tenderheaded: A Comb-Bending Collection of Hair Stories. Juliette Harris and Pamela Johnson, eds. Pocket Books, 2001.

Twisted: The Tangled History of Black Hair Culture. Emma Dabiri. Harper Perennial, 2020.

Unyielding Roots: What Is Your Hair Story? Kiana Davis, ed. Tree Roots Strong Publishing, 2021.

Children's Books

ABC My Hair and Me. Miyosha Streets. Illustrated by Sarah Gamal. Self-published, 2019.

Ask Uncle Neil: Why Is My Hair Curly? Neil Thompson. Illustrated by Cathy Bolio. Teach the Geek Kids, 2018.

Bad Hair Does Not Exist. Sulma Arzu-Brown. Illustrated by Isidra Sabio. Afro-Latin Publishing, 2015.

Beautiful, Wonderful, Strong Little Me! Hannah Carmona Dias. Illustrated by Dolly Georgieva-Gode. Eifrig Publishing, 2019.

Bippity Bop Barbershop. Natasha Anastasia Tarpley. Illustrated by E. B. Lewis. Little, Brown Books for Young Readers, 2009.

Black Hair Coloring Book for Girls Ages 4–8. Fearless Confidence Coufeaux. Self-published, 2021.

Color My Fro: A Natural Hair Coloring Book for Big Hair Lovers of All Ages. Crystal Swain-Bates. Illustrated by Janine Carrington. Goldest Karat Publishing, 2013.

Cool Cuts. Mechal Renee Roe. Doubleday Books for Young Readers, 2020.

Curls. Ruth Forman. Illustrated by Geneva Bowers. Little Simon, 2020.

Guide for the Extra Kinky Coily Girl Who Thought Baby Hairs & Sleek Up-Dos Would Spring Forth. By Jouelzy. Illustrated by Sharee Miller. CreateSpace Independent Publishing, 2016.

Hair as Big as My Dreams. Destinee Sierra. Illustrated by Jasmine Kenya. Self-published, 2020.

Hair Like Mine. Jenaine Bazzell. Illustrated by Haytham Karim. J. V. Bazzell Publishing, 2021.

Hair Like Mine. LaTashia Perry. Illutrated by Bea Jackson. G Publishing, 2015.

Hair Like Mine Coloring and Activity Book. LaTashia Perry. G Publishing, 2016.

Hair Love. Matthew Cherry. Illustrated by Vashti Harrison. Kokila, 2019.

Happy Hair. Mechal Renee Roe. Doubleday Books for Young Readers, 2020.

Happy to Be Nappy. bell hooks. Illustrated by Chris Raschka. Little, Brown Books for Young Readers, 2017.

How I Wear My Crown. Ka'ala Kaio Mahlangeni-Byndon. Illustrated by Bunch Ketty. CreateSpace Independent Publishing, 2017.

How I Wear My Crown Coloring Book. Ka'ala Kaio Mahlangeni-Byndon. Illustrated by Bunch Ketty. CreateSpace Independent Publishing, 2017.

I Love My Hair! Natasha Anastasia Tarpley. Illustrated by E. B. Lewis. Little, Brown Books for Young Readers, 2001.

I Love My Hair Affirmations Coloring Book for Black and Brown Girls with Natural Hair. Illustrated by Hatice Bayramoglu. Color My Culture, 2021.

It's Time to Comb Your Hair. Tanisha Singleton Thompson, Veriteady Thompson, and Klere Kado Thompson. Illustrated by Jamil Burton. Bowker, 2021.

Latina Como Yo. Rukia Kufakunoga. Illustrated by Graphii. Self-published, 2021.

Latina Looks Like Me. Rukia Kufakunoga. Illustrated by Graphii. Self-published, 2021.

Love Your Hair! Dr. Phoenyx Austin. Self-published, 2015.

Milly Loves Her Natural Hair: K–6 College and Career Readiness Workbook. Dr. Tuesday Mahoney. Kyra Williams, ed. Self-published, 2020.

My Afro! My Hair! Sabrina N. Henry. Illustrated by Emily Hercock. Self-published, 2020.

My Afro: Twin Best Friends. Tiana-Rose Akoh-Arrey. Conscious Dreams Publishing, 2021.

My Big, Curly Fro. Alyssa McClelland. Melanin Merch, 2020.

My Hair. Danielle Murrell Cox. HarperFestival, 2020.

My Hair. Vithlene Olivier-Lamartiniere. Bryony Van der Merwe, ed. Illustrated by Danh Tran Art. Self-published, 2021.

My Hair Is Beautiful . . . Because It's Mine. Paula Dejoie. Black Butterfly Children, 1997.

My Hair Is MAGIC! M. L. Marroquin. Illustrated by Tonya Engel. Page Street Kids, 2020.

Nappy Hair. Carolivia Herron. Illustrated by Joe Cepeda. Dragonfly Books, 1998.

Pelo Bueno. Yolanda Arroyo Pizarro. EDP University of Press, 2018.

Pelo Malo No Existe. Sulma Arzu-Brown. Illustrated by Isidra Sabio. Afro-Latin Publishing, 2014.

Stella's Stellar Hair. Yesenia Moises. Imprint, 2021.

Natural Hair Events in the United States

California

Afrolicious Hair Expo
https://artfullyyourz.wixsite.com/afrolicious

District of Columbia

Natural Hair Fest DC Metro
Designed to promote a way of life that nurtures natural hair growth and proper care regimens
https://naturalhairfest.wpcomstaging.com/natural-hair-fest-washington-dc-metro

Florida

Capital City Natural Hair & Health Expo
Helping each patron see their own reflection of beauty, naturally
https://www.mandisa-ngozi.com/CCNHHE-Spring

COIL-ture Freedom Festival
Celebrating the narrative of the significant role natural hair plays in the lives of Black people
https://coilturefreedomfestival.com/about

Curlfriends Expo/South Florida Natural Hair Expo
https://curlfriendsexpo.com

Fabulously Unique Natural Hair and Beauty Expo
Bringing to life the passionate movement of natural beauty
https://fabunaturalhairexpo.com

The Natural Experience Inc.
Annual natural hair, health, and beauty expo of Saint Petersburg
https://www.eventbrite.com/e/the-natural-experience-inc-tickets-153545836731

Georgia

Atlanta World Natural Hair, Health & Beauty Show
http://atlantanaturalhairshow.com
The Loc Fest
Educating, raising awareness, and unifying the Loc Community
https://www.thelocfest.com

Illinois

Natural Hair Fest Chicago
One-day festival celebrating the art and beauty of hair
https://naturalhairfest.wpcomstaging.com/natural-hair-fest-chicago

Louisiana

Baton Rouge Natural Hair Expo
Promoting healthy hair and skin care
https://www.facebook.com/batonrougenaturalhairexpo
New Orleans Natural Hair Expo
Celebrating and promoting the natural-hair community and culture
https://www.neworleansnaturalhairexpo.com

Maryland

Natural Hair Care Expo
https://naturalhaircareexpo.com

Michigan

Detroit Hair Care Expo/Naturals United Fest
Educating people around the world to love and embrace their natural hair
https://www.detroitnaturalhairexpo.com
Natural Hair Fest Detroit
Meet professionals who specialize in natural hair care, as well as other like-minded festival goers
https://naturalhairfest.wpcomstaging.com/natural-hair-fest-detroit

Minnesota

Annual Twin Cities Natural Hair & Beauty Expo
Aiding individuals in their natural-hair journey
https://www.facebook.com/mnnaturalhairexpo/events/?ref=page_internal

Mississippi

Mississippi Natural Hair Expo
Educating, inspiring, and empowering women who wear their hair in its natural state
https://mississippinaturalhairexpo.com

Missouri

Frizz Fest
Natural beauty festival encouraging self-love and inspiring confidence
https://frizzybynature.com/about-frizz-fest/
The Saint Louis Natural Hair & Black Cultural Expo
Promoting natural hair, healthy living, and beauty concepts for the African family
http://www.stlnaturalhairexpo.com

Nevada

Las Vegas Natural Hair & Wellness Expo
Bringing together naturals in the community to learn about natural hair, health, and wellness
https://www.beautynailhairsalons.com/US/Las-Vegas/2178158572420611/Las-Vegas-Natural-Hair-%26-Wellness-Expo-Vegasnhe

New York

Afro-Latina Festival
Paying tribute to the African roots of people from Latin America and the Caribbean
https://www.afrolatinofestnyc.com/trending/tag/natural+hairhttps://www.afrolatinofestnyc.com/

Curlfest
    Celebrating the magic of natural beauty
    https://www.curlfest.com
HUE Beauty & Natural Hair Affair
    Supporting brands and businesses showcasing products for us!
    http://www.huebeautyandnaturalhairaffair.com
Loc Fest
    A celebration of loc'd hair and culture
    https://www.locfestnyc.com
Natural Hair Fest
    Welcome to a world of natural hair and beauty culture
    https://www.eventbrite.com/e/naturalhairfestival-nyc-2022-tickets
    -61585760668?aff=erelexpmlt

North Carolina

Natural Hair Fest Charlotte
    Celebrating the art and beauty of hair and promoting proper care and
    maintenance regimens
    https://naturalhairfest.wpcomstaging.com/natural-hair-fest-charlotte

South Carolina

Charleston Natural Hair Expo
    Celebrates those who embrace the various textures of their hair
    https://www.charlestonnaturalhairexpo.com

Tennessee

Memphis Naturals
    Learn and connect with other naturals in the City of Memphis and sur-
    rounding areas.
    https://www.meetup.com/es-ES/NaturalsinMemphis
Naturals in the City Hair and Wellness Expo
    Natural hairstyling, natural products, and a natural holistic way of living
    http://www.naturalsinthecity.com/about

Texas

Armed Forces Natural Hair & Health Expo

Let's celebrate the beauty and awareness of natural hair

https://www.eventbrite.com/e/10th-annual-armed-forces-natural-hair
-health-exp-tickets-165005334397?fbclid=IwAR0M_2luVzWdv7JR7edU
__5LnT0paOI329Rb6k5HF5z7cpCfEsmr55TsgPQ

Blossom & Sol Fest

Vibe out and discuss natural hair, culture, and appropriate cultural representations of ourselves

https://www.blossomandsolnaturalhairfestival.com

HUE Beauty and Natural Hair Affair Austin

The first and only natural-hair event during SXSW

http://www.huebeautyandnaturalhairaffair.com

Kinky Curly Coily Fest

Natural-hair festival featuring performances

https://do512.com/events/2021/6/27/kinky-curly-coily-fest-tickets

A Few of the Largest Natural Hair Conventions Outside of the United States

Bahamas

CurlyCru Natural Hair Festival

Celebrating those who choose to wear and admire natural hair among men and women of the Bahamas

https://www.eventbrite.com/e/curlycru-natural-hair-festival-tickets
-73702364757?aff=efbevent&fbclid=IwAR1uS2g4NihPawxTQCWHvs
_9N4-ni3lDy3GhGUZVvdiHzLt4j3XDPyTYCVA

Canada

Edmonton Natural Hair Show

Inspiring people of all ages to embrace their natural hair as part of what makes them uniquely beautiful

https://www.facebook.com/EdmontonNaturalHairShow/

France

Natural Hair Academy
> One of the largest natural-hair conferences in the world
> https://nhaparis.com

Salon Boucles d'Ébène
> http://salonbouclesdebene.com/concept

Great Britain

Curlytreats Fest
> Providing access to information, education, activities, support, products, and services to help women and girls with their natural hair
> https://curlytreats.co.uk/

Nigeria

Afro Hair Culture & Beauty Festival/African Hair Summit
> A festival of unity, culture, and natural African hair and beauty
> https://africanhairsummit.org/

Salons Specializing in Natural Hair Care

Alabama

Amelia Salon
Hayah Beauty
The Loc Oasis
Randall's Grooming Lounge & Salon Suites
Salon Lisa Brown
Swoope Hair Natural Hair Lounge

Alaska

Glamour Braids & Weaves

California

Braid Street LLC
The Curl Consultant
GoodBody

The Institute of Fine Braidery Arts
Loving Your Natural Self
Naza

Connecticut

Brown Skin Women

District of Columbia

Curls Understood
Kustummaid Tailor Hair Studio
Loc Love
Natural Kinks
Sisterlocks by AzizaMawiyah
Uzuri Braids

Florida

Casanova Beauty
Divine Design Natural Hair Solutions
Ethnic Hair Care Salon
Janice Beauty Salon
Mandisa Ngozi Art & Braiding Gallery
Natural Glow Supply & Salon
Natural Trend Setters
Natural Tresses
Naturally U Hair Studio
Sanctuary Salon & Med Spa
She's a Natural Salon Studio

Georgia

Adell's Natural Hair Salon
Hi Texture Salon
Huetiful Salon
Kinky Curly Beauty's Hair Studio LLC
Natural Hair Academy

Pre'Vail Natural Hair Salon
Rockafro Natural Hair Designs

Hawaii

Braids Hawaii

Illinois

Hair Bar
Huetiful Salon
Loc Goddess

Indiana

Brown's Elite Hair Salon
Elite Hair
Kurly Koils
Soul Sisters Natural Salon

Iowa

Mai African Hair Braiding

Kentucky

C & R Beauty Bar

Louisiana

Baby Bangz
Beauty by See
Beyond Flaws
HeadQuarters Barber & Beauty Salon
Nolabraider Natural Hair & Braids Salon
Strawberri Curls

Maryland

Creative Hair Expressions
Diaspora Salon

Dreadz N' Headz Natural Hair Care Center
Fabulous Salon
Healthy Hair Center
Locspiration Natural Hair & Beauty Salon
N Natural Hair Studio
Urban Natural Hair

Massachusetts

Bebe's African Hair Braiding Salon
The Curl Bar
Liz's Hair Care
The Loft Hair Studio
Salvaged Roots Hair & Beauty
Studio 27 Salon
STYLLISTIK Salon
Zahara Locs

Michigan

Amazing Kinks
Happy to Be Nappy Natural Hair Salon & Spa
Locks 4 Life Natural Hair Salon
Melinda Denise Hair Care
Naturalistas Botanic Hair Spa
Textures by Nefertiti
U Natural Hair Dreadlock Services LLC

Minnesota

Loc Starz Natural Hair
Malobe Natural Hair Salon

Missouri

NAPPS Natural Hair Salon
Naturally Unique Salon
Your Natural Image

Mississippi

Natural U Hair Salon
Simply Natural Hair Care Salon

Nebraska

More Hair by Kessa

Nevada

Rare Naturals Hair Sanctuary
Raw Remedies LLC

New Hampshire

Natural Hair and Braids LLC

New Jersey

Jesula's Natural Hair Spa
Knotty Roots Natural Hair Care Studio
The Natural Hair Studio
Potent Transitions
Textures & Kinks

New Mexico

Kamaria Creations

New York

Bohemian Soul Natural Hair Salon
Curl & Co. Hair Studio
Hair to Go Natural
Harlem Natural Hair
Heaven on Earth Beauty Salon
Lovejoy Natural Hair Salon
New Beginnings Natural Hair Salon
Vanity Hair Studio

North Carolina

Anew You Transitional Salon
HC Natural Hair
Nubian Natural Hair Gallery
Styles by Lisa
Taji Natural Hair Salon

Ohio

Curlversity
Designerae
LaToyia Dionne Natural Hair & Wellness Spa
Nature's Outer Beauty Salon
Puff Apothecary
Synergi Salon
Styles of Success Beauty Loft

Oklahoma

Naturally UniQue
SheesDreamy Hair Studio

Oregon

Conscious Coils
Dean's Beauty Salon and Barber Shop
Dread Rock Salon

Pennsylvania

Duane Hair Salon
Rasa Salon

Rhode Island

The Loft Hair Studio

South Dakota

Diamond Locs

Tennessee

A Natural Affair Beauty Lounge

Texas

Huetiful Salon
Kris Koffee Beauty
Naturally Me Hair Salon

Utah

Essence of Ebony

Virginia

Da Knotty Roots
Deeply Rooted Hair Salon
Thrive Hair Bar

Washington

Good Hair Salon
I AM Loc Shop
Mr. Naturalz Salon

West Virginia

Hair on Locke

Organizations

Black Girl Curls
> Dedicated to the curls and the culture
> https://www.blackcurlmagic.com

The Black Hair Syllabus
> While not an organization per se, this is a good listing of teaching resources—all about Black hair!
> https://www.blackhairsyllabus.com/black-hair-and-education

Coilettes
> Guiding little girls through life by building confidence and love for who they naturally are
> https://www.instagram.com/coilettes_/

Curls Understood
> Taking the mystery out of curls
> https://curlsunderstood.com/about

Embracing My Natural Inc.
> Empowering girls and women to embrace their natural hair
> https://www.embracingmynatural.org

Frizzy by Nature LLC
> Nonprofit organization encouraging self-love and inspiring confidence among women
> https://frizzybynature.com/

Funky University
> Supporting women, men, and children in their quest to showcase their beauty naturally
> https://unclefunkysdaughter.com/funkyuniversity.html

The Halo Collective
> Building a future in the UK without hair discrimination
> https://halocollective.co.uk

Mane Moves Media
> Inspiring Black women worldwide to embrace their natural hair, beauty, and brilliance
> https://www.manemovesmedia.com

NAACP Legal Defense and Educational Fund Inc. CROWN Act page
> Advocating for the CROWN Act to become law in all fifty states
> https://www.naacpldf.org/crown-act

Nappy Head Club
> A community of healing exploring the reclamation of our Black identity
> https://medium.com/nappy-head-club

Natural Partners in Crime
> Creates unique events for the natural-hair community
> https://naturalpartnersincrime.com/about

Naturally Curly
> Our mission: be the most trusted and engaging community for women with textured hair
> https://www.naturallycurly.com

PsychoHairapy
> A global mental health and hair movement
> https://www.psychohairapy.org

Urban Bush Babes
> A publication creating the definitive source for natural hair, fashion, health, arts, and culture
> http://urbanbushbabes.com/category/hair

Films

As It Grows, Dalian Adofo (2014)

The Big Chop, Derek D. Dow (2016)

Braided: An American Hair Story, Angel Lenise, Julie Schott (2017)

Detangling the Stigma: A Natural Hair Documentary, Roseline Chavannes (2019)

Good Hair, Jeff Stilson (2009)

The Grapevine TV, Ashley Akunna (2015)

Hair Love, Matthew Cherry, Everett Downing, Bruce Smith (2020, Best Animated Short Film Oscar)

Happy Hair Conversation, Brooklyn Independent Media (2014)

The Hidden Cost of Black Hair, Economist (2021)

Kickin' It with the Kinks, Cynthia Butare (2015)

Kinks, Locs, and Love, Lawrence Green (2015)

Nappily Ever After, Haifaa al-Mansour (2018)

Natural Hair: The Movie, Reginald Titus Jr. (2019)

"No, You Cannot Touch My Hair," Mena Fombo, TEDx Bristol (2017)

Our Hair-itage: A Natural Hair Documentary, Crystolyn Macklin (2016)

"The Psychology of Black Hair," Johanna Lukate, TEDx Cambridge University (2018)

"Roots of America's Black Hair Problem," *HuffPost* Live (2014)

"Understanding Afro–Puerto Rican and Other Afro-Latin@ Cultures," Center for Puerto Rican Studies (2012)

Going Natural

If you are considering taking the leap from a permed, relaxed, weaved, or other style to a natural style, these materials can help you transition in a contemplative, deliberate, and gradual way.

Being Natural Hair Care Journal: Black Hair Growth Book, Planner, Log. Miss Tan Designs. Self-published, 2021.

Black Hair Care Journal: Reach Your Hair Goals! Promise Books. Self-published, 2021.

Black Hair Growth Tracking Journal: 52-Week Hair Care Journal for Women of Color. Girl Glam. Self-published, 2021.

The Black Woman's Hair Bible: Everything You Have Always Wanted to Know About Your Hair but Didn't Know Who to Ask. Lisa C. Johnson. CreateSpace Independent Publishing, 2014.

Cocoa Butter & Hair Grease: A Self-Love Journey Through Hair and Skin. Dr. Donna Oriowo. 2019.

For the Love of N.A.P.P.Y: When Self-Love and Hair Journaling Heals the Soul. Camille L. Holmes. Self-published, 2019.

Hair Journey Journal. J. L. Tate. Self-published, 2021.

Hair Secrets: A Journal for Your Natural Hair Journey. Ken'Yada Nicole Mullins. Self-published, 2021.

I Think I Like My Natural Hair. Stephanie Shider. Self-published, 2015.

If You Love It, It Will Grow: A Guide to Healthy, Beautiful Natural Hair. Dr. Phoenyx Austin. Self-published, 2012.

It's the Hair for Me: A Natural Hair Journal. Jannell. Treasure Chest Journals, 2021.

Kinky Coily Natural Hair Journal. Pamela Samuels Young. Goldman House Publishing, 2014.

Loc'd Natural Hair: Hair Care and Growth Journal. Shanice DK Designs. Self-published, 2021.

My Great Hair Chronicles: Natural Hair Journaling Today. Renee Abeo Williams. Self-published, 2021.

My Hair Care Log. Kimberly Alston. Self-published, 2021.

My Healthy Hair Journey: Journal for Natural Hair. LaMonica J. Williams. Self-published, 2018.

My Loc Reflective Journal: A Meditation on My Locing Journey. Natalie Boyle. Self-published, 2020.

Own Your Natural: Your Personal Guide to Beautiful, Healthy Natural Hair. Simeko Hartley. Self-published, 2021.

The Science of Black Hair: A Comprehensive Guide to Textured Hair Care. Audrey Davis-Sivasothy. Saja, 2011.

Tarchelle B's Natural Hair Journal: 4 Weeks to Figuring Out What Your Hair Loves. Tarchelle Bryant. CreateSpace Independent Publishing, 2016.

Thrive, Hair, Thrive: A Workbook to Help You Thrive in Your Hair Care Journey and Develop a Kick-Butt Hair Care Routine! Andrea D. Boyd. Self-published, 2019.

The Ultimate Do-It-Yourself (DIY) Hair Care Journal. Angie. Blurb, 2021.

Ultimate One-Year Natural Hair Journal. A. Monica Santos. CreateSpace Independent Publishing, 2017.

CONTRIBUTORS

Dr. Bárbara Abadía-Rexach is a communication scholar, sociocultural anthropologist, and Afro Puerto Rican feminist and antiracist leader. Bárbara is assistant professor of Afrolatinidades at San Francisco State University's Latina/o Studies Department. Her work explores racialization from different cultural productions in Puerto Rico and its diasporas, and within the Latinx communities. She is the author of the book *Musicalizando la raza: La racialización en Puerto Rico a través de la música* (Ediciones Puerto). Her articles include "Summer 2019: The Great Racialized Puerto Rican Family Protesting in the Street Fearlessly," "Centro y periferia: Las identidades en el nuevo movimiento de la bomba puertorriqueña," and "The New Puerto Rican Bomba Movement." She is one of Colectivo Ilé's community organizers and a member of the Black Latinas Know Collective. Bárbara produces and moderates the *Negras* radio program at Cadena Radio Universidad de Puerto Rico. She is a collaborator of the Spanish digital platform Afroféminas and the Puerto Rican feminist and solidarity journalist project Todas.

Margalynne Armstrong, JD, joined the Santa Clara University School of Law faculty in 1987 and serves on the boards of several community organizations. Prior to joining the law faculty at Santa Clara, Margalynne practiced public employment law, served as a staff attorney with the Legal Aid Society of Alameda County, and directed the Academic Support Program at the University of California, Berkeley, School of Law. While she attended the University of California, Berkeley, she served as associate editor of the *Ecology Law Quarterly*. She has worked for four decades to help BIPOC law graduates pass the California bar exam and has received the Public Interest Award from the California Association of Black Lawyers and the Matthew O. Tobriner Public Service Award from the Legal Aid Society of San Francisco. She is widely published in the areas of housing, racial discrimination, and constitutional law. Her recent publications include the article "Are We Nearing the End of Impunity for Taking Black Lives?" and, coauthored with Stephanie Wildman, new materials for the 2021 reissue of *Privilege Revealed* (NYU Press). She is a lifetime member of the California Association of Black Lawyers.

For over fifteen years, **Sulma Arzu-Brown** has been working professionally as a champion for diversity and inclusion. She has been involved with this work since well before the term became a trending topic. A proud Garifuna Afro-Latina immigrant from Honduras, in 2005 she began working with the Garifuna Coalition USA. Sulma also worked for a New York–based organization that assisted formerly incarcerated fathers (who were predominately Black and Latino) in returning to the workforce. Sulma has also worked as the director of operations for the New York City Hispanic Chamber of Commerce. Her publications include the award-winning *Bad Hair Does Not Exist!/Pelo Malo No Existe!* (Afro-Latin Publishing) and *My Hair Comes with Me: Shifting the Paradigm of What Success Looks Like* (CreateSpace Independent Publishing). Sulma's work appears in *O, The Oprah Magazine*; *Black Enterprise*; *HuffPost*; Univision's *Despierta América,* and Remezcla.

Carmen Bardeguez-Brown is the author of the poetry collection *Straight from the Drums: Al Ritmo Del Tambor*. Her work was showcased in the award-winning documentary *Latino Poets in the United States*. She has been featured in many well-known cultural institutions such as the Nuyorican Poets Café, Mad Alex Foundation, Smoke, the Soho Arts Festival, Long Wood Gallery, the Kitchen, La Casa Azul, New Year's Alternative Poetry Marathon, the Capicu Cultural Series, the New York Poetry Festival at Governors Island, Bowery Poetry Club, Caribbean Theater Words Festival, and Caribbean Theater Panel on Afro-Latino writers, among others. Her work has been performed by Felipe Luciano's Poets' Choir and Butch Morris Conduction series #27 and at the Whitney Museum and Art in Progress Cantieri Del Contemporaneo at Cosenza, Italy. Her work appears in *Aloud: Voices from the Nuyorican Poets Cafe* (Henry Holt) and in magazines such as *A Gathering of the Tribes, Long Shot, Fuse, Phati'tude,* and *Centro Voices,* and in Woman Writers in Bloom Poetry Salon. Carmen produced a poetry CD entitled *Straight from the Drum*, an assortment of poems that encapsulate her Afro Caribbean poetic rhythm.

Tyrice Brown, MA, goes by the artist name Blacksmoothie, a pseudonym representative of her flavor as a Black-centric artist with an eclectic style. Her most recent work is featured in the international anthology *Our Spirits Carry Our Voices* and the Bay Area collection titled *Colossus: Home*. She has worked with nonprofits from the West Coast to Virginia in supporting the mission of race and gender equity. She is the content curator for West Oakland to West Africa, a poetry exchange program that connects members of the African diaspora and Africa through creative writing.

MK Chavez, a Black Latinx writer and educator, is the author of *Mothermorphosis* (Nomadic Press), *Dear Animal* (Nomadic Press), and several chapbooks, including *A Brief History of the Selfie* (Alley Cat Books) and *Virgin Eyes* (Zeitgeist Press). MK curates the reading series Lyrics & Dirges and is codirector of the Berkeley Poetry Festival. She serves as poetry editor at *Bronzeville Quarterly* and has been a visiting instructor at Stanford University, San Francisco State University, and Mills College. MK is a recipient of the Alameda County Arts Leadership Award, the PEN Oakland Josephine Miles Award, and the 2021 San Francisco Foundation/Nomadic Press literary award. She has received residencies from Hedgebrook, Caldera, CantoMundo, Community of Writers, and VONA. MK's work appears in the *San Francisco Chronicle*, *Story* literary magazine, *Cipactil*, *Penumbra Art and Literary Journal*, *Eleven Eleven*, *Rivet* literary journal, and *Foglifter*. Her poetry also appeared in the Academy of Poets Poem-A-Day series and at Golden Gate Park's Voice of Trees projects.

Iris Crawford is an independent journalist, poet, and prose writer with a background in social, environmental, and climate-justice grassroots organizing. Her work has appeared in the Oaklandside, *Oakland Reporter*, Bay Area Local News Matters, the *Bold Italic*, Nati Earth, PBS's *Rewire*, People's World, the Plug, and elsewhere. She has worked with the Maynard Institute of Journalism Education's Oakland Voices program, and in 2020 she was a Dezie Woods Jones public policy fellow with the Berkeley/Oakland chapter of Black Women Organized for Political Action. A first-generation Guyanese American, Iris is committed to amplifying the voices of BIPOC (Black, Indigenous, and people of color) communities.

Lyndsey Renee Ellis, MFA, a writer from Saint Louis, Missouri, is a Barbara Deming Memorial Fund grantee, a San Francisco Foundation Literary Award winner, a Voices of Our Nations Arts Foundation (VONA) alumna, and a Squaw Valley Writers alumna. Her work appears in *Joyland*, *Stockholm Review of Literature*, Entropy, the *Jamaica Observer*, Shondaland, *St. Louis Anthology*, and *Black in the Middle: An Anthology of the Black Midwest*. Lyndsey is a prose editor at Great Weather for MEDIA. She currently serves on the board of directors at Paul Artspace and Exceptional Women in Publishing (EWIP). Lyndsey's debut novel, *Bone Broth*, was released in 2021.

Dr. Priscilla Ferreira is an assistant professor in geography and Latinx and Caribbean studies at Rutgers University–New Brunswick. She has been organizing with communities of color inside and outside the university over the past twenty years. Her current research engages collaborative work with Black women residents in majority-Black geographies in Rio de Janeiro to map Black community economies and understand how they enact grassroots urban planning and community-driven development initiatives.

Kim Coleman Foote, is a writer of fiction, creative nonfiction, and experimental prose and is the recipient of several fellowships, including from Phillips Exeter Academy, the National Endowment for the Arts, NYFA, Center for Fiction, Illinois Arts Council, and Fulbright. Her residencies include MacDowell, the Anderson Center, and Hedgebrook. Foote's work has appeared or is forthcoming in *The Best American Short Stories 2022, Iron Horse Literary Review, Ecotone*, and the *Rumpus*. She is currently working on a book fictionalizing her family's experience of the Great Migration and an African female–centered novel about the transatlantic slave trade. She has also written a memoir about the Black diaspora experience in Ghana. Originally from New Jersey, Kim received an MFA in creative writing from Chicago State University.

Dr. Regis M. Fox is associate professor of English at Florida Atlantic University. Her primary research interests include nineteenth-century American literatures, feminist theory, and African American literary and cultural studies. Her work appears in *Women's Studies: An Interdisciplinary Journal*, the *Journal of American Studies*, and *A Determined Life: The Elizabeth Keckley Reader*. A former McKnight Junior Faculty Fellow, Regis is author of *Resistance Reimagined: Black Women's Critical Thought as Survival* (University Press of Florida).

Jewelle Gomez is a Cape Verdean, Ioway, and Wampanoag writer, activist, and author of the double Lambda Award–winning novel *The Gilda Stories* (Firebrand Books). *Gilda Stories* is the first Black, lesbian, feminist vampire novel, and it has been in print for more than thirty years. Her adaptation of the book for the stage, *Bones & Ash: A Gilda Story*, was performed by the Urban Bush Women company in thirteen US cities. The script was published as a Triangle Classic by the Paperback Book Club. *Waiting for Giovanni*, her play about James Baldwin, and *Leaving the Blues*, her play about Alberta Hunter, have been produced in San Francisco and in New York City.

Jewelle is the recipient of a literature fellowship from the National Endowment for the Arts, two California Arts Council fellowships, and an Individual Artist Commission from the San Francisco Arts Commission. Her fiction, essays, criticism, and poetry have appeared in numerous periodicals, including the *San Francisco Chronicle, New York Times, Village Voice, Ms.* magazine, *Essence* magazine, *The Advocate, Callaloo,* and *Black Scholar.* Her work has appeared in such anthologies as *Home Girls; Reading Black, Reading Feminist; Dark Matter: A Century of Speculative Fiction from the African Diaspora;* and *The Oxford World Treasury of Love Stories.* She was the winner of the 2020 Legacy Award from the Horror Writers Association.

Jasmine Hawkins is a Philly-based educator, writer, and community organizer serving as president and cofounder of the nonprofit Urgent 365 Inc., an organization derived from her 2015 poetry chapbook *Urgent Conversations: Race, Reality, and Responsibility.* She uses writing-centered arts programming to help Black youth and young adults unpack and uproot unhealthy habits, narratives, and mindsets in order to uncover their true identity and unleash their God-given potential. Recognized for her art-based community endeavors, Jasmine is the recipient of the 2020 Bartol Foundation Micro-Grant and the Leeway Foundation 2020 Art and Change Grant. Her writing is featured in *Mogul Millennial* and *The Dreamer's Anthology.* In addition, a forty-day devotional is forthcoming.

Dr. Sherry Johnson tells stories that engage memory and Black writing between Canada and the United States. She is a writer, researcher, and scholar of literature, particularly at the intersection of Black women's lives and their writing, African American visual culture, and film studies. Currently an associate professor and director of the master of arts program in English at Grand Valley State University, she teaches courses in African American literature, multicultural American literature, neo-slave narratives, and critical approaches to literary study. Her work appears in the *American Studies Journal, African American Review, Dictionary of Caribbean and Afro–Latin American Biography, MELUS*, and other publications.

Dr. Shatima Jenique Jones is a visiting assistant professor in the Gallatin School of Individualized Study at New York University and is interested in the intersection of race, space, gender, and culture. Shatima is writing a book manuscript, under contract, for University of Chicago Press, called *The Headmasters of Brooklyn: Barbering, Blackness, and Brotherhood*. It focuses on how Black people interpret and perform their racial identity, the processes by which they create community based on these understandings, and the significance of place and space in shaping these sentiments. The bulk of Shatima's research employs ethnographic methods to uncover what Black people believe constitutes an authentic racial identity, how they signal this to others in everyday interaction, and how racially exclusive places shape understandings and performances of race. Shatima has embarked on a new ethnographic project focusing on women's hair salons in order to explore gender differences in racial performance.

Judy Juanita's poetry and fiction have been published widely, and her plays have been produced in the Bay Area and New York City. She has taught writing at Laney College in Oakland since 1993. In 1968, while attending San Francisco State, Judy served as editor in chief of the *Black Panther,* the newspaper of the Black Panther Party. *Virgin Soul* (Viking, 2013) was her novel debut. Judy's writing is archived at Duke University in the John Hope Franklin Research Center for African and African American History & Culture, alongside the archives of student activists from the Student Nonviolent Coordinating Committee. Eleven of her plays are archived at the Jerome Lawrence & Robert E. Lee Theatre Research Institute, Ohio State University (OSU), where her full-length play *Theodicy* was a prizewinner in the Eileen Heckart Senior Play Competition in 2008.

Dr. Raina J. León is a Black and Afro Boricua writer and teacher educator from Philadelphia and a founding editor of the *Acentos Review*. Her poetry, nonfiction, fiction, and scholarly work appears in well over one hundred journals and anthologies. She has published four poetry collections: *Canticle of Idols, Boogeyman Dawn, sombra: dis(locate),* and *black god mother this body,* along with the chapbooks *profeta without refuge* and *Areyto to Atabey: Essays on the Mother(ing) Self.* Raina's interests include Afrofuturism, genealogy and walking in relationship with our ancestors, ecopoetics, writing for change, writing for healing and health, and mothering. Raina was only the third Black woman and the first Afro Latina to achieve the rank of full professor at Saint Mary's College of California. She was only the fourth Black woman and first Afro Latina to get tenure there.

Dahlma Llanos-Figueroa, MLS, is author of *Daughters of the Stone* (Thomas Dunne Books), which was a finalist for the 2010 PEN America Literary Awards. The hardcover edition of *Daughters of the Stone* was shortlisted as a 2010 finalist for the PEN/ Robert W. Bingham Prize. Her second novel, *A Woman of Endurance*, was released in April 2022. The Spanish-language edition, *Indómita*, was released in May 2022. Her short stories have been published in anthologies and literary magazines such as *Breaking Ground: Anthology of Puerto Rican Women Writers in New York 1980–2012*, *Growing Up Girl: An Anthology of Voices from Marginalized Spaces*, *Afro-Hispanic Review*, *Pleaides*, *Latino Book Review*, *Label Me Latina/o*, and *Kweli Journal*. She lives in New York City.

Having been in love with hair her whole life, **Dr. Afiya Mbilishaka** grew up as her family's hairstylist, graduating from "salon" lawn chairs at cookouts to hosting a minisalon in her college dorm room. A clinical psychologist, Afiya served as a full-time therapist at Columbia University before becoming a professor at the University of the District of Columbia. She is founder and CEO of PsychoHairapy, an organization featuring hair as an entry point to mental health care. Afiya is a natural hairstylist and partners with N Natural Hair Studio in Silver Spring, Maryland, where she loves creating art with locs, braids, twists, and Afros.

Dr. Adrienne Danyelle Oliver, MFA, a writer, hip-hop scholar, and educator living in Oakland, California, began her natural-hair journey in 2004 while living in Little Rock, Arkansas, where negative perceptions of natural hair were alive and well at the time. She survived her early career as a scholar transitioning to twists and then a 'fro, and Adrienne ultimately arrived at dreadlocks. Adrienne's academic work appears in *Storytelling, Self, Society* and *Systemic Collapse*. She uses creative writing to theorize about a more just education system that honors hip-hop culture. Her creative work has been published in *Digital Paper* and *The Womanist*. Beyond her work as an interdisciplinarian, she mentors other educators as a Bay Area Writing Project teacher consultant, training others to use hip-hop sensibilities to cultivate imaginative and inclusive instructional practices. Adrienne has been a VONA fellow and leads a virtual writing and healing circle for Black women. In her spare time, she likes to write poetry, play music, dance, and sing in the mirror à la Issa Rae.

For nearly a decade, Nigerian American writer and mental health advocate **Kelechi Ubozoh** has worked in the California mental health system in the areas of research and advocacy, community engagement, stigma reduction, and peer support. She began her career as an investigative reporter in New York City and was the first student reporter ever published in the *New York Times*. She has been featured in *The S Word* documentary and in *O, The Oprah Magazine*. Her book, *We've Been Too Patient: Voices from Radical Mental Health* (North Atlantic Books & Penguin Random House), is a collection of diverse stories of radical healing that considers the recent movement toward reform in the mental health field, including the consumer movement, peer support, and trauma-informed care.

Artist

Sal Steiner is a San Francisco–based artist whose work celebrates the way hair twists, bends, curls, braids, and weaves a wonderful world of magic. He finds ways to evolve in art and in life while weaving his dark side to dance with his creativity. A seeker of truth and love, Sal finds ways to play with and test the bounds of life's constructs while nourishing a willingness to learn and be humbled. In his Interwoven: Headscapes series, some of which are featured in this book, Sal uses his love of tiny lines to scribble out masterful depictions of hair. Each hair he draws pulls him into a deeper meditation, a rhythmic trance that leaves him searching for the next detail. Black hair has surfaced as Sal's main focus, highlighting the ways in which people wear their hair for self-empowerment or as statements. His series coincided with the growing momentum of the Black Lives Matter movement. The absence of a face draws the viewer in to the fine details, while challenging them to look beyond.

Editor and Contributor

Lyzette Wanzer, MFA, is a San Francisco author, editor, and writing workshop instructor. A flash fiction connoisseur and essay aficionado, her work has appeared in *Natural Bridge, Los Angeles Review, Callaloo, Tampa Review, The MacGuffin, Ampersand Review, Journal of Advanced Development, Fourteen Hills, Journal of Experimental Fiction, Pleiades, Flashquake, Glossalia Flash Fiction, Potomac Review, International Journal on Literature and Theory, Fringe Magazine,* and many others. She is a contributor to *Lyric Essay As Resistance: Truth From the Margins* (Wayne State Press, 2023), *Civil Liberties United: Diverse Voices from the San Francisco Bay Area* (Pease Press, 2019), and *Chalk Circle: Intercultural Prizewinning Essays* (Wyatt-MacKenzie, 2012). Her articles have appeared in Essay Daily, the Naked Truth, and the *San Francisco University High School Journal.* Lyzette is the current judge of the Soul-Making Keats

Literary Competition's Intercultural Essay category and the Women's National Book Association's Effie Lee Morris Writing Contest's nonfiction category.

Lyzette has been invited to present her work on panels and/or at conferences across the country, including the American and Popular Culture Association (PCA/ACA), the Association of Writers & Writing Programs (AWP), the Association for the Study of African American Life and History, the College English Association (CEA), the Louisville Conference on Literature & Culture Since 1900, Litquake Festival, the San Francisco Writers Conference, and others.

Lyzette is a member of the National Writers' Union, in which she served on the Northern California chapter's steering committee for five years; the Authors Guild; American and Popular Culture Association; and AWP. She has also served on the fellowship adjudication panel for the Writers Grotto. Lyzette has been awarded writing residencies at Blue Mountain Center (New York), Kimmel Harding Center for the Arts (Nebraska), Playa Summer Lake (Oregon), Horned Dorset Colony (New York), Virginia Center for Creative Arts, Writers' Colony at Dairy Hollow (Arkansas), Headlands Center for the Arts (California), PlySpace (Indiana), the Banff Centre for Arts and Creativity in Canada, and the Anderson Center (Minnesota). She is the recipient of grants from the Center for Cultural Innovation, San Francisco Arts Commission, Yerba Buena Center for the Arts, Black Artist Foundry, California Arts Council, and California Humanities, a National Endowment for the Humanities partner. Lyzette is working on *Building a Career as a Literary Artist of Color*, a professional development workbook for BIPOC creative writers. Contact Lyzette at www.LyzetteWanzerMFA.com.